Marketing in the Not-for-profit Sector

The Marketing Series is one of the most comprehensive collections of books in marketing and sales available from the UK today.

Published by Butterworth-Heinemann on behalf of The Chartered Institute of Marketing, the series is divided into three distinct groups: *Student* (fulfilling the needs of those taking the Institute's certificate and diploma qualifications); *Professional Development* (for those on formal or self-study vocational training programmes); and *Practitioner* (presented in a more informal, motivating and highly practical manner for the busy marketer).

The Chartered Institute of Marketing

Formed in 1911, The Chartered Institute of Marketing is now the largest professional marketing management body in Europe with over 60 000 members located worldwide. Its primary objectives are focused on the development of awareness and understanding of marketing throughout UK industry and commerce and in the raising of standards of professionalism in the education, training and practice of this key business discipline.

Books in the series

Marketing in the Not-for-profit Sector

Margaret Kinnell and Jennifer MacDougall

Published on behalf of
The Chartered Institute of Marketing

Butterworth-Heinemann
Linacre House, Jordan Hill, Oxford OX2 8DP
A division of Reed Educational and Professional Publishing Ltd

℞ A member of the Reed Elsevier plc group

OXFORD BOSTON JOHANNESBURG
MELBOURNE NEW DELHI SINGAPORE

First published 1997

© Margaret Kinnell and Jennifer MacDougall 1997

British Library Cataloguing in Publication Data
Evans, Margaret Kinnell
   Marketing in the not-for-profit sector. – (CIM professional
   development series)
   1. Nonprofit organizations – Marketing
   I. Title   II. MacDougall, Jennifer   III. Chartered Institute of
   Marketing
   658'.048'0688

ISBN 0 7506 2234 2

Data manipulation by David Gregson Associates, Beccles, Suffolk
Printed in bound in Great Britain by Biddles Ltd, Guildford and King's Lynn

Contents

Acknowledgements

We are grateful to those many organizations and individuals who have provided the data and insights which have informed our study. Their collaboration has been invaluable. In particular we should like to thank those who supported the case study investigations: Tim Richmond of Pannell Kerr Forster and Bob Salisbury of Garibaldi School; Martyn Allison, Deputy Director and subsequently Director of Leicester City Council Leisure Services and Richard Watson, Principal Assistant Director; Pat Coleman, Director of Birmingham City Council's Library Services in the Department of Leisure and Community Services and her successor, John Dolan, and Dawn Wise, Marketing Officer. Irene Martindale was also a staunch support in the organization of data gathering.

CHAPTER 1

Introduction

Summary

Not-for-profit services marketing has become more important in the UK and more widely practised as a consequence of the market environment created by a range of legislation and the development of a new ethos. While not-for-profit organizations have existed for centuries, they have only recently featured in the consideration of business practices. Social marketing began the implementation of marketing in not-for-profits, but arguments against the value of marketing for public services have also been advanced. However, government policies that have introduced compulsory competitive tendering and European legislation that has enforced competitive tendering processes have been important in supporting a customer-centred culture.

Introduction

Services marketing in the not-for-profit sector has become increasingly significant over the last few years. Sectors particularly affected by the legislation which has created the new market-led conditions, such as education, health, social services, leisure and libraries, are turning to marketing practices as they develop a more customer-focused philosophy. Charitable and religious organizations are also employing marketing principles more widely in their operations. Quality concerns are fuelling this market-led approach to managing all aspects of services and effectiveness is now measured by user satisfaction as much as by the efficiency of the operation. The need to develop and demonstrate effectiveness through the provision of quality services within limited budgets to meet customer expectations has provided much of the impetus behind these trends. Services which have traditionally relied on government support through national and local taxation and which have based service provision on long-held values and assumptions have had to face the challenges of marketplace economics. In this book we shall be exploring the impact of marketing practices on a range of organizations and identifying how relationship marketing has become of significance to meet this challenge, while at the same time supporting organizations in providing quality services.

Fundamental changes within the political and social environment in which services operate have led to the new approach. These include the creation of the internal market in the National Health Service (NHS) and social welfare agencies, the imposition of compulsory competitive tendering (CCT) in local government, the effects of the Education Reform Act 1988, the European free market agreement and the influence of European Union directives, the introduction of market testing in central government, and the impact of recession on a shrinking resource base. Charities and religious organizations face particular problems associated with changes in social and cultural patterns and in the financial accountability of their operations. Overall there has been an emphasis in recent years on quality and performance in line with the Conservative government's Citizen's Charter initiative, and new relationships are being forged between service providers and service enablers, relationships which are likely to continue despite the change of government in the 1997 General Electiob.

Definitions and context

Not-for-profit organizations have been in existence much longer than the for-profit sector but have only been formally defined quite recently.

Hansmann (1980) states that an organization can only be not-for-profit if, after wages and expenses have been taken into account, it is prohibited from dispersing any additional revenue to management or any other controlling personnel such as trustees. There should be no relationship between the control of the operation and the distribution of profits. The not-for-profit sector comprises a wide-ranging and disparate number of organizations from arts bodies to healthcare, charities, churches and local authority leisure services. As O'Hagan and Purdy (1993) explain, there is a distinction to be made also between the public and the private non-profit-making enterprise. While private not-for-profit organizations rely on sales income, donations, grants and/or volunteers, public bodies are supported by public money in the form of taxation from local and central government sources and/or funding from other public bodies. Typically, however, goods or services provided by not-for-profit organizations such as education, health and the arts have both public and private aspects (James, 1987).

The broadening of the marketing concept from the traditional business environment to involve other areas such as education, health, and social programmes was heralded by a paper from Kotler and Levy (1969). They felt that the traditional marketing approach used by commercial organizations would provide a useful framework for not-for-profit organizations of many kinds and that the aim was not whether they introduced marketing or not but whether it was used effectively. Over the last twenty-five years many academics and researchers have come to the conclusion that marketing is fundamentally concerned with the exchange processes and relationships between human beings. Foxall (1989) discusses this generic definition of marketing and doubts whether it can encompass all aspects of human exchange as claimed by some writers (Bagozzi, 1975; Levy, 1978). He prefers the definition of marketing as a process of matching supply and demand, arguing that this is a more logical and straightforward expression of marketing activity.

Social marketing was the term introduced originally in 1971 as the 'design, implementation, and control of programmes seeking to increase the acceptability of a social idea, cause, or practice in a target group' (Kotler, 1980, p. 20). This type of marketing is usually associated with not-for-profit organizations such as those examined here – state-run health and education services, local government library and leisure services, charitable and religious organizations, and voluntary bodies. The aim is to achieve social change (improving standards of health and education, increasing recreation opportunities and fitness, putting across an ideology) within a reasonable amount of time by using marketing practices to motivate the public, at the same time improving the efficiency of the organizations involved. Although there is still resistance to marketing with its hard-sell image, marketing is basically a voluntary exchange between different sections of society (Razis and Razis, 1993).

Writers such as Kotler and Zaltman (1971) claimed that even fundamental social changes like safer driving and family planning could be
facilitated through the use of marketing techniques such as analysis
and planning. It can also be argued, however, that those organizations
involved in social marketing are dealing with totally different market
conditions from the traditional commercial sector. Social marketers
such as those involved in social services or health promotion can face a
situation where there is unlimited demand or an excess of demand over
supply. These types of organizations are not often in competition with
each other and their customers do not usually have any alternatives to
turn to. It has been argued that such organizations cannot be consistently marketing-oriented when they do not have the same pressures as
private commercial businesses (Foxall, 1989). Local authority services
such as street cleaning, police and firefighters are provided in return
for taxes paid by the consumer. However, it is not always clear how
much actual choice the consumer has, apart from the democratic process, in the choice or type of service delivered.

Other major differences between the private and public sector include
the identification of customers, which is usually more straightforward
for business organizations than for the public sector. In terms of education, for example, consumers can be seen as students, pupils, parents,
future employers, or society in general. Similarly, local authorities have
no exact equivalent of an internal balance account and success or failure can be very difficult to assess, for example in terms of social welfare.
Political pressures on local authorities are exerted as well as other internal and external constraints common to both the public and private sector such as economic and environmental pressures. Services marketing
is also distinguished by a range of characteristics from traditional
goods marketing which are well documented elsewhere, and include
intangibility, perishability, and the inseparability of a service from personnel providing it (Cowell, 1984).

As McCort (1994) describes, the rate at which not-for-profit organizations, particularly voluntary, religious and charitable institutions, are
adopting the marketing concept and integrating fully the principles
and practices which could benefit their operation is slow in many
cases. The cultivation and development of long-term relationships with
consumers is recommended as a useful strategy to overcome the difficulties encountered by the unique characteristics of not-for-profit services.
A relationship marketing strategy is particularly appropriate for voluntary, religious and charitable organizations, McCort suggests, in dealing
with the characteristic dual nature of their public – the donors and the
beneficiaries. The development and maintenance of long-term relationships with donors is crucial for the survival of these organizations. The
motivation and encouragement of donors to continue their loyalty and
support with intangible benefits is a challenging process and can be

facilitated by building on the value of the relationship rather than the transaction itself.

The competitive environment

Conservative government policy has been based on the premise that the UK public sector needs to be reduced in favour of the more efficient market-led private sector. To expedite these aims private sector management practices have been introduced into many public services including health, education and local government. This policy propounds the view that value for money is achieved through open competition which uncovers inefficiency and bad practice.

In the modern marketplace, encompassing both the private and public sector, the emphasis is on the need to acquire and retain customers. The competitive advantage, therefore, will go to those not-for-profit organizations which can achieve the most successful relationship with their targeted customers. However, applying marketing techniques in the public service sector is not without its detractors. Some see it as having a manipulative element creating consumer needs artificially which are satisfied to the organization's benefit. This in turn could lead to increased demand for public services, placing unnecessary strains on government finances (Graham, 1993). In spite of the detractors, however, the consensus among the majority of academics and practitioners is that marketing has an important contribution to make to the not-for-profit public sector.

Competitive tendering and contracting out have been in existence for many years in terms of public procurement policy (for example, in the case of specific Department of Health and Ministry of Defence purchases), but in 1980 the Conservative government began a programme of compulsory competitive tendering (CCT) in local government (the Local Government Planning and Land Act 1980, the Local Government Act 1988, and the Local Government Act 1992). These measures required local authorities to examine and clarify their corporate objectives and to review development of policies and programmes. While research shows that general aims and objectives have been set, in many cases there has been a lack of attention given to setting specific goals and developing evaluation methods (Palmer, 1994), and the widely projected economic benefits are not conclusive (Wilson, 1994). While savings may be made in relation to increased efficiency this may be at the cost of greater unemployment, reduced pay, and more part-time staff.

The Education Reform Act 1988 strengthened the role of central government and gave greater financial autonomy to schools through the introduction of local management of schools (LMS), removing control from local authorities. CCT in the National Health Service began in 1983 when the Griffiths Inquiry recommended a general management approach to health service delivery. The 1989 review of the NHS, *Working for Patients* (Department of Health, 1989), led to the establishment of independent hospital trusts and the internal market between purchasers and providers of health services. The overall effect of this legislation and other related publications such as *Raising the Standard* (Citizen's Charter Unit, 1992) has been to extend competitive tendering to services of all kinds from the traditional catering and cleaning contracts to recreation, libraries, education, health, community and social care.

The European dimension is an important consideration when reviewing the recent development of public sector services. The Single European Act laid down regulations that most public procurement must be conducted through competitive tendering processes open to a European-wide market. In addition, the European Union has an important influence on the allocation of jobs, the levels of pay, and pension and redundancy rights of public sector employees (Wilson, 1994). Privatization in the UK and Europe-wide has accelerated since 1992 and has obvious implications for strategic planning and marketing in these organizations.

The political environment and the enabling authority

Public accountability, consumerism and decentralization have reflected the drive towards a market-led approach to the provision of public services in recent years. The publication of *The Citizen's Charter* set out the rights of the public to 'expect high quality services, responsive to their needs, provided efficiently at minimum costs' (Citizen's Charter Unit, 1992, p. 5). The introduction of marketing practices in not-for-profit organizations is based on the assumption that the quality of services will thereby be improved, as shown in the Charter Mark initiative (Cabinet Office, 1992).

Local government authorities in adopting strategies to improve the quality and efficiency of services are increasingly becoming enabling authorities. Rather than providing services directly some authorities are supplying the resources and direction needed for outside contractors to do so instead. The effects of this development on the marketing of services is complex and depends on the type of service concerned. One of the developments arising from recent legislation is the establishment of arm's-length companies which perform services previously carried out by local authorities. These organizations provide an entrepreneurial input, additional capital, and can reduce duplication of time and expenditure by pooling resources in a semi-autonomous organization, while still being controlled by the local authority. An example of this type of organization is the tourism development action programmes (TDAPs) described by Palmer (1994). The problems associated with arm's-length organizations include the possibility of becoming too commercially oriented, thereby losing sight of the democratic process, policies and social agenda behind them.

The necessity of recognizing significant internal differences in the way local authority services operate is emphasized by Palmer (1994) who offers a framework for classifying services. This is based on two dimensions concerning the complexity of the service provided in terms of numbers of specialist operations and interdepartmental relationships involved and on the nature of the environment in which the service is provided, whether it is a totally planned or a competitive, market-led environment. Where a service is both complex and used in a market-led environment such as recreation and leisure services, it is essential that the local authority develop a marketing orientation in all its activities or lose out to private competitors.

Adopting a marketing approach in the not-for-profit public sector has been accepted as essential if services are to survive in the modern political and economic environment in order to facilitate priority setting and fulfil the needs of targeted consumer groups. While local government personnel need to adopt a marketing approach to all aspects of service delivery, marketing personnel must be able to adapt their methods to the public sector. In the local government environment strict political guidelines must be followed and all actions are subject to a high level of public accountability. This can place constraints on marketing activity and risky undertakings are not to be entertained. In spite of these restraints public sector marketing is increasing in terms of manpower and skills sophistication (Latham, 1991).

A customer-centred culture

The challenge of public sector marketing is to overcome the historical lack of a customer-centred culture and to encourage the growth of objective setting and evaluation. One of the persistent dangers of the competitive market-led economic environment is the tendency to overlook the specific needs of customers in the compulsion to improve efficiency and cost-cutting. In public sector services there are many obstacles obscuring the way to a truly customer-focused culture. These may be of political origin ranging from the interference or dominance of central government to the confusion between local political wrangling and management policies. The need to ensure cost-effectiveness at the expense of quality is a strong pressure on many organizations and may often result in unsatisfactory short-term plans which reveal a lack of commitment.

As we have discussed, consumerism and customer rights are at the forefront of the new market-led economy and the not-for-profit sector must improve service delivery and quality in order to survive. Developing a customer culture at the core of the corporate strategy is essential and involves attention to the person-to-person encounters which form the heart of service provision. In a suggested model of strategic processes for service organizations Mattsson (1994) recommends that managers should initiate and sustain a programme of defining, attracting, involving and satisfying customers. These processes concern all types of operations within the organization and form the basis of service provision. In order to improve service quality all aspects of these processes must be examined and evaluated on a continuous basis. Defining customers involves:

- segmentation according to needs and behaviour;
- determining quality criteria (environment, encounters, equipment, etc.);
- distinguishing core and additional services;
- designing the service process.

Attracting customers includes

- dialogue with the most demanding customers;
- fixing realistic benchmarks to monitor performance;
- offering guarantees of high quality and value for money;
- encouraging customers with a matching mental model of the service;
- attracting customers with realistic expectation levels.

The process of involving customers begins with the reward and motivation of both customers and employees or volunteers equally. The need is for a server as leader management mentality or 'servant leadership' to be developed. In addition, information systems should be used to handle customer and process information which is effectively based on benchmark quality criteria. Appraisal practices should include continuous evaluation of service processes.

The satisfaction of customers is the most important goal of the not-for-profit public service or voluntary organization. In order to fulfil customer requirements their reactions to service delivery must be noted, recorded and acted upon. It is important to react immediately to some customer experiences/complaints, which means a flexible and empowered staff at all levels. Staff and the organization as a whole should learn from customer reactions and remedy past mistakes. Also, examples of quality service should be made available to customers and staff to underline the improvements achieved (Mattsson, 1994).

The processes outlined above include a range of communication initiatives involving both staff and customers of the organization. Staff training, particularly in the area of customer care, is essential to ensure a responsive organization, as is communicating through internal newsletters, meetings and surveys. Equally important is maintaining good contacts with customers and/or donors through newsletters, a corporate identity, information on services and guaranteed quality services offered by the organization.

Market research is another important tool in maintaining a customer-centred culture and in the continuous evaluation of service quality. Customer surveys should be carried out regularly and complaints dealt with promptly and monitored by management. Access to the organization by the public should be flexible and as open as possible, including suggestion schemes, open meetings, advice panels, and local offices or centres where possible.

Marketing quality

Marketing quality is vital in the not-for-profit public and voluntary sector as it focuses the organization's attention on identifying and satisfying customer needs; it will be considered in more depth in the next chapter. Total quality management (TQM) has traditionally been a tool of statistical quality control and assembly-line factory and similar processes. The principles of TQM and continuous improvement have been adapted however in recent years to the public service sector (Swiss, 1992). Important elements transferred to the public sector include many of the marketing tools we have mentioned in this chapter, for example customer reaction, performance monitoring, continuous improvement and staff empowerment and participation.

The introduction of TQM initiatives has not been without its failures, as a number of surveys have shown (Povey, 1993). Reasons for lack of TQM success in the business world include not enough effort made to measure performance and set benchmarks, and insufficient customer involvement and staff empowerment. In spite of this, many organizations still approach quality management from a product or service viewpoint rather than from the customer's position. Adopting a marketing orientation throughout the organization facilitates a customer-centred approach and focuses on meeting and satisfying their needs. Marketing personnel have a major role to play in quality management, particularly in a not-for-profit organization where the customer should be the central focus and where interpersonnel relationships form the basis of the service.

Aims and scope of the book

The purpose of this book is to present an overview of the complex environment within which managers in not-for-profit services are operating and to identify the key issues which affect their services. Relevant marketing principles to aid the development and control of quality management are described, providing models for this sector which take account of the necessary social and professional values and ethics inherent in many of the services. Sector-specific concerns are examined through case studies and scenarios.

Following this first chapter, in which an outline has been provided of the context within which not-for-profit services marketing has been developing, in Chapter 2 there will be a critical survey of relevant theoretical approaches and the identification of models for managers. Relationship marketing will be covered in more depth here, and the wider issues of marketing management for the not-for profit sector also considered. The issues and principles highlighted in this chapter and Chapter 2 are explored in depth in the following chapters.

The next part of the book is concerned with organizations in the public sector and Chapters 3 and 4 look at managing change in schools and quality marketing in further and higher education. The impact of local management of schools and grant-maintained status on marketing for schools are examined, while the experience of the college and university sectors on the links between quality assurance programmes and marketing practices are also considered. Chapter 5 looks at the internal market in the National Health Service and its impact on management practices, specifically the issues centring on market-led approaches. In Chapter 6 local authority leisure services and the impact of compulsory competitive tendering and quality programmes on marketing practices are described. Library and information services and the role of marketing in performance review are outlined in Chapter 7, while Chapter 8 is concerned with relationships between service providers and purchasers and quality issues in local government social services.

The next part of the book deals with organizations in the voluntary sector. Chapter 9 studies charities and voluntary organizations and the management of their marketing activities, attitude marketing, direct marketing techniques, corporate image and the limits of marketing. In Chapter 10 we examine churches in the marketplace, with emphasis on the fund-raising and membership issues which marketing has been used to address. Chapter 11 provides a conclusion which draws together the issues examined in the studies of each sector within the book as a whole, especially quality concerns in marketing management. It also summarizes relevant concepts and identifies problem areas raised.

Chapter 12 comprises a set of brief case studies with issues and questions for students and tutors. These will be drawn from the preceding chapters and bring cases together for use in tutorial discussion and/or coursework exercises.

References

Bagozzi, R.P. (1975) Marketing as exchange. *Journal of Marketing*, **39** (4), 32–9.

Cabinet Office (1992) *The Citizen's Charter: Charter Marks scheme 1993*. Guide for Applicants, Central Office of Information, London.

Citizen's Charter Unit (1992) *Raising the Standard: Britain's Citizen's Charter and public service reform*, Foreign and Commonwealth Office.

Cowell, D.W. (1984) *The Marketing of Services*, Butterworth-Heinemann, p. 23.

Department of Health (1989) *Working for patients*, Cm 555, HMSO.

Foxall, G. (1989) Marketing's domain. *European Journal of Marketing*, **23** (8), 7–22.

Graham, P. (1993) The use of marketing positions in government departments and public sector organizations in Australia. *Australian Journal of Public Administration*, **52** (2), 164–172.

Hansmann, H.B. (1980) The role of nonprofit enterprise. *Yale Law Journal*, **89**, 835–901.

James, E. (1987) The nonprofit sector in comparative perspective. In Powell, W.E. (ed.), *The Nonprofit Sector: A research handbook*, pp. 397–415, Yale University Press.

Kotler, P. (1980) *Marketing Management: Analysis, planning and control*, Prentice-Hall, p. 20.

Kotler, P. and Levy, S.J. (1969) Broadening the concept of marketing. *Journal of Marketing*, **33** (1), 10–15.

Kotler, P. and Zaltman, G. (1971) Social marketing: an approach to planned social change. *Journal of Marketing*, **35** (3), 3–12.

Latham, V. (1991) The public face of marketing. *Marketing*, 28 November, 22–3.

Levy, S.J. (1978) Marcology 101 or the domain of marketing. In Britt, S.H. and Boyd, H.W. (eds), *Marketing Management and Administrative Action*, McGraw-Hill.

McCort, J.D. (1994) A framework for evaluating the relational extent of a relationship marketing strategy: the case of nonprofit organizations. *Journal of Direct Marketing*, **8** (2), 53–65.

Mattsson, J. (1994) Improving service quality in person-to-person encounters: integrating findings from a multi-disciplinary review. *The Service Industries Journal*, **14** (1), 45–61.

O'Hagan, J. and Purdy, M. (1993) The theory of non-profit organizations: an application to a performing arts enterprise. *The Economic and Social Review*, **24** (2), 155–67.

Palmer, A.J. (1994) Providing complex local authority services in competitive markets – the role of arm's-length organizations. *Local Government Studies*, **20** (1), 78–94.

Povey, B. (1993) Continuing improvements. *Total Quality Management*, **5** (6), 37–40.

Razis, V. and Razis, N. (1993) An analysis of the value of marketing to non-profit organizations: the case of child safety. *Health Marketing Quarterly*, **11** (1/2), 163–89.

Swiss, J.E. (1992) Adapting total quality management to government. *Public Administration Review*, **52** (4), 356–62.

Wilson, J. (1994) Competitive tendering and UK public services. *The Economic Review*, April, 31–5.

Further reading

Cowell, D.W. (1984) *The Marketing of Services*, Butterworth-Heinemann.

Kotler, P. and Levy, S.J. (1969) Broadening the concept of marketing. *Journal of Marketing*, **33** (1), 10–15.

McCort, J.D. (1994) A framework for evaluating the relational extent of a relationship marketing strategy: the case of nonprofit organizations. *Journal of Direct Marketing*, **8** (2), 53–65.

CHAPTER 2

Relationship marketing

Summary

Relationships between customers, stakeholders and the organization, which need to be managed over the long term, are the basis for successful marketing in the not-for-profit sector. Delivering quality to customers is an essential element in managing relationships. This entails understanding customers' behaviour and ensuring their loyalty. Marketing management involves several key marketing concepts and the application of strategic marketing techniques, including the management of the marketing mix.

Introduction

Every service organization, whether in the profit or not-for-profit sector, is concerned with its overall quality, with its role towards its clients or customers and especially the development and maintenance of a reputation for excellence. This holds good for the total service portfolio as well as individual product lines. In developing marketing for not-for-profit organizations, the quality imperative is therefore a key issue and because quality is seen to be an essential component of the effective organization, the concept of the 'customer' is particularly apt. Customers normally pay directly for a service, while those receiving services from organizations such as churches, hospitals or state-run schools may contribute only indirectly through taxation. However, their patronage is equally vital to organizational success and customer relationships across the for-profit and not-for-profit sectors share many common features. In addition, and again in common with other business organizations, the role of other interested parties or 'publics' ('any group that has an actual or potential interest in or impact on a company's ability to achieve its objectives', Kotler, 1988) in the not-for-profit organization is also important. These 'publics', or stakeholders, could include financial institutions, the media, government, community action groups, local residents, the general public, and the staff of the organization.

An example of the complex relationships between an organization, its customers and stakeholders can be seen in the case of a school. Relationships need to be managed over the long term and take account of the totality of activities, to ensure the quality of service. A secondary school will seek superior performance at every level of its public examinations. Employment success and entry to further or higher education will be yet further important quality criteria for pupils, parents and also the local education authority and government, to whom schools are also accountable. The customers for the school will, of course, include the pupils themselves and their parents, but employers, colleges and universities could also be included in this category or be considered as significant stakeholders. In order to satisfy both customers and stakeholders' interests every class in the school and each element of the school's service will be relevant to its overall success: including the library, catering, sports facilities and information technology provision. Each member of staff contributes to and derives their livelihood from the school and therefore has a direct stake in its achievements. The quality of education offered by the school will thus be seen as a whole-organization, total portfolio concern which has to be managed continually in order to satisfy the long-term aspirations of the pupils and their parents, the staff and all the other stakeholders in the school: the local community, local education authority, government. The community will be looking not only for direct evidence of success through examination results but also in the type of citizens produced by a school. Pupils' contribution to building that community, through their behaviour and attitudes as well as through their ability to support the economy by gaining employment, is increasingly being considered important. This extensive level of school service to a community and to generations of parents and their children is developed over many years. Building relationships with clients (pupils and parents) and also with the relevant stakeholders, and sustaining these over a substantial period of time, is therefore the key aspect of managing and marketing quality services. A school becomes successful and maintains its position through establishing and retaining a reputation for the excellence demanded by all of those with an interest in its success: clients/customers and stakeholders.

Like schools, many other service organizations depend on developing this kind of commitment from those who both fund and patronize them. Success only breeds success where the service not only offers excellent products in the short term but *continues* to do so long term, and convinces both its customers and stakeholders of its relevance to them.

In this chapter, relationship marketing, sometimes described more simply as 'building bridges' (Kotler and Andreasen, 1996) to ensure a continuing link between the service and its various customers and stakeholders, will be discussed in the context of developing quality services. Definitions of relationship marketing have evolved in recent years as a reaction against over-use of the marketing mix – the '4 P's' which are discussed below (Gummesson, 1987; Gronroos, 1990a, b). Instead, it was seen as important to establish, strengthen and develop customer relations: always asking the question 'does the customer want a relationship?' (Blois, 1996). A marketing relationship is:

> a managed context within which formal transactions between a consumer and a supplier (in the form of a manufacturer, retailer or service provider) to that consumer are supplemented by voluntary and reciprocated actions by both parties. Consumers (and suppliers) are assumed to voluntarily enter into and remain in relationships of this type because they perceive that they will in some way be better off as a result of doing so (Christy, Oliver and Penn, 1996).

It is easy to see why not-for-profit organizations would seek long-term relationships, as the cost of achieving these will be less than that of obtaining similar purchases or patronage from customers through a series of discrete transactions. The value of ongoing relationships for customers may be less obvious to them, and it is here that the quality of their interactions with the organization will need to be considered. For many consumers of not-for-profit organizations such as education, health or social services an organization's ability to develop and sustain a quality relationship will be an important element in their product.

Marketing and quality management are therefore seen as complementary management functions in effective not-for-profit organizations, and the expanding literature in both areas provides important lessons for managers. Quality, like relationship marketing, has become a particular growth area in management science, and there is increasing interest in developing theory and applying quality management principles to the not-for-profit service sector. However, there is a problem in charting a pathway through the maze of sources (Line, 1995). This chapter is intended to provide such a pathway and to introduce those marketing and quality concepts which will be further developed in the main body of the book.

Quality and marketing

Quality management is based on sound management practice operating on a human level. It acknowledges the primacy of both the customer and of staff at all levels in the organization. It is democratic and dynamic, and therefore ideally suited to a not-for-profit environment. It has been described as a way of working, as a philosophy or as the way things should be done and is:

> the total composite product and service characteristics of marketing, engineering, manufacture, and maintenance through which the product and service in use will meet the expectation of the customer (Feigenbaum, 1983)

and a total approach to quality management (TQM) is:

> a management philosophy embracing all activities through which the needs of the customer and the community and the objectives of the organization are satisfied in the most efficient and cost effective way by maximizing the potential of all employees in a continuing drive for improvement (British Standards Institution, 1991).

Much of what is involved in managing quality in services, whether in for-profit or not-for-profit organizations, has to do with customer service. This includes the service itself; the way it is served; after-delivery service and support. Service excellence can be defined as a 'balance between purpose, people and process' (Taylor, 1992), in which purpose comprises the mission of the organization; process is the systems which have to meet the needs of customers and people are the staff who understand and value the customers they serve.

The focus is firmly fixed on providing a service or product which is valued by the user over the long as well as the short term and of which the staff can feel proud. The emphasis is not on what managers perceive their customers or users want but on establishing exactly what customers themselves want, and trying to go some way towards providing it. Quality is often described as being 'simply meeting the customer requirements', but it also includes a holistic view of the product or service. A range of definitions indicates the breadth of issues requiring attention in delivering a quality service (Oakland, 1995):

> The totality of features and characteristics of a product or service that bear on its ability to satisfy stated or implied needs;
> The total composite product and service characteristics of marketing, engineering, manufacture and maintenance through which the product and service in use will meet the expectation by the customer;
> Conformance to requirements.

In order to ensure that quality management has meaning in relation to comparable services provided elsewhere, whether or not these are in competition, requires an element of benchmarking, or 'the continuous process of measuring products, services and practices which will lead to sustained and superior performance' (Bullivant, 1994). A continual awareness of how a service stacks up against accepted standards has to be built into the quality assurance systems of the organization, and seen as an essential element in the marketing strategy. Higher education in the UK has been transformed by the activities of two elements of quality assurance: teaching quality assessments and the research assessment exercise. League tables have established expectations on the part of stakeholders (particularly government) as well as customers, of acceptable levels of performance and are used extensively by universities in their marketing activities.

Consistence in service delivery is also seen as essential, in order to sustain a relationship between the customer and the service, and to develop and maintain relations with suppliers and other stakeholders. Stakeholders of not-for-profit organizations are often highly influential in determining policy and allocating funding and will therefore be a significant feature in relationship marketing. Communicating effectively with each of the groups of stakeholders requires varied messages according to their particular preoccupation. For example, in a local authority, elected members are of considerable importance in allocating funding and setting policy for departments. However, the committee to which a department reports will also have competing and often contradictory agendas which stem from the variety of political and personal interests represented by its members. A local authority manager will therefore need to communicate to those interest groups in different ways to achieve their support. Political skills of a high order are part of the communication process.

The 'quality chain' is also an important concept for not-for-profit organizations. If one link in the chain from supplier to customer is faulty, there is breakdown in the service and in the perception of that service from the customer's viewpoint. The quality chain not only operates between the organization and external suppliers, internal links are also important to ensure that each part of the organization's activities harmonize. Timeliness of supply may be essential for the customer and has to be related to promises made in promotional materials.

To the customer who has ordered Christmas cards and gifts from a charity catalogue, no matter how attractive and glossy the production which stimulated the purchase nor how effective the targeting which ensured delivery of the catalogue, if the order arrives late, its value to that customer is nil. Marketing of the products will have failed. Equally, if the order is not delivered as specified and a substitute is offered – perhaps even something as minor as an alternative colour for a silk scarf – the customer experiences disappointment and will be wary of buying from this source again. Another failure of marketing.

Creating the expectation, experience and the perception of excellence in the minds of customers and stakeholders is the means to developing a relationship based on trust that the organization will consistently deliver what it promises.

Customer behaviour

The link to marketing is therefore quite explicit. Quality management is concerned with how the consumers or users of a service experience a service and how their perceptions are transformed into marketing management practices. Knowing and satisfying customers' needs underpins the marketing concept and is vital to business success, whether in the profit or not-for-profit sector. If the marketing function is to create and use profitably those marketing mixes, or tools (discussed further, below),which will respond effectively to the requirements of customers then a quality approach which focuses on the customer has to be in place for marketing to succeed.

Judgements about satisfaction or dissatisfaction come from the forming of expectations. Customers have expectations of the benefits and performance of a service. Comparing the results of experiencing or consuming the service with those expectations will lead to (Foxall and Goldsmith, 1994):

- a 'positive disconfirmation' of the service's performance (the service exceeds expectations);
- or to confirmation (the service meets expectations);
- or to 'negative disconfirmation' where the service fails to provide the expected benefits.

While the organization naturally will seek to ensure at least that the minimum performance expectation requirements are met, there is a question as to whether exceeding expectations is necessarily in the best interests of the organization. Oversatisfying customers may well be the means of beating the competition. However, especially in those not-for-profit organizations where the competition comes not only from another organization but also from the opportunity time or cost spent on other activities, it may be better to 'underpromise' and 'overdeliver' as a means of raising customer expectations (Peters, 1988).

To return to the case of the charity mail-order catalogue, it is good practice to set a longer delivery time than can actually be provided, in order (a) to anticipate potential supply delays and postal problems and (b) to enable the charity to exceed its own standards. A further example is that of a parish church which found that by only promising a small crêche for children during morning service, but then actually delivering a well-run nursery class with activities, stories and refreshments parents were encouraged to bring younger children to services. Through combining this with baptisms held at family services which involved all the congregation attendances rose and the decline in active church membership of families with young children was halted. The success in running the class also gave confidence to volunteers that they could develop further activities, with a 'virtuous circle' of activity–success–development being created.

There are certain guiding principles which can be applied to any organization in meeting the needs of customers. Studies of a range of service organizations have indicated that all customers perceive similar elements in service quality, although the relative importance of each varies from one service to another (Berry, Parasuraman and Zeithaml, 1985). These key elements have been identified as:

1   *Reliability*   This means that the organization performs consistently and dependably, honouring its promises. For not-for-profit organizations this will include keeping membership records accurately, delivering services to time, sending subscription reminders correctly.
2   *Responsiveness*   The employees – including volunteers – should be ready to deliver the service, including promptly responding to customers.
3   *Competence*   The necessary skills and knowledge for the service to be performed should be available to customers. Front-line personnel, administrative support and any research capacity should each have the requisite competences.
4   *Access*   The service must be easily contactable and approachable. As well as ensuring convenient location and times of access, telephone waiting times and waiting to receive the service should be minimized.
5   *Courtesy*   Politeness, consideration and respect, together with a friendly manner, are involved.
6   *Communication*   Informing customers in terms they understand

and listening to them in order to explain the service are included. Varying communications will be required by the different target groups.

7   *Credibility*   How far the service can be trusted and believed involves consideration of the good name of the organization and what it stands for, the personal qualities of staff and the nature of the transactions between the organization and its customers.

8   *Security*   This means that the service should be free of danger, risk or doubt, and includes the safety of any machinery or equipment used in delivering the service as well as financial security and the confidentiality of transactions.

9   *Understanding the customer*   The organization takes the trouble to understand its customers' requirements, provide individual attention and recognize repeat customers or members. This is an essential element in successful relationship marketing.

10 *Tangibles*   The physical elements of the service such as facilities, credit cards, stationery, the appearance of staff and equipment should be fit for their purpose.

This work of Berry, Parasuraman and Zeithaml confirmed that of Gronroos (1983), who identified the importance of varying perceptions of service quality among customers. Despite the agreement of these theorists that the customers' expectations of a service have to be at least matched for a quality service to be perceived, modelling service marketing has been a difficult undertaking. Expressing the different kinds of quality in a service context is much more problematic than the experience of product marketing. When a manufactured product like an automobile is offered to a customer, the transaction of purchasing is relatively unimportant: the quality of the end-product is paramount. However, in a service such as education the complex interactions between teachers and pupils *are* the product, and perceptions of the quality of the school include all the personal encounters between pupils, staff and parents as well as the tangibles such as the school buildings, equipment and facilities. The customer is interested in the 'expressive performance' or the pyschological element of the service, as well as its 'instrumental performance' or its technical aspects. While this concept was first applied to product marketing, Gronroos tested it in the service context and found that 'the perceived service is the result of a consumer's view of a bundle of service dimensions, some of which are technical and some of which are functional in nature' (Gronroos, 1990a). This might be expressed in the following way, in a model which uses a range of theoretical approaches (see Figure 2.1).

An example of how this model can be applied is that of a medical information service. When reviewing approaches to quality assurance in database searching, it was found to be important to define the success of the search not only in terms of how many successful 'hits' the cus-

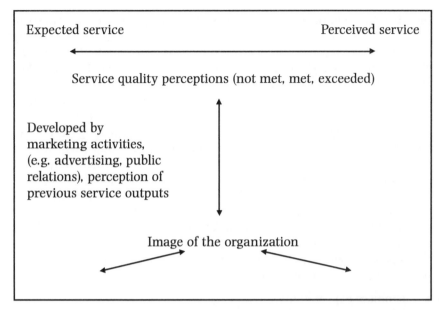

Expected service   Perceived service

Service quality perceptions (not met, met, exceeded)

Developed by
marketing activities,
(e.g. advertising, public
relations), perception of
previous service outputs

Image of the organization

Figure 2.1   Service quality and perceptions of performance

tomer received (instrumental performance) but through the manner of
service delivery (expressive performance). It was found that a quality
information service depended on three elements (Shedlock, 1988):

- the answer (which had to be accurate in terms of the information on
  sources given to the customer);
- the process (which had to be efficient and timely);
- the delivery (the style in which the information is communicated to
  the customer).

The total image of the information service, which impacts on customers'
expectations of service, is therefore composed of both the expressive
and the instrumental aspects of the service.

Another element which has been found to bear on customers' perceptions of quality in the product sector is that of branding. However, a
not-for-profit organization like a school or a hospital information service
cannot rely on a brand name alone to provide its image. Image can be
influenced by traditional marketing activities such as advertising, but
this has to be handled sensitively so that unrealistic assertions about
service quality are not made. If there is a gap between customer expectations of the service and its performance, the quality of the service will
be misperceived. The SERVQUAL model assesses the impact of expectations on service quality (Parasuraman, Zeithaml and Berry, 1985) but
has problems associated with it, especially in regard to public, as distinct
from private services (Buttle, 1996). Most difficult of all is the problem
that many customers or potential customers for public services such as

health, education or information services may have low expectations of what services can or should offer them. Only the professionals running such services may have sufficient knowledge of the potential and the standards to which the public has a right. Their responsibility as professionals will include that of determining the level of service that their customers should receive, and ensuring there are sufficient resources to meet those needs. Equally, there are public policy questions determined or influenced by the various stakeholders (e.g. central government, local authorities, professional associations, pressure groups) which have to be considered as part of the service offering and which may be at odds with some consumers' – and indeed some professionals' – expectations. A health service has a duty to provide the most cost-efficient service to the whole of the community and difficult clinical as well as management decisions about what levels of services should be offered have to be faced. There are several models which attempt to improve the quality of services, but one of the greatest barriers to their implementation is the reconciling of these variables:

- customers' expectations;
- professionals' expectations;
- stakeholders' expectations;
- service capability.

While understanding and believing customer expectations are therefore starting points for success in the development of quality, they are not sufficient on their own (Ghobadian, 1994).

This was found when the Royal Shrewsbury Hospital carried out a preliminary study to ascertain whether BS 5750 could be applied in the National Health Service. While there were aspects of the service which were amenable to some objective quality assurance measures, e.g. waiting times, there were others which were not so readily measurable because of the complexity of the interactions between departments and functions and the need to reconcile different healthcare professionals' views on service delivery. The operation of the outpatients' clinic depended on the X-ray department and on the variable nature of patients' needs, which meant that consultation times could not always be anticipated. While the criteria of the British Standard could be applied in principle, in practice these had to be substantially modified to accommodate the essential human factors of patients' needs and professional expectations (Rooney, 1988).

Managing customer loyalty

Another aspect of this role of the customer in quality management is that of 'brand loyalty' among consumers. In order to maintain loyalty organizations need continually to assess how well their service or product is performing in relation to the competition and ensure that they meet any challenges. Successful service organizations avoid the complacency associated with a long history of service and maintain a freshness in their response. 'Delighting the customer' is one means of sustaining such loyalty over the long term. For one internationally renowned hotel this meant not 'pandering or grovelling to guests' but simply 'doing the basics – a welcoming smile, a confident, warm-sounding voice, an offer of help' plus 'that little bit extra' (Taylor, 1993). This is, of course, the nub of the problem. How does an organization anticipate what extra they need to offer to delight their customers? To a hotel chain it includes details like having firm pillows or down pillows, still spring water or carbonated water and communicating an individual customer's wants to their hotels around the world. Over a period of time, the hotel staff get to know their regular guests and specifically ask them what their needs are. Recognizing a returning guest is important.

While each organization's customers will have needs that are specific to the service being offered there are, however, some principles which can be used to guide not-for-profit marketers in developing the delight factor and which can be applied to their customers. Lynch (1993) offered the seven 'secrets' of the delight factor. These can be adapted for not-for-profit organizations:

1 *'Personalize the experience'* This can be achieved through the use of personalized services and associated products. Personally addressed computerized letters have become commonplace and sometimes counterproductive, but other ways of personalizing can be developed. Some aid charities have developed personal giving by individuals to named individuals on the model of Action Aid, which recognized the need of many donors to feel directly involved in providing benefits to aid recipients.

2 *'Delight breeds delight'* Creating the experience of delight is more likely to be successful if it can be shared with others – especially relatives, friends or colleagues – or if the organization creates a shared experience by acknowledging significant events. Churches which remember the wedding anniversaries of those couples they have married and send greetings are not only helping to create a sense of delight but are also developing a long-term relationship.

3 *'What delights people is what delights people'* There has to be sensitivity in managing the delight experience, as individuals will vary in their tastes. A four-stage process is suggested:

- initiation
- exploration
- reinforcement
- symbiosis.

By this stage the customer and the organization will have recognized their interdependency by developing a closer relationship. Charities frequently develop relationships with their supporters through involvement in local groups. These have the greatest success by not 'forcing the pace' with new recruits.

4   *'Less can be more'*   There is an inevitable law of diminishing returns as customers expect more and more of the organization, so that many small surprises, such as the remembering of anniversaries, are more effective than one big one. Remaining a jump ahead of the customer's expectations can also be a problem, so that a sequence of surprises has to be planned to be effective. A church which only remembers the first wedding anniversary of those couples it has married and then jettisons them will produce a negative rather than a positive relationship.

5   *'Blend novelty and nostalgia'*   Creating situations in which both nostalgia and the novel are provided uses the appeal to customers' sense of the past and their interest in what is innovative. Fundraising campaigns by not-for-profit organizations should recognize this by offering activities which cater for the range of tastes.

6   *'Technology helps and hinders'*   Technology can be used to lower the price and raise the quality of a service, but there has to be human intervention fully to satisfy customers' needs. Information services now make extensive use of information technology in accessing and delivering information, but the role of the information specialist in helping users to navigate information remains crucial.

7   *'There is no end to delight'*   Keeping customers satisfied by exploiting all the opportunities for delighting them will be increasingly important for organizations which are operating in a competitive environment.

Most important of all, when embarking on delighting customers the question : do customers really want such a relationship? has to be asked.

Repeat buying and loyalty to the organization are particular features of customers of service organizations and they are of especial relevance where a professional service is being delivered. Consumer preferences therefore have to be understood in order to manage demand as well as to forestall competition. In a general practice each doctor will have a unique image in the mind of a patient, partly due to patients' personal preferences. There may be GPs who see fewer patients than their colleagues, due to less demand for consultations. Partly, though, this comes about through patients' ignorance of the particular strengths of each doctor. Generally, it has been found that customers are loyal to a single brand in the product field and continue to be so unless marketing efforts persuade them to switch. Promotion of the benefits of another brand is important in persuading non-customers and other customers to change their allegiance (East, 1990). This principle holds good for the delivery of not-for-profit services. Identifying and advertising the particular expertise of the doctors and ancillary staff in a general practice will be a means of helping patients to pinpoint which doctor will provide the type of advice and support they require, and at what level – in other words, 'switching brands' to the most suitable person for treatment and at the same time ensuring the optimum use of valuable professional time. By developing their communications with patients about those treatments which nurses, physiotherapists and health professionals other than doctors can supply, a practice can deal more effectively with an increased volume of activity and the complex health needs of their patients.

Building loyalty among customers for services has been described as 'frequency marketing' and has developed from the acceptance that promotion of the benefits of a particular product or service is a means of attracting and keeping brand loyalty. This kind of relationship marketing is especially concerned to identify, maintain and increase the custom from best customers, through long-term, interactive, value-added relationships. It involves the development of complementary promotional programmes which both tie in the customer more tightly to the organization and exploit the revenue potential of add-on services. Credit cards linked to a particular charity have become an important revenue-earner for some of the larger charities, and newsletters, tie-in purchases carrying logos, discounts, and other privileges are further examples of frequency marketing techniques.

Marketing management

All that has been discussed indicates that a quality-conscious organization has to engage thoroughly with a range of marketing activities. While marketing theories and principles were first developed to meet the needs of for-profit organizations making products, they are now widely applied throughout every organization that sees itself as customer oriented. It has been convincingly argued that marketing is a pervasive societal activity that has meaning beyond the narrow confines of the business environment and several key marketing concepts have been identified as relevant to the management of marketing activities for not-for-profit organizations (Kotler and Levy, 1969; Shapiro, 1973).

The marketing mix

The set of marketing tools has been reduced by McCarthy (1981) to the four P's: product, price, place, promotion. However, even with this oversimplified model there are many potential choices for applying the mix, given the complexity of each of the tools:

Product
quality features
optional features
service features
style
Price
list price
allowances
discounts
Place
distribution channels
geographical coverage
location transport
Promotion
advertising
personal promotion/relationships
promotional campaigns
public relations

Balancing the mix for each target segment involves decisions on the nature of the product/service to be offered, pricing policies, distribution and the type of promotion. Some elements of the mix can be changed quickly, while others take longer to develop, and this has to be taken into account in deciding where and how to target resources. A university can rapidly produce a new promotional brochure, but developing new degree programmes and teaching materials takes both much longer and a considerable proportion of available effort. Despite the criticism that there has been an overemphasis on the simplistic '4 P's' they do still retain their value for not-for-profit marketers if seen in this wider context:

1 *The product*   Every organization produces products, which can be:
    physical products
    services
    persons
    organizations
    ideas.
2 *Customers*   Every organization has to deal with many groups or stakeholders who are interested in their products, including:
    suppliers
    consumers
    directors
    'publics'
    the general public.

3 *The self-interest aspect of the transaction or exchange* The customer and the provider believe they are receiving greater value than they are giving up.
4 *The marketing task* This stresses the importance of satisfying customer needs. Marketing plans are designed by management to satisfy all the groups under the heading 'customer'.
5 *The marketing mix* These are the tools that marketers use and include:
product/service development
channels of distribution
pricing
communication.
6 *Distinctive competence* The organization concentrates on what it does best and so maximizes its effectiveness.

The concepts are closely linked, so that while self-interest impels customers to seek for the best way to fulfil their needs, the organization searches for the most efficient way to satisfy customers through the marketing task. Marketing therefore focuses on the nature of the transactions involved. The marketing mix describes a range of those tools available for satisfying customers and relating to other stakeholders, and the idea of distinctive competence means that organizations, with their limited resources, most usefully attempt to meet those needs which they can best serve.

The product

This takes many forms, and is more complex than the traditional product of a for-profit organization.

Physical products are often produced by not-for-profit organizations, particularly to support fund-raising. For example, even small parish churches will produce leaflets, a parish magazine and postcards for sale, and the larger cathedrals run sophisticated retail outlets with a range of associated goods: religious artefacts, gift items, stationery, books. Leisure services sell sports equipment and large municipal libraries frequently have publishing and bookselling activities which raise revenue.

Intangible services are more usually associated with not-for-profit organizations. They offer benefits and values which are perceived by the customer, but are often difficult to articulate and may include spiritual wellbeing, relaxation, emotional satisfaction.

Persons may be the subject of the organization's marketing. Evangelists like Billy Graham and politicians are examples of this focusing on the key people assets.

Organizations exert a great deal of effort in marketing themselves and their core activities. Charities such as Oxfam have worked hard over decades to publicize their work in a variety of countries and for a wide range of needs.

Ideas are a key aspect of many of the organizations considered in this book. Churches of all denominations exist for the purpose of evangelizing and sustaining their religious message; charities are as much concerned with promoting the needs of their targets to governments as with fund raising; and educators are in the business of promoting the values of education and lobbying for political support at both local and national levels, to ensure adequate funding.

Customers

This core concept has been considered above in the context of delivering a quality not-for-profit service. In managing marketing activities, it is essential that the organization is aware of the varying agendas and needs of the different groups, both customers and the various stakeholders. These are more complex than is usually found in for-profit organizations, where managing sensitive political and societal issues may be but is not invariably the key to effectiveness.

Self-interest

We have discussed this aspect of marketing in considering the behaviour of customers and how an organization can develop and sustain customer loyalty over the long term. Self-interest is particularly important in the not-for-profit sector as, typically, the kinds of services being offered together with the relationships desired are durable, that is they are expected to last more than three years. This characteristic was identified by Greenfield (1966) and remains an important consideration when considering how each transaction builds into a long-term relationship. It is also important for identifying how marketing concepts previously reserved for products can be implemented for services. Perishable transactions include such services as cinema shows or sports events, while the durable include education and health. However, there are few services which do not contain some element of the durable in their outcomes (Wilson, 1972).

The marketing task

The marketing planning process has tended in many organizations to focus on short-term tactical planning rather than the longer-term strategic planning which assesses the marketing needs for years rather than merely months ahead (Kinnell and Macdougall, 1994; McDonald, 1995). Building long-term relationships is such a key aspect of the operations of not-for-profit organizations that a strategic approach to marketing is essential. A strategic marketing plan will contain the following elements (McDonald, 1995):

- a mission or purpose statement;
- a financial summary;
- a market overview;
- the key market segments with a strengths, weaknesses, opportunities and threats (SWOTs) analysis for each;
- the key issues which need to be addressed in the planning period;
- a summary of the SWOTS;
- assumptions;
- objectives and strategies;
- resource requirements.

Focusing on the customer profile will form much of the activity; this offers particular challenges in a not-for-profit environment. The Pareto effect, known as the 80/20 rule, where 20 per cent of the customers account for 80 per cent of the business means that organizations need to identify the 20 per cent of customers and potential customers where targeting most of their resources would bring the most efficient outcome. Those segments which will best repay the organization's expenditure of time and effort may not, however, be the only segments which the organization *should* be targeting to meet its overall corporate objectives. A public library could profitably just expend its efforts on children and the middle-class elderly, who make up a considerable proportion of library users. Adolescents, though, especially those with low reading scores, are seen as an important target group precisely because at present they make up such a proportionately low percentage of users. The mission of the public library is to provide a service to all of its community, and effectiveness, not just efficiency, dictates that those presently using libraries least should be prime marketing targets.

Marketing objectives should therefore relate to the corporate objectives of the organization, to its core mission and to the values it espouses. Strategic planning and the consequent setting of marketing objectives are described as 'the managerial process of developing and maintaining a viable fit between the organization's objectives and resources and its changing market opportunities' (Kotler, 1988). For many not-for-profit organizations market opportunities will be represented by those groups not presently being effectively served by the organization. Churches and religious organizations were established to proselytize and to save sinners, not just to minister to the faithful. Ansoff's (1957) product/market expansion grid can be profitably used to gauge whether organizations – even churches – could gain more market share from their current products in existing markets (market-penetration strategy), whether they can develop new products of potential interest to their existing market (product-development strategy) and then whether there are opportunities to develop new products for new markets (diversification strategy):

	Current products	New products
Current markets	1 Market-penetration strategy	3 Product-development strategy
New markets	2 Market-development strategy	4 Diversification strategy

Understanding the nature of the competitive threats to the organization is important in the not-for-profit sector, just as with for-profit businesses. This means that the nature of the business and the expectations of customers have to be fully understood and placed in the context of the organization's position in the marketplace. Gaining and sustaining market share is vital. In for-profit businesses there has to be a balance between leadership on cost (i.e. being the lowest-cost supplier) and leadership through having highly differentiated products (i.e. offering uniqueness) (Porter, 1980). In a school there would be need to estimate how far the school should offer additional subjects in the curriculum such as instrument tuition or a wide range of languages to attract new pupils and how the costs of these would impact on the core elements of curriculum delivery (teachers' salaries, textbook provision, technology).

Distinctive competence

What distinguishes highly successful organizations is their success in providing clearly differentiated products for their target markets. Quality is one of the best of all differentiators and, as we have seen, not-for-profit organizations rely heavily on the quality of the relationships they develop with their customers. Services have been characterized as being along a continuum in terms of customer interaction and customization. The challenge for managers is not only to define but also to manage these interactions and to provide the most relevant support for customer/organization relationships. Hospitals, for example, are relatively low in labour intensity, so that the role of information technology is important in managing capacity, scheduling and financial management. General practices, while still in the 'business' of healthcare, are, by contrast, much more highly customized, with a greater degree of personal interaction between doctors, health professionals and patients. Information technology is increasingly important in supporting the management of practices, but has not assumed the central role of information management and technology strategy in health service trusts.

Whatever the organizational setting, the quality of the customer's experience will depend on how effectively the distinctive attributes of the service are offered, and particularly on how the relationship between the customer and the organization has been nurtured and supported.

Conclusion

The complexity of the task facing marketers in not-for-profit organizations in developing and managing effective relationships with their customers and stakeholders has been outlined in this chapter. Understanding what quality service means for the organization and identifying the behaviour of its customers is an essential first stage in developing a marketing strategy. Equally, an organization which is committed to meeting the needs of its customers will need to retain a clear sense of its corporate objectives, to be aware of the 'business' it is in and the competitive threats it faces. Relationship marketing demands long-term, sustained effort in developing and implementing a marketing strategy, with the customer at the core of the activity and a willingness to use the full range of marketing techniques available. Through this approach, the marketing mix becomes a set of essential tools for developing strong and mutually rewarding relations between the organization, its customers and stakeholders.

References

Ansoff, I. (1957) Strategies for diversification. *Harvard Business Review,* September–October, 113–24.

Berry, L.L., Parasuraman, A. and Zeithaml, V.A. (1990) Quality counts in services, too. In Clark, G. (ed.), *Managing Service Quality,* IFS Publications, pp. 3–11.

Blois, K.K.J. (1996) Relationship marketing in organizational markets: when is it appropriate? *Journal of Marketing Management,* **12**, 161–73.

British Standards Institution (1991) *Quality vocabulary: Part 2. Concepts and related institutions,* BSI, BS 4778, Part 2.

Bullivant, J. (1994) *Benchmarking for Continuous Improvement in the Public Sector*, Longman, p. 1.

Buttle, F. (1996) SERVQUAL: review, critique, research agenda. *European Journal of Marketing*, **30** (1), 8–32.

Christy, R., Oliver, G. and Penn, J.(1996) Relationship marketing in consumer markets. *Journal of Marketing Management*, **12**, 175–87.

East, R. (1990) *Changing Consumer Behaviour*, Cassell.

Feigenbaum, A.V. (1983) *Total Quality Control*, 3rd edn, McGraw-Hill.

Foxall, G.R. and Goldsmith, R.E. (1994) *Consumer Pyschology for Marketing*, Routledge, p. 22.

Ghobadian, A. (1994) Service quality concepts and models. *International Journal of Quality and Reliability Management*, **11** (9), 43–66.

Greenfield, H.I. (1966) *Manpower and the Growth of Producer Services*, Columbia University Press.

Gronroos, C. (1983) *Strategic Management and Marketing in the Service Sector*, Marketing Science Institute, Chapter 14.

Gronroos, C. (1990a) Relationship approach to marketing in service contexts: the marketing and and organizational behaviour interface. *Journal of Business Research*, **20**, 3–11.

Gronroos, C. (1990b) A service quality model and its marketing implications. In Clark, G. (ed.), *Managing Service Quality*, IFS Publications, pp. 13–18.

Gummesson, E. (1987) The new marketing-developing long-term interactive relationships. *Long Range Planning*, **20** (4), 10–20.

Kinnell, M. and MacDougall, J. (1994) *Meeting the Marketing Challenge: Strategies for public libraries and leisure services*, Taylor Graham.

Kotler, P. (1988) *Marketing Management: Analysis, planning, implementation and control*, 6th edn, Prentice Hall, pp. 33, 141–2.

Kotler, P. and Andreasen, A.R. (1996) *Strategic Marketing for Non-profit Organizations*, Prentice Hall.

Kotler, P. and Levy, S.J. (1969) Broadening the concept of marketing. *Journal of Marketing*, **33** (1), 10–15.

Line, M.B. (1995) Needed: a pathway through the swamp of management literature. *Library Management*, **16** (1), 36–8.

Lynch, J.A. (1993) *Managing the Delight Factor*, IFS International, pp. 209–16.

McCarthy, E.J. (1981) *Basic Marketing*, Irwin.

McDonald, M.H.B. (1995) *Marketing Plans: How to prepare them, how to use them*, 3rd edn, Butterworth-Heinemann.

Oakland, J.S. (1995) *Total Quality Management: Text with cases*, Butterworth-Heinemann, pp. 4–5.

Parasuraman, A., Zeithaml, V.A. and Berry, L.L. (1985) A conceptual model of service quality and its implications for future research. *Journal of Marketing*, **49**, Fall, 41–50.

Peters, T.J. (1988) *Thriving on Chaos*, Knopf, p. 96.

Porter, M.E. (1980) *Competitive Strategy: Techniques for analyzing industries and competitors*, Free Press, Chapter 2.

Rooney, E.M. (1988) A proposed quality system specification for the National Health Service. *Quality Assurance*, **14** (2).

Shapiro, B.P. (1973) Marketing for nonprofit organizations. *Harvard Business Review*, **51** (5), 123–32.

Shedlock, J. (1988) Defining the quality of medical reference service. *Medical Reference Services Quarterly*, **7** (1), 49–53.

Taylor, L.T. (1992) *Quality: Total customer service*, Century Business, pp. xv–xvi.

Taylor, L.T. (1993) *Quality: Sustaining customer service*, Century Business, pp 134–56.

Wilson, A. (1972) *The Marketing of Professional Services*, McGraw-Hill, p. 7.

Further reading

Bullivant, J. (1994) *Benchmarking for Continuous Improvement in the Public Sector*, Longman.

Gummesson, E. (1987) The new marketing-developing long-term interactive relationships. *Long Range Planning*, **20** (4), 10–20.

Kotler, P. and Andreasen, A.R. (1996) *Strategic Marketing for Non-profit Organizations*, Prentice Hall.

Shapiro, B.P. (1973) Marketing for nonprofit organizations. *Harvard Business Review*, **51** (5), 123–32.

CHAPTER 3

Managing change in schools

Summary

The Education Reform Act 1988 introduced a much greater emphasis on the market in education, with Local Management of Schools and enhanced parental choice in schooling. Concern for the loss of democratic control has been voiced, but schools are faced with the need to operate in an increasingly competitive environment and to provide measures of their performance. Schools have also become customers for services and have to manage their budgets to buy back services previously provided centrally. The role of marketing has therefore become more significant, to support school development planning.

Introduction

The passing of the Education Reform Act 1988 signalled a concern bordering on obsession with the quality of schooling in England and Wales and a change to the system of funding and controlling schools. One of the peculiarities of the UK education system is this continuing national cultural basis for education, despite long-standing political union, while the actual delivery of state education has always been a matter for the local education authorities. There has not been the anxiety over standards nor the concern for a rigid legislative structure to control the curriculum and management of schools in Scotland or Northern Ireland that has been shown for England and Wales. It is important at the outset, therefore, to recognize the varying context within which the marketing of schools has been undertaken across the UK in recent years. The changes imposed on English schools have been gradually assimilated into the rest of the UK, but the changes elsewhere have been neither so sudden nor so dramatic in their impact on the management of schooling as they have in England and Wales.

In addition to the state sector in the UK, there are also around 2500 independent schools which educate at present around 600 000 children (although the numbers appear to be growing) and which provide education independently of local and national government structures. Their funding comes from fees and endowments and while some run like private businesses, most of the larger and better-known operate as charitable foundations. Approaches to marketing from the independent sector also have some bearing therefore on the education sector generally; their long experience in developing relationships with parents and sponsors is now being emulated by state schools.

There are about 26 000 state nursery or primary schools, and 5000 secondary schools, attended by over 90 per cent of all children. Different kinds of state school are in existence, resulting partly from the history of church involvement in education and partly from the terms of the 1988 Act:

- local education authority schools;
- voluntary schools, originally provided by voluntary bodies, usually churches, which are now part local authority and part voluntary funded;
- grant-maintained schools which have opted out of local authority control and are funded directly by central government;
- special schools run by local education authorities for children with special educational needs.

The Education Reform Act 1988 had a profound and wide-ranging impact on schools, and its provisions were further enhanced by the Education Act 1993 which abolished the requirements to establish an education committee in a local authority, following the arguments presented in a Government White Paper (Department for Education and The Welsh Office, 1992). The 1988 Act was the most sweeping reforming legislation since the Education Act 1944 which established the pattern of post-war schooling and set up the grammar, secondary modern and technical schools. These remained as the basis for secondary schooling until the comprehensive movement of the 1960s halted selectivity at the age of 11 and brought the almost blanket rejection of the 11-plus examination. Some areas have retained selection at 11 for entry into those few grammar schools which have survived, but the majority of children do not undergo formal selection procedures on entry into secondary education.

The 1988 Act did not remove this anomaly of vestigial selectivity, but instead created mechanisms to enable schools to opt out of local authority control and become grant maintained and also to curb the powers of local education authorities in managing the budgets of schools. The complexity of provision was therefore retained, while changes to the basis of funding have created the most significant of the marketing opportunities for schools. As we discuss below, though, there are mixed views on the extent to which a truly commercial marketplace exists. Paradoxically, the potential for marketing has also caused problems in the provision of some services to schools. Changes to the curriculum with the enforcement for the first time of a National Curriculum across England and Wales have also brought with them threats as well as opportunities for schools.

Demographic changes, too, have been significant. Secondary schools have been closed in recent years or merged, due to the falling numbers of pupils aged 11–18, so that the choices available to parents for single-sex schools or co-educational schools have been disappearing in many parts of the country in recent years. By 1992, there were just 250 girls-only schools left in the UK and the numbers continue to decline (Baker, 1992).

In this chapter the complex environment within which schools operate will be discussed and the marketing opportunities available to them considered. The arguments for and against a marketing ethos in education also require analysis, as there remain concerns among educators at the new values which it is felt have been imposed on schools. Because many of the threats have appeared for secondary schools, due to falling rolls, the emphasis will lie with them. The most difficult challenge facing secondary head teachers and governors has been that of managing change effectively in an increasingly competitive situation. While marketing techniques have particular relevance in this sector, there remain questions about the extent to which they should be used, and also which are the most helpful.

Markets and democratic control

Many of the arguments for a more consumer-oriented and market-led education service, which underpinned the 1988 Act and subsequent legislation, relate to the problems identified not only in UK schools but also in the USA (Rosario, 1986). There, too, it was argued that schools were failing because local democratic controls were stifling and coercive, rather than balancing the needs of all children and enabling a market to emerge. Enabling parents to choose the school they wanted for their child and developing competition between schools emerged as the most important issues. Power struggles at the local level were felt to have created victors who imposed their values on the system and lobbied for their own particular emphasis in both curriculum content and peda-gogical styles: 'bilingual education', 'the socialization of immigrants', 'what history to teach' (Chubb and Moe, 1990). It was considered that a market should be created because 'institutions work when people choose them' (Ranson, 1993). While it was acknowledged that a market-driven system also had its imperfections and had to be operated with due regard to professional needs, it was argued by Tooley (1988), looking at the UK situation, that a combination of market mechanisms, good management and strong leadership and teamwork from the teaching profession would offer more effective schooling.

The Conservative government's development of a new market-centred education system based on this philosophy has, though, created criticism of the basis for a market-led approach. So-called 'free choices' in schooling have been argued as having created more problems for the delivery of education than they have solved. It has been found that rather than empowering customers, the new system has instead em-powered educational providers who are able to be more selective of their pupils. The customer focus of marketing in other service organiza-tions, which target specific market segments, is felt not to be applicable to education. An education service has to balance the needs of all pupils in a community and organize schooling for everyone, catering for all abilities, and all religious and cultural groups. Segmentation of the market by some schools, on a free-for-all basis is therefore not deemed socially or organizationally desirable. When schools enter niche markets they promote an image of themselves which is distinctive and com-petitive and can result in a hierarchy of esteem which may reduce opportunity for the many in an area (Tomlinson, 1988).

These are more than philosophical arguments: they confront all head teachers and governors as they work within the new market-oriented environment created by the legislative framework. City technology col-leges, for example, which were established following the 1988 Act, have faced particular criticisms of their elitist and IT-centred approach which could be seen to deny opportunity to children within their catchment area whose parents are seeking a more rounded educational offering for them. Despite these criticisms of the market, though, schools such as Garibaldi School in Mansfield, described in detail in Chapter 12, have exploited to the full the opportunities offered not only by a more customer-oriented philosophy but also the tools and techniques of marketing to improve their product and serve the whole of their community more effectively. There is also evidence from the case of Kent that perceptions of competitiveness among schools predate the 1988 Act and that a market-driven ethos was already well established: perceptions of the relevance of a marketing philosophy had been growing during the 1980s following the Education Act 1980 which had confirmed parents' rights to choose a school for their child. In 1987, MORI was commissioned by Kent County Council to undertake a study of public attitudes to services, including education. They found that local consumers were dissatisfied with the limited choice of schools, and that schools themselves generally already felt they were in competition with one another.

> Schools saw that a competitive edge could be gained through marketing and 'flagships'. A flagship, in this instance, refers to alternative uses of school property. They were special projects that raised the profile of the school as well as generating income such as bookshops and IT suites (Common, Flynn and Mellon, 1992).

Defenders of a market-based education service would argue that, at a period when the numbers of potential pupils of secondary schol age are falling, schools are inevitably competing for students. Gaining a competitive edge is therefore an inherent part of managers' concerns, and marketing provides the essential tools to help achieve this.

Local management of schools

Undoubtedly, the implementation of Local Management of Schools (LMS), with the emphasis on consumer choice following the 1988 Act, has focused schools even more firmly on the significance of marketing. The principle set down in the Act was simple. Schools' budgets were to be largely devolved directly to them to spend as they saw fit, given that funds had to be found for the following:

- staffing;
- internal building repairs and maintenance;
- cleaning;
- books, stationery, equipment;
- postage and telephones;
- rates and rent;

- energy;
- examination fees.

Schools now became the strategic business units, rather than local education authorities, and there was an assumption that financial planning became an integral part of the school's overall planning processes, including curriculum planning. There was also the option for schools to come out of local authority control completely, and become 'grant-maintained', that is, to receive their funding directly from central government rather than through the local education authority. While fewer schools took this route than the Conservative government had hoped, the possibility of becoming virtually an independent school within the public sector created further choices for governing bodies and parents. For even the majority of schools who have decided to stay within the local education authority's ambit, there has, though, been much greater freedom of action as well as greater responsibility than ever before. Schools – their head teachers and governing bodies – now have both the authority and largely the accountability for their actions, particularly in relation to how they spend their budgets.

This has had obvious attractions for schools, but there were some problems associated with the new regime. For 'winning' schools, able to attract and retain pupils – especially post-16 – the change to a rigid system of formula funding, which meant that funding was in line with pupil numbers, could offer the security of level or enhanced funding. But for schools in difficult inner-city areas who have found it difficult to recruit new pupils, there is the prospect of a downward spiral of low attainment levels, falling rolls and continuing low funding. Garibaldi School is an example of just such a school which faced this scenario following the 1988 Act, but whose head teacher and senior management team have turned this situation around. For similar schools in areas of deprivation which have not succeeded in meeting these challenges the consequences have been stark.

The Ridings School in Halifax, West Yorkshire, which was the subject of much media interest during the autumn of 1996 (BBC, 1996) when its teachers threatened to strike because of pupil unrest, had been created from two schools with falling numbers. There was still a selective system in operation in West Yorkshire, which meant that The Ridings, described by its former head teacher as a 'sink school', was competing for pupils with grammar schools and other comprehensives. Higher-ability children from its feeder primaries were being 'creamed off' to other more successful schools, which created a sense of low self-esteem in those who attended The Ridings. This exacerbated a cycle of poor attainment, low expectations and behaviour problems among pupils. While an inspection undertaken by the Office for Standards in Education (Ofsted) identified poor teaching, and a lack of effective management in the school and from the education authority as contributory factors, the context within which The Ridings was established and was having to attract pupils was also not a 'level playing field'. It is apparent that, with the 1988 Act, a market has been created which has offered choices to some parents and children, but that the operation of this market has been variable across the country. Unlike the environment in which Garibaldi operates – a wholly comprehensive system where no selection is practised at the end of primary schooling – The Ridings had to contend with its potentially most able pupils entering local grammar schools. In West Yorkshire, where The Ridings school lacked the management effectiveness which had been achieved in Garibaldi School, the consequence was that choices actually became more limited for those parents whose children were not able to gain admission elsewhere.

The operation of LMS has also caused problems for the provision of services to schools, services which used to be centrally provided and which still directly impact on the quality of education. Schools library services, for example, provided for decades by public library authorities acting as agents for local education authorities, are now threatened with closure in some areas. Their budgets have been devolved to schools and buying-in to these centralized services has become an option that many schools have rejected (Heeks and Kinnell, 1992). The effect of this has been to force these services to take on a commercial role and to enter the new education marketplace alongside commercial suppliers such as booksellers. The ways in which services originally provided for schools were handed over to them for funding support underpinned the whole marketing ethos of LMS. Schools were to be responsive to the choices made by parents, and, at the same time, were themselves to be exercising choices about which services they bought from the local education authority. Schools had become customers as well as providers.

Education services

Education services which had previously been provided to all schools by the education authority from centralized funding became delegated to schools. In the early 1980s Cambridgeshire education authority pioneered the original concept of local financial management, before LMS was imposed nationally, and so was well placed to provide for the progressive delegation of full financial and staffing powers to schools, which it did from April 1991 to April 1993. The Education Department was restructured to meet the changing needs of schools and colleges and the old area administrative arrangements were replaced by named officers with functional responsibilities. Schools were allocated budgets which represented not just their share of the LMS budget for the year but also their share of the total council budget for the Education Service. While schools would be required to pay back to the authority those sums which were necessary for the authority's statutory duties (for example, 'statementing' of pupils with special needs), all resources for support services were delegated to schools to spend as they wished, not necessarily on education authority services. These services were wide-ranging, and included: personnel, legal, payroll, management, curriculum, and library services. The continued provision and scale of these services, which now began to operate as business units, were determined by their competitiveness and the preparedness of schools to buy the services from their delegated budgets. The schools library service, for example, which supported curriculum delivery in schools and had operated from within the education authority, then became a semi-independent unit and embarked on a promotional campaign to schools in order to convince them to buy back into the service as part of the wider education authority marketing drive for all of its services (Cambridgeshire County Council, 1992). Booklets were circulated to schools outlining the various products offered by the central services, with information on:

- the price of each service;
- a brief description of each service;
- a summary of those statutory services that continued to be funded centrally;
- a list of contacts for further information;
- an order form;
- a questionnaire to give head teachers the opportunity to comment on services.

The schools library service, which had been operating as a county-wide service since the local government reorganization of 1974, had become one of the best resourced in the country (Heeks and Kinnell, 1992). It had a high national profile and was therefore one of the first of Cambridgeshire education authority's services which it was felt could develop an appropriate marketing strategy in the new circumstances.

It was set up as a business unit in April 1991 and began to operate on commercial lines. With a potential market of all the education authority and grant-maintained schools within the county, each of whom had previously been able to access the service, there was a considerable effort to maintain the existing high level of support. By 1993, only a few schools were not buying into the service, and buying-back continued to be high. Following its establishment as a business, publications and consultancy work were also targeted to a wider, national market and software was beginning to be sold to several other schools library services.

Tangibilizing the benefits provided to schools was a particular concern at the beginning of the promotional campaign. Many schools were aware of the benefits of the service:

- loans of books and other materials for pupils and teachers;
- advice on resource selection and purchases;
- support for the organization and use of learning resources;
- development of learning and information-handling skills;
- advice on information technology within the school's library resource centre;
- planning and design of library resource centres;
- advice on the management and development of the centres;
- information, advice and in-service training for teachers, governors, librarians and ancillary staff.

These now had to be translated into terms which would be meaningful to schools, and which related to their concerns both as customers for the service and providers of education. In order to continue to delight their customers – i.e. the schools – the schools library service had to focus on three key issues (Smith, 1993):

- the availabilty of easily accessible expert, quality advice and support in schools when it was required;
- the availability of large quantities of the widest range of quality learning resources when they were required;
- the efficient provision of the resources into the school by the quickest methods of at-the-door delivery and collection.

As schools were in competition for pupils, in terms of both numbers and abilities, the excellence of their facilities was an important element in their marketing strategy. Parents ask about the range of support offered in schools, including the library, when comparing schools. The schools library service was therefore able to exploit this concern of schools to offer the best possible facilities, in order to promote its services. Before 1991, it had not been considered necessary to communicate the benefits of a service which was self-evidently so valuable. There was an assumption that the service existed and that schools who wished to use it would do so.

After 1991, the levying of charges directly from schools required consultation with the customers (schools, head teachers, governors) and the provision of more accurate and explicit information and statements of levels of service. Value statements, detailing the financial value received by an individual school from the schools library service, were helpful to decision makers; these demonstrated that schools often received as much as ten times the resources from buying into the service, and that it was more economical to borrow than try to buy books. Other promotional activities were also established by use of the local media: press, radio and television, with the support of the County Council's Press and Public Relations Section. A logo and letterhead were designed to develop a corporate identity, with business cards for senior staff, and information folders. The high national profile of staff continued to develop through contributions to professional conferences, advisory groups and articles in the professional press. The result has been the survival of this service, when others around the country have failed. Whether an enhanced level of service provision has been the result is more difficult to ascertain. Customer surveys indicate a high level of satisfaction on the part of schools, but comparing pre- and post-1991 provision is difficult, as the basis for the questions changed. Value for money became a consideration which had previously not entered into the relationship between the service and its customers.

Schools' customers and stakeholders

The Cambridgeshire case shows that an environment in which schools became customers themselves has been the means of focusing on those relationships which are important to schools. Most significant following the 1988 Act has been the building of links with the local community and especially with parents and potential pupils. Following the Act, the consumer had become all-important. This created difficulties in the minds of some professionals, who had been accustomed to delivering education as a result of their training and professional experience. Public providers of services such as social services, health and education have eschewed marketing practices partly because of this perception that professional judgements will be at risk and also open to scrutiny – of a political as well as professional kind. However, the greater accountability being asked of all services in the public sector has meant that schools, like other services, have had to accept the rights of their customers to question the quality of services which they pay for through taxation and to expect politicians who are accountable to the public to exert controls and measures to monitor and develop standards.

In order to market itself successfully, a school, like any other organization, has to identify customer expectations and to provide a service which meets them. As we argued when considering relationship marketing, though, there remains the responsibility of educators and other service providers in not-for-profit organizations to ensure that standards exceed those which are the result of low expectations on the part of poorly informed consumers. Professional judgement has to be a key component of the development of the product, as the customer may simply not know what can be achieved. This is particularly true in communities which, like that of Garibaldi School, may not have experienced what a good school can and should do for children. Also, what parents and pupils expect from a school before they register may change after they have gained experience of it (Stillman and Meychell, 1986). An investigation into the main factors which were important to parents and children, largely composed of professionals' views (teachers and governors) but which also used inputs from parents and pupils, has identified a list that can be used by schools in determining their appeal and considering how they meet general expectations, although the point was made that each community will have specific needs. For secondary schools the factors included (Dennison, 1989):

- the quality of the buildings;
- location of the school;
- history and traditions of the school;
- characteristics of the catchment area;
- the caring attributes of the school;
- the organization of parents' evenings and other visits to the school;
- examination and test results;
- the quality of the teaching, including the implementation of a home-work policy;
- the range and quality of extra-curricular activities;
- published reports of the school from government and local authority inspections;
- length and arrangement of the school day;
- links with feeder schools;
- links with employers, further and higher education;
- children's behaviour outside school;
- children's behaviour inside school;
- school uniform policy;
- the unoffical grapevine of comment about the school;
- quality of information sent to parents;
- quality of the school brochure;
- number of feeder schools receiving the brochure;
- adverse comments made about competitor schools;
- attitude of the media towards the school;
- volume of good publicity about pupil achievements, etc.;
- level of school involvement in and with the community;
- the profile achieved by the head, staff and governors of the school.

The product: quality and performance

In a service like a school, which relies on high levels of contact between the immediate customers (children and parents) and the school, and the development of relationships with a wide range of stakeholders, controlling the delivery of the product is a particular problem. Services which are characterized by high customer contact are regarded as inevitably limited in the efficiency they can achieve, because of the uncertainty that people introduce into processes (Chase, 1992). The heterogeneity which is inherent in the output of education services also means that conformity is difficult to achieve. Even when it has been decided what constitutes quality of educational delivery, the extent to which this can be efficiently provided and effectiveness can be measured is therefore problematic.

The list of factors above go some way to providing performance indicators that have relevance to customers, but the difficulty arises when translating these into measures which can then be meaningfully applied. In the educational context, a performance indicator has been defined as 'a statement against which achievement in an area or activity can be assessed', but indicators 'are also useful for setting goals and clarifying objectives . . . there is a place for both quantitative and qualitative indicators. For the purpose of school improvement, performance indicators should reflect a synthesis of local education authority, national and local aims and be constructed in such a way as to provide signposts for development' (Hopkins and Leask, 1989). Indicators for schools are therefore being expected to satisfy at least two, competing, demands: assessment and goal setting .

The National Curriculum introduced following the 1988 Act, which all state schools in England and Wales had to teach, had a profound impact on the delivery of education and on the ways its effectiveness was to be measured. For many teachers the new curriculum was felt at the outset to be a constraining influence on them, for others it was seen as a positive means of reassessing their teaching and the role of the school in furthering wide objectives, not just the narrow delivery of subject knowledge. There was a new emphasis on overarching skills such as information technology and also on the basic reading and numeracy skills which had been considered to be falling behind those of the UK's competitors. However, in a study of the impact of the National Curriculum on schools (Weston, Barrett and Jamison, 1993) it was found that there were real problems for schools in developing a coherent curriculum from the ten separately designed subject blocks of the National Curriculum. It was felt that there was too much prescription, with schools having to adhere to strict guidelines which were designed to ensure rationalization and assist the measurement of specific educational targets, but without adequate consideration of how the curriculum as a whole would be experienced by individual children. Coherence between elements of the curriculum was particularly difficult to achieve in secondary schools. Teachers, some of the key stakeholders in schools, were not wholeheartedly in favour of a change which imposed a rigid framework and ran counter to the previous autonomy of schools in devising a curriculum to meet the needs of their pupils. While curriculum development had always taken account of the constraints of public examinations: GCSE, 'A' Levels, City and Guilds, etc., for pupils from the ages of 11–16, secondary schools had been left relatively free to design their programmes to meet objectives set by the school, in liaison with the local education authority. For the first time in the history of education in the UK national standards of attainment were set which compelled schools to consider how subjects were being delivered across the age ranges, and to compare their results with those achieved elsewhere. Examination league tables became important as a means of schools proving their effectiveness in the terms determined by government.

There were a number of difficulties for schools in implementing the measures. Schools have many more purposes than most commercial organizations, and determining the key indicators for a school's activities has been a particular problem. Part of the problem is that schools have not adequately prioritized their objectives (Gray and Jesson, 1990), but they have also had measures imposed upon them which have been quantitative rather than qualitative. There has been an emphasis on measuring what could be measured rather than evaluating what should be valued. An influential report, for example, suggested that one of the considerations which should influence government's choice of measures should be: 'ease of collection and monitoring of data (automated where possible)' (Coopers and Lybrand, 1988; Hedger, 1990).

Some of the most important ways in which 'schools make a difference' and are effective are not so readily measurable. Research on school effectiveness has shown that a school's values and its leadership are important components of success. The more effective schools have a sense of mission which is visible, if difficult to define. A study of six such American high schools showed that they had explicit ideologies which were shared and understood by teachers and pupils (Gray, 1993). All the stakeholders and customers owned the values and helped in creating the culture. The role of the head teacher and senior staff appeared to be crucial, as borne out by the experience at Garibaldi School, where a charismatic and visionary head teacher also played a major part in developing a mission for the school, with the support of teachers and governors. It is notable that in a study of leadership in schools, head teachers perceived LMS to be helpful in enhancing both school autonomy and their management role (Grace, 1995), which emphasizes the likelihood that leadership will grow in significance.

However, what most of the measures introduced since the 1988 Act (e.g. examination successes, truancy rates) have captured are the results not only of effective management but also of the impact on a school's performance of the social mix in an area. Weighting these scores to take account of social deprivation has proved particularly complex. The concept of measuring how effectively a school adds value to its pupils is beginning to be considered, but has not yet been implemented nationally.

A role for marketing?

There is a clear role for marketing in support of schools' drive to improve their product and to demonstrate effectiveness. Analysing a school's product can be seen as part of market research, but is also a means to developing relationships with customers. Successful independent schools continually monitor the performance of their pupils to check on the effectiveness of their product, and use these results and measures including examination performance and numbers gaining university entry as the means both to demonstrate their success and to build on their relationships with parents. Parents are involved in their children's performance through extensive reports, meetings, and celebrations of achievements: feedback from parents is expected and welcomed. This is also true of successful state schools. In Garibaldi School, parents were regularly invited to provide views on the school's strengths, weaknesses, opportunities and threats in collaboration with teachers and governors. Parents were involved both as customers and as partners in the delivery of education, so that when a pupil was disruptive, their parents were invited to participate with them in lessons – an effective means of ensuring control. In Cambridgeshire, the Cambridge Accountability Project used questionnaires to parents to receive feedback on their perceptions of a school and its various services and this was fed into school development planning (Davies and Ellison, 1991). An effective information system provides not only data on customer satisfaction and views on development but also information about the market itself: its structure, location, trends. Existing databases of pupils can be used to support marketing by revealing changes in recruitment patterns, and potential for promotion (Pardey, 1991).

The impetus of LMS has been to require schools to produce development plans which require this kind of marketing information. They are likely to be most effective when they offer (Smetherham, 1989):

- statements against which achievements can be assessed;
- signposts in support of the planning and decision-making process;
- organizational targets against which progress can be measured.

With the responsibility for planning now in the hands of head teachers and governors rather than the local education authority, there is also need for each school to have a marketing strategy. This will consider how the school can position itself in the marketplace in order to attract pupils and also to sustain competitiveness, and what marketing efforts need to be developed, especially relationship marketing.

So complex is the environment for schools following the changes introduced in the 1988 Act that marketing tools and techniques have become increasingly relevant. It is probable that even with a change of government the emphasis on competition and on accountability will remain; the move to a consumer-oriented education service appears unstoppable. Despite criticism that an overemphasis on marketing has been detrimental to equity in provision, school managers are likely, increasingly, to see marketing as an important element of their strategic management needs. As the examples in this chapter have shown, marketing principles are being applied to a wide range of issues now confronting schools, in their new roles as both customers and providers.

Issues

1 The legislative context for educational provision in England and Wales and the complexity of other aspects of the operating environment.
2 The establishment of a market and its impact on providers and customers.
3 Local management of schools and the provision of services to schools.

Questions

1 How has the operating environment changed for schools in England and Wales since 1988?
2 To what extent is a true market for secondary education now operating?
3 How significant is the role of the school as the strategic business unit, compared with that of the local education authority?
4 Who are the key customers and stakeholders?
5 What are the major elements making for a quality school, from the point of view of both customers and stakeholders – are there different expectations by each group?
6 How can quality be measured?
7 To what extent is marketing planning in place in the examples offered in this chapter?
8 What is the relevance of the marketing mix to schools?

References

Baker, M. (1992) *A Parents' Guide to the New Curriculum*, BBC Books.

BBC (1996) *Panorama* programme, 4 November.

Cambridgeshire County Council Education Service (1992) *Education Support Services: secondary schools. A guide to help schools make their buying decisions for the academic year 1992/3*, Cambridgeshire County Council.

Chase, R.B. (1992) The customer contact approach to services: theoretical bases and practical extensions. In Lovelock, C.H. (ed.), *Managing Services: Marketing, operations and human resources*, 2nd edn, Prentice Hall International, pp. 43–8.

Chubb, J. and Moe, T. (1990) *Politics, Markets and America's Schools*, Brookings Institution.

Common, R., Flynn, N. and Mellon, E. (1992) *Managing Public Services: Competition and decentralization*, Butterworth-Heinemann, pp. 81–2.

Coopers and Lybrand (1988) *Local Management of Schools*, HMSO.

Davies, B. and Ellison, L. (1991) *Marketing the Secondary School*, Longman, pp. 67–70.

Dennison, W.F. (1989) The competitive edge – attracting more pupils. *School Organization*, **9** (2), 179–86.

Department for Education and The Welsh Office (1992) *Choice and Diversity: A new framework for schools*, HMSO, Cm 2021.

Grace, G. (1995) *School Leadership: Beyond education management*, Falmer Press, pp. 115–41.

Gray, J. (1993) The quality of schooling: frameworks for judgement. In Preedy, M. (ed.), *Managing the Effective School*, Paul Chapman/Oxford University Press, pp. 23–37.

Gray, J. and Jesson, D. (1990) The negotiation and construction of performance indicators: some principles, proposals and problems. *Evaluation and Research in Education*, **4** (2), 93–108.

Hedger, J. (1990) Performance indicators: an internal management tool? *Head Teachers Review*, Spring, 6–8.

Heeks, P. and Kinnell, M. (1992) *Managing Change for School Library Services*, British Library.

Hopkins, D. and Leask, M. (1989) Performance indicators and school development. *School Organization*, **9** (1), 3–20.

Pardey, D. (1991) *Marketing for Schools*, Kogan Page, pp. 91–120.

Ranson, S. (1993) Markets or democracy for education. *British Journal of Educational Studies*, **41** (4), 333–352.

Rosario, J.R. (1986) Excellence, school culture, and lessons in futility: another case against simplistic views of educational change. *Journal of Curriculum Studies*, **18** (1), 31–43.

Smetherham, D. (1989) Developing high performance through institutional development plans. *School Organization*, **9** (1), 157–67.

Smith, M. (1993) Cambridgeshire schools library service. In Broome, M. and Ashcroft, M. (eds), *The 'Business' of Schools Library Services*, Capital Planning Information.

Stillman, A. and Meychell, K. (1986) *Choosing Schools: Parents, LEAs and the 1980 Education Act*, NFER-Nelson.

Tomlinson, J. (1988) Curriculum and the market: are they compatible? In Haviland, J. (ed.), *Take Care, Mr Baker*, Fourth Estate.

Tooley, J. (1988) *A Market-led Alternative to the Curriculum: Breaking the code*, Institute of Education.

Weston, P., Barrett, E. and Jamison, J. (1993) Curriculum coherence: reviewing the quest. In Preedy, M. (ed.), *Managing the Effective School*, Paul Chapman/Oxford University Press, pp. 68–76.

Further reading

Common, R., Flynn, N. and Mellon, E. (1992) *Managing Public Services: Competition and decentralization*, Butterworth-Heinemann.

Davies, B. and Ellison, L. (1991) *Marketing the Secondary School*, Longman.

Gray, J. (1993) The quality of schooling: frameworks for judgement. In Preedy, M. (ed.), *Managing the Effective School*, Paul Chapman/Oxford University Press, pp. 23–37.

CHAPTER 4

Quality marketing in further and higher education

Summary

The environment in which universities and colleges practise marketing is both complex and threatening, with competition now a major issue. Funding is a particular problem, but defining the product also presents difficulties, as the goals of universities are very varied. The market has widened considerably to include targets who were previously not accessing higher and further education. Developing relationships with the range of customers and stakeholders has beome a more significant aspect of marketing, and defining objectives and measuring performance is now complex. The example of marketing to overseas students highlights the range of issues faced by institutions and the need to develop a more strategic, relationship-focused approach.

Introduction

Like schools, colleges and universities have experienced and are continuing to face dramatic changes to their environment and to the ways in which their operations are conducted. The most significant change of all has been one of culture. From being organizations which relied on tradition and a secure income from funders – whether local education authorities in the case of colleges and the old polytechnics or the funding councils for universities – they have been forced to become enterprises which can, if they fail, go out of business. This possibility is highly challenging for the FE and HE sectors where security, especially job security, was previously taken for granted.

Education reforms have meant that local education authorities have not only lost much of their power over schools; from April 1993, they also lost control altogether of further education colleges, which were then incorporated as free-standing, independent institutions funded by a national funding body. As with schools, new funding formulae meant that money followed students. Touche Ross's Education Sector Group, who undertook a survey of the further education sector for the Department for Education commented that:

> Effective marketing capabilities will be essential to the success and prosperity of FE colleges following incorporation. Not only will colleges be competing to attract students, they will depend increasingly on diversifying their activities and income base so as to finance their future developments (Sargent, 1993).

Prior to this, local education authorities had prevented colleges openly competing with each other, and with schools, whose sixth forms were important to the maintenance of strong curricula and excellence in teaching. From 1993 onwards, local colleges have seen their positions as monopoly providers eroded as schools, too, have sought to maintain falling rolls and as other training providers have come into the marketplace – supported by the local Training and Enterprise Councils. Even before 1993, marketing activity was becoming more significant in the colleges sector, with the publication of guides to basic marketing techniques for college managers (Davies and Scribbins, 1985; Baber and Megson, 1986) and the establishment in 1991 of the Further Education Marketing Unit. There had been a lack of significant marketing expertise in colleges, though, before 1993: one estimate, from HEIST, a non-profit organization whose mission is to provide marketing and public relations support to the FE and HE sectors was that of the UK's 400 FE colleges, only a half had a marketing manager or equivalent and of those only a quarter were professional marketers.

Universities have also seen changes to their funding structures, with the transformation of the former polytechnics into universities in 1992 and their removal from local education authority control to that of the funding bodies for the sector as a whole. (Again, as with schooling, this is nationally distinct; Scotland, Wales and Northern Ireland are funded by separate means, although government policy has had similar impacts across the sector.) They now have the right to award their own degrees, thus creating a more competitive environment in home and overseas student recruitment, research funding, industrial and commercial sponsorship, the development and validation of courses from within their own institutions and for other institutions. The overseas market had traditionally been dominated by the 'old' universities and was seen as a particularly important area for competition.

Compared to colleges, universities already had a significant marketing function, and many of the new universities had particularly well-developed marketing units staffed by professional marketers. With their close links to industry and a vocational orientation, marketing was seen by them as a core activity, particularly to ensure effective competitiveness in the new context. The old universities, on the other hand, tended to have less centralized marketing functions, with student recruitment, relationships with former students, corporate fund-raising and the development of degree programmes handled separately. Coordinating these activities and recognizing them as 'marketing' was more of a problem in these institutions.

In this chapter the context in which marketing is being developed by the FE and HE sectors will be explored, especially with regard to issues of quality assurance. Maintaining the quality of the product is regarded as key to successful marketing in a sector where international competitiveness demands that British institutions retain their reputation for excellence. One of the difficulties which university managers face, however, is that new course development and the maintenance of standards is seen as an academic rather than a managerial activity. Developing relationships with university staff – key stakeholders in the business of higher education – is therefore an essential part of successful marketing. As many of the more interesting recent developments have taken place in universities, especially in the field of international marketing, the examples and cases in this chapter will be largely taken from them.

The marketing environment

Funding

The most threatening feature for both FE and HE institutions at present is the uncertain financial situation. Most universities are about to fall into deficit in the financial year 1997–8, according to an analysis by the Higher Education Funding Council for England (Higher Education Funding Council, England, 1996). The sector's £49 million surplus for 1995–6 will be reduced to a deficit of £13 million in 1996–7 and £58 million by 1999–2000. This means that universities' reserves will be needed to offset annual deficits, which will result in a lack of support for changes, and the need to reduce staffing levels in some institutions (by an estimated 1200 for the sector as a whole), the deferring or cancelling of capital programmes, cutting of maintenance and limits on new equipment. Capital expenditure is expected to fall between 1995–6 and 1999–2000 by 60 per cent.

There are wealthy institutions like Oxford and Cambridge which have endowments from patrons and considerable funding from the research councils and industry that will enable them to weather the financial stringencies government has imposed upon the sector. However, for the majority of the 181 HE institutions the funding situation is acknowledged to be parlous, with unit costs received per full-time equivalent student falling from almost £7000 per head in 1989–90 to just over £4500 per head in 1996–7 (Nye, 1996). Undergraduate students' fees are still paid out of public funds in the UK, so that universities are reliant on government to support their teaching activity, which is the largest element of their business. The situation is complicated by the fact that subjects like medicine, engineering or science are more expensive to teach, and so universities with more students in those areas will receive proportionately higher funding from their funding council than institutions with a preponderance of students in the humanites or social sciences. Equally, a university with more part-time students is likely to receive less money. There is concern at the poor levels of funding and a realization that government is unlikely to provide higher fees, with some contribution inevitably expected from students (Rigby, 1995). The Dearing Committee has been established to review the options, and to make recommendations on the shape, structure, size as well as funding of HE and FE, but the publication of its report was likely to be deferred until after the 1997 general election.

The product

The sector has dramatically expanded its delivery of teaching since the Robbins Report of 1963 led to a massive expansion of what was then an elite system of higher education which had relatively high entry requirements, usually measured by 'A' Level grades. From 400 000 students in 1965–6 the sector now has just over one and a half million full-time equivalent students, a participation rate of over 30 per cent of the population. This increased popularization of higher education took place particularly during the 1980s when 'public sector higher education' (PSHE) which was delivered by the polytechnics and colleges took on the role of providing higher education for all who might benefit from it, and dubbed the 'popular model of higher education' (Ball, 1988).

It has been argued that both models of education are needed – the elite and the popular – but with the restructuring of the sector to encompass the old polytechnics and the traditional universities the popular model is now growing in importance. The old universities have taken on many more of the features of the former polytechnic sector. An emphasis on external validation of quality, which the Council for National Academic Awards had provided for the polytechnics, has evolved into the Higher Education Quality Council (HEQC), whose mission is 'to contribute to the maintenance and improvement of quality, at all levels, in institutions of higher education in the United Kingdom.' The HEQC undertakes teaching quality assessments of subjects across the whole sector and is also involved in a range of other activities. Its Graduate Standards Programme, for example, is setting out to consider academic standards for first degrees and the means by which these may be articulated and assured (Higher Education Quality Council, 1995). Unlike schools, universities are still responsible for devising their own curricula and establishing and maintaining standards, but the introduction of a quality assurance system which began in the polytechnic sector and the increasing need for accountability to both funders and customers (students, parents, employers) has intensified the concern to both maintain and demonstrate quality.

A real difficulty for marketers concerned with quality in higher education institutions lies with the definition of their product. One assumption is that it mainly comprises the teaching programmes they offer. When assessing the quality of what they provide, though, government – still their major funder through support of the teaching and much of the research activity – will be assessing their overall activity, not just teaching and research programmes. Universities themselves will also have a view as to what are their 'products', a view formed by the academic community as well as by the institutions' managers (not necessarily one and the same). Four concepts have been identified in relation to this defining of the quality products of universities (Barnett, 1992):

1   Higher education as the production of qualified personnel. Students are the products, which have utility value on the labour market.
2   Higher education as a training for a research career. This is framed by those members of the academic community who are active in research. Research outputs such as publications and research income form the most important measures.
3   Higher education as the efficient management of teaching provision. Higher staff : student ratios and declining units of resource are

some of the measures used, with assumptions made that a high throughput and maximization of resources are indicators of quality.

4 Higher education as a matter of extending life chances.

Consumers of higher education see this as an important role, as it offers them the opportunity to participate more fully in society and provides them with access to its benefits. We will be assessing these varying views of universities' roles when considering goals and performance and how these may be related to a marketing strategy. It is helpful to emphasize at the outset that universities are not monolithic institutions with one simple product, and that their complexity makes the marketing task more difficult than in many other not-for-profit organizations.

The market

One of the greatest changes in universities has been in the kinds of people they have targeted and perceptions of the market for degree programmes. Under the elite model, the targets were traditionally school-leavers with three 'A' Levels, many of them from the old grammar and independent schools. Recruits were expected to demonstrate not only a willingness to learn and have innate ability but also a track record of successful academic achievement. During the 1980s, PSHE began to recruit more of its students from groups who had missed out on traditional public examinations, and whose abilities were measured in less conventional ways: through work experience, vocational examinations offered by City and Guilds or BTec, and professional training. Institutions targeted a wider student base, including women, mature students, ethnic minorities. To meet the needs of these groups, more flexible patterns of teaching and learning, with modular degree programmes and semesterized teaching timetables, were also developed.

However, at the same time as institutions were enhancing access and offering flexible learning, funding support for students was declining. There was concern therefore that a popular model of provision might not be sustained, due to the financial difficulties faced by students. A student loans system now operates, but students are still in debt after their studies and there is some evidence that more of them are leaving university early because of debt.

The overseas market continued to be important, especially for postgraduate education: students from countries outside the EU made up nearly a quarter of all UK postgraduates in 1995. As full-cost fees are charged for the overseas market, there is a huge incentive to institutions to recruit as many students as possible, but the UK also faces intense competition from HE providers in the USA, Australia and Canada, and from countries like Malaysia, which are now developing their own programmes, in order to educate students more cheaply at home.

Customers, stakeholders and relationship marketing

Customers for FE and HE institutions are, first, the students. Increasingly, parents are being regarded in the same light, for many of them are supporting students, through postgraduate fees and maintenance. Employers are another important customer group, with whom institutions need to make strong alliances. Frequently, they are also involved with colleges and universities as partners through industrial placements and in projects which students undertake. The stakeholders are numerous and include:

- government;
- funding bodies;
- research councils;
- professional bodies;
- employers' associations;
- trades unions;
- banks and other financial institutions.

FE and HE institutions are fully engaged in the movement from a transaction-based focus to the management of relationships between themselves and their customers, and with their numerous stakeholders. Payne and Ballantyne (1991) suggest six markets as a means of expanding marketing to account for such complexity and of bringing both customers and stakeholders fully into the marketing strategy. They can be related to FE and HE in the following ways:

1 *Customer markets* Establishing long-term relationships is the emphasis, rather than individual transactions. For a university this may mean rejecting an individual student from an overseas source, because of their poor qualifications and/or English skills, in order to sustain a quality output and retain the confidence of the funder. Building links over time through a sustained delivery of quality education will be the aim.

2 *Referral markets* It will be important to have referral sources, or advocates for the institution. UK subsidiaries in overseas countries can act as advocates for an institution, while university and college alumni often provide the best recommendations and advocacy to potential students.

3 *Supplier markets* Building trust between the institution and its suppliers, including: the business community, financial institutions, alumni, is essential as they play an important role in delivering quality products.

4 *Employee markets* Developing customer service through relationships with all staff in the institution is vital. Every transaction

within an institution between a member of staff and a student makes up the student's learning experience: catering staff, porters, technicians, library personnel, as well as lecturers, constitute the product from the student's viewpoint. Relationship marketing will therefore pay attention to human resource management and developing a strong sense of the organization's mission and the delivery of quality by its staff.

5   *Influencer markets*   Institutions will seek to develop relationships with government and other funders in order to influence policy. Other potential influencers include the general public, accrediting organizations and the business community.

6   *Internal markets*   Within the institution, each individual and department has a supplier and a customer and managing these relationships effectively is a key part of the marketing task. Academic departments will be receiving support ('supplies') from the admissions office, financial services, computer services, the estates office, etc. They will also have customers: their students. Managing interactions between their students and suppliers will comprise much of a department's activity and also needs to be viewed from a wider organizational standpoint to ensure that systems operate effectively both for suppliers, customers and the students.

Goals and performance

With so many complex relationships being managed, it has become difficult to define institutional goals with precision. In all organizations, there are competing power blocs and a number of factors in the environment which will influence values. The nature of the business universities and colleges are in is a product of the expectations of academics, government, society, students, employers and other stakeholders. Of all the general influences, it is suggested that the organization's *culture* is the most significant (Johnson and Scholes, 1989) and it is the one that is least easy to capture.

During the 1980s, as part of the reforms of higher education, universities were obliged to produce mission statements and strategies and studies were undertaken to highlight the issues and to determine how the culture of universities could be translated into policies and goals (Leverhulme, 1981; Lockwood and Davies; 1985). With recent concerns to sustain and raise the quality of higher education the debate has continued, with concern among many academics that the scholarly role of universities should remain at the core of their activities and continue to be an expression of HE culture.

Stakeholders' views have been important, but not always either well focused or congruent. A 1988 study found that the general public 'has only a marginal and spasmodic contact with universities' and that there was a poor perception of their performance with the result that 'public discussion has been about little else but reforming them' (Allen, 1988). This situation has continued, with the result that the poor state of university funding has been largely depoliticized because the public is very little concerned with the fate of the sector. Employers have voiced the need for more vocationally oriented graduates, with closer relationships between industry and a more responsive attitude on the part of universities. Professional bodies exert varying degrees of influence. The Pharmaceutical Society and the engineering professional bodies demand specific inputs in courses to ensure students' professional accreditation, while the accountancy profession has six bodies with a separate pattern of examinations and different criteria for recognizing degrees. However, as students receive little credit for their first degrees, they need only take a few more examinations set by the professional body to ensure entry into the profession.

Academic staff also have varying views on the roles of universities, which reflect the confusion of other stakeholders. Research activity is for many of them the primary focus of university life, and credence is given to this by university managements, who still see research performance as a key indicator when deciding on staff promotions.

These conflicting and confusing views of what universities are about and the goals they should espouse have been unhelpful in the debate on quality and how it should be measured. A more fundamental view of the role of quality higher education is offered by Goodlad (1995), who sees the primary aim as being 'to take individuals, teacher or taught, within it to the highest level of what is known or knowable within the limits of time, money and human capability'. Universities are seen as the 'primary custodians of the rites of passage of modern society' and places where individuals are 'nourished, developed and celebrated'. This provides a more open and inclusive concept of the goals of universities and an acceptance that more than one model of the delivery of higher education is acceptable. It has been shown that decisions based on good or poor indicators of quality can drastically affect the fortunes of institutions (Shattock, 1994). A broad consensus which accepts diversity of provision is important, therefore, so that performance is measured across the spectrum of activities properly undertaken by universities and colleges. Competitiveness is also likely to be enhanced by variation.

Distinctiveness and variety, which characterized institutions before the end of the binary divide, are still very apparent although current measures do not easily accommodate them. The delivery of teaching in an Oxford college, with its reliance on a staff-intensive tutorial system and resource-rich library services, and where research activity is a primary focus, differs greatly from that in De Montfort University, formerly Leicester Polytechnic. Here, success depends on large classes and a high staff : student ratio, together with electronic delivery of library and information services to provide the most economic learning support. Research is also a much less significant activity. Each institution is successful, but doing different things both in teaching and research. Their contrasting communications to the market indicate just how different: De Montfort has invested in a high-profile mass advertising campaign in cinemas and on TV, while Oxford colleges make greater use of their alumni through targeted campaigns for fund-raising. The Oxford reputation provides the communication to potential students. Applying the same measures of quality to asses the value of what both institutions do is inevitably problematic.

The HEQC has attempted to deal with these complexities by focusing on quality assurance mechanisms which concentrate on the form that such educational delivery takes rather than its content. In a request for documentation from institutions they identified the systems which should be monitored, rather than the impact of these systems on students' learning experiences and on the other roles of the institution – notably its research activity. They sought documented policies and practices on a range of procedures, including:

- undergraduate and postgraduate admissions access;
- credit accumulation and transfer;
- modularization;
- new course or programme design and approval;
- programme or course reviews;
- departmental reviews;
- resource allocation for courses and programmes;
- validation of other institutions' courses;
- franchise arrangements for courses taught off-campus;
- academic staff appointment procedures;
- interaction with accrediting bodies.

To support their Teaching Quality Assessments, the Higher Education Funding Council for England offered institutions guidance for the self-assessments which had to precede the Assessors' visit. These were similarly difficult to intepret, as they did not indicate how evidence was to be judged under the headings (Higher Education Funding Council, England, 1993):

- aims and curricula;
- students: nature of intake, support systems and progression;
- quality of teaching;
- students' achievements and progress;
- staff and staff development;
- resources;
- academic management and quality control.

Identifying and comparing research quality between institutions has been even more problematic for the funding councils. The counting of output which formed the basis for the 1992 Research Assessment Exercise was heavily criticized from within and beyond the sector as too simplistic and so in the 1996 Research Selectivity Exercise it was decided to use just a self-selection of four outputs per member of academic staff returned as 'research active'. These were then rated by panels of their peers.

While grave doubts have been expressed from within the sector about the capacity of both teaching and research quality assessments to measure the quality of higher education, they have nevertheless been seen as important in HE marketing. An 'Excellent' rating for teaching and a Grade 5 (the highest for research performance) will usually be remarked on in promotional literature and advertisements for staff. Colleges use similar inspections of their teaching as indicators of their quality in promotional literature.

Marketing applications

Marketing principles have been applied across the range of FE and HE activities, as we have seen, especially through the development of relationship marketing. Quality is a key concept. Recruitment of overseas students has been one of the most significant areas in which marketing has been used, and in which quality of educational delivery figures prominently. It also points up the problems when tactical rather than strategic marketing is undertaken by universities and the need to develop a longer-term view of the marketing activity.

The Loughborough and Nottingham experiences

Universities and colleges have had a long tradition of educating students from abroad. UK higher education has always enjoyed a high reputation internationally but it was only in the 1980s that the cost of overseas students' fees made the marketing of programmes an important issue for institutions after full-cost fees were imposed on overseas students in 1979. Before then, it had been accepted that a level of subsidy was needed to encourage international access to UK education and recruitment flourished alongside that of home students. In the mid-1980s it became apparent that maintaining recruitment was a difficulty due to competition from other countries as a result of the increased fee levels. At the same time, the underfunding of the HE system was beginning to be felt and universities began to set clear targets for maintaining and enhancing their overseas student recruitment. Government has set quotas for the recruitment of home undergraduate students – the maximum aggregate student number (MASN). If instutitions exceed their allocated MASN they are financially penalized. Overseas student recruitment is one financially rewarding area for which universities can theoretically recruit limitless numbers and therefore became an attractive means of supporting core activities, supposedly at marginal cost to institutions.

Loughborough and Nottingham Universities were the subjects of a comparative study in the late 1980s which investigated the longer-term strategic marketing implications of this move to more commercially oriented recruitment of international students, that is, students from beyond the European Union who attract the full-cost overseas fees, which are around double those charged to home, including EU, students (Kinnell, 1990). Loughborough, one of the newer 'old' universities which was originally a College of Advanced Technology, was renamed a University of Technology. In 1995 it finally lost 'Technology' from its title to become Loughborough University. Loughborough is particularly well known for its engineering and science departments, and for sports science, with the social sciences and humanities fields now becoming recognized in an institution which is seeking to shed its image as 'just' a technological institution. Nottingham is a much older and more traditional institution, one of the most respected of the old universities which for several years has been the most favoured choice of all UK universities among school leavers. It has a wide academic base, with strong departments across the range including a leading medical school and agricultural science department.

In common with other universities their decision to target overseas students was incorporated into strategic plans and policy which were developed by university committees: at Loughborough an Inter-school Working Party for the Recruitment of Overseas Students and at Nottingham the Senate Committee for Overseas Student Recruitment. However, in both institutions it was clear that while policy was set at the centre, and coordinated at university level, most of the recruitment activity was implemented at the Departmental or Faculty level, with the delivery of courses and research programmes to students very much a grassroots concern. In both universities – and this is a common feature of many universities – academic departments operated as largely autonomous strategic business units, although strategy was defined by the centre and coordination and many of the administrative systems were provided by central administration. Student registration and the billing of students was one such central activity.

Relationships with the major stakeholders was carried on at both levels: university and department. These included foreign governments, overseas institutions, alumni, the British Council and the Association of

Commonwealth Universities. The British Council's market surveys of significant markets (Singapore, Indonesia, Brunei, South Korea, etc.) were used to identify potential recruitment, together with the universities' relationships through alumni and industrial contacts. The interactions between stakeholders was also important, but less easy to influence directly other than through the development of a long-term perception of the quality of courses offered and of the students' learning experiences while at Loughborough and Nottingham. Collaboration between Nottingham University and the then Nottingham Polytechnic to promote Nottingham as a place to study was also developed: although they were to some extent competing for students, because of their very different subject emphasis there was seen to be value in a common approach to the overseas market. Much of the recruiting was achieved, though, by the initiatives of the individual departments at Loughborough and Nottingham: admission tutors were targeting additional markets as a result of contacts of one kind or another (such as external examining in an overseas institution). It was felt that this approach, based as it was on strong professional contacts was helpful in avoiding the pitfalls of rapidly increasing numbers without a sound educational basis for student selection.

As part of the study, an audit was undertaken of existing marketing practices, through data gathered from students and staff. The range of issues covered included communications, the delivery of programmes, language support, accommodation, competitors, and organizational objectives. Although Loughborough and Nottingham were the subjects, experiences from other universities were also used to develop a wider view of the implementation of marketing practices in universities.

Communications

Information to potential students was not being sent out as one package; some came from the Centre, some from departments. There was no coherent message coming from institutions. There was also an underestimation of the communication needs of students, many of whom had not visited the UK before. They needed basic information on eating habits and foods, British habits and particularly the British system of personal responsibility for learning, together with information on how overseas students might expect to be aided on arrival, to alleviate anxiety.

The delivery of programmes

As the type of course offered by the institution was one of the most important factors for students, how programmes were delivered was of tremendous importance to them. Orientation courses, offered on both campuses, were particularly valued for anticipating students' language and study problems and helping them to settle quickly into the learning environment. There was general satisfaction with the content of courses, but more constructive feedback was needed by students – research students particularly commented on the importance of their relationship with their supervisor. Sensitive personal contact between staff and students was seen to be a key area.

Language support

An important element in the product was language support: some students were using English as their third language and it was agreed that even the basic language qualification which the universities required to ensure a sound level of understanding was not sufficient for coping with a higher education course. The language support facilities offered on both campuses were therefore of great importance to both students and staff in enabling students to learn effectively.

Accommodation

Settling into appropriate accommodation was absolutely crucial to students, but was felt not to be sufficiently understood as a key issue by universities. Overseas students without suitable acommodation immediately available on arrival felt transient and disoriented, a particular problem for postgraduate students on one-year courses who had little time in which to settle down to work.

Competitors

A major source of competition was from American institutions: Jordanian students, for example, were choosing American universities over British ones and Australia's share of the Singapore undergraduate market was also growing. Competition between British universities was also intensifying, a growing trend more recently, with the new universities entering the market more aggressively. It was clear, though, that excellence in the delivery of programmes was the best differentiator and that a reputation for quality, which both Loughborough and Nottingham had established with their customers over many years, was paying dividends as their market share had held up.

Organizational objectives

While financial goals were driving the increased international student recruitment from the centre of institutions, other objectives were also important. Universities are complex institutions set up to achieve wide educational objectives and there were many reasons other than financial expediency at work in the recruitment processes. Staff shared a common belief in the importance of overseas students for the cultural life of their institutions and were also concerned to retain the educational quality on which their reputations rested. While the concepts of relationship marketing were not articulated by staff, they were being implemented in the goals set for recruitment, which was intended to be a long-term activity sustained through the delivery of high-quality programmes to students with sufficient ability to cope with rigorous standards.

Implementation of a marketing system

An analysis of the implementation of marketing showed, though, that while tactical marketing practices were in place, a strategic view of marketing was not. Targets for overseas recruitment were being set at university level, but also in departments or faculties and, while university committees were set up to consider recruitment, more coordination was needed. It was also not clear that recruitment planning was encompassing all the areas of the product which students and staff had identified as key to the overall activity of overseas student recruitment. The concept of recruitment was narrowly defined as ensuring students were admitted to the university successfully. Language teaching provision, academic and non-academic support from services like the library, and accommodation, were not coordinated specifically with the needs of international students in mind. This was partly because services were also dealing with other students' needs and it was difficult for some of them to target one group of students without seeming to disadvantage others. However, there was little evidence that planning of services was taking sufficient account of the specific needs of overseas students – particularly with regard to communications within campuses and the information needed successfully to implement a marketing programme.

Several recommendations were made at the conclusion of the study which were applicable to all institutions undertaking intensified recruitment of overseas students. The Loughborough and Nottingham experiences were being replicated elsewhere. It was particularly noted that universities needed to adopt a more strategic approach to their marketing activities. Accurate costing of overseas recruitment to the institution was not being undertaken. There was a view that overseas recruitment was only a marginal cost to universities, but the study showed that support services, staff time, technical support and accommodation all needed to be costed into the equation. Coordination of admissions polices and communication; staff training; customer feedback also required attention.

Conclusion

Since this study, there have been major developments in both institutions and in many other universities to develop a more coherent approach to recruitment and a more strategic, long-term vision of marketing potential. Competition from the new universities has stimulated more marketing activity and intensified the professionalism with which universities – and colleges – approach their marketing. Recognition of the value of established relationships between institutions and their customers which are built on trust that the product is of higher quality than that offered by the competition has become particularly significant. Price is important, but not the deciding factor when students and their sponsors select an institution. Marketing for the short term is being replaced by the building of sustainable competitive advantage. A more strategic aproach to marketing for higher education was indicated, in the face of the intense competitive and environmental threats facing both universities and colleges.

Issues

1   The change from a relatively secure, stable environment to a turbulent and threatening one.
2   The problems caused by inadequate funding and the need for new funding mechanisms.
3   The increasing importance of relationship marketing, particularly for the overseas market.

Questions

1   What are the key features of the operating environment for universities and colleges?
2   Who are the major stakeholders?
3   How should universities maintain the quality of their product?
4   What is the product being provided by universities?
5   How would you apply a product/market expansion grid to the university sector?
6   How important is culture to an understanding of a university's marketing objectives?
7   To what extent are current measures of quality appropriate to the university sector?
8   From the examples offered in this chapter, assess the extent to which effective marketing is being practised in relation to overseas markets.
9   What should form the main elements of a marketing strategy for a university?

References

Allen, M. (1988) *The Goals of Universities*, Society for Research into Higher Education and Open University Press, pp. 79–97.

Baber, M. and Megson, C. (1986) *Taking Education Further: A practical guide to college marketing success*, MSE Publications.

Ball, C. (1988) Keynote speech. In Eggins, H. (ed.), *Restructuring Higher Education: Proceedings of the annual conference 1987*, The Society for Research into Higher Education, Open University Press, pp. 3–12.

Barnett, R. (1992) *Improving Higher Education: Total quality care*, The Society for Research into Higher Education and Open University Press, pp. 18–20.

Davies, P. and Scribbins, K. (1985) *Marketing Further and Higher Education: A handbook*, Longman, for The Further Education Unit and Further Education Staff College.

Goodlad, S. (1995) *The Quest for Quality: Sixteen forms of heresy in higher education*, The Society for Research into Higher Education and Open University Press.

Higher Education Funding Council, England (1993) *Description of the template used in June 1993 to analyse the self-assessments and claims for excellence received in May 1993*, Higher Education Funding Council Quality Committee.

Higher Education Funding Council, England (1996) *The analysis of 1996 financial forecasts*, HEFCE.

Higher Education Quality Council (1995) The graduate standards programme. *HEQC Update*, **8** (1), 6–7.

Johnson, G. and Scholes, K. (1989) *Exploring Corporate Strategy: Text and cases*, Prentice Hall, pp. 113–44.

Kinnell, M. (ed.) (1990) *The Learning Experiences of Overseas Students*, The Society for Research into Higher Education and Open University Press.

Leverhulme Foundation (1981) *The Structure and Governance of Higher Education*, Society for Research into Higher Education.

Lockwood, G. and Davies, J. (1985) *Universities: The management challenge*, Society for Research into Higher Education and NFER-Nelson.

Nye, M. (1996) How to read the signposts. *The Times Higher Educational Supplement*, 27 September, iv–v.

Payne, C.M and Ballantyne, D. (1991) *Relationship Marketing*, Butterworth-Heinemann.

Rigby, G.(1995) Funding a changing system. In Schuller, T. (ed.), *The Changing University?* The Society for Research into Higher Education and Open University Press, pp. 139–49.

Sargent, V. (1993) Back to school. *Marketing Business*, March, 18–21.

Shattock, M. (1994) *The UGC and the Management of British Universities*, The Society for Research into Higher Education and Open University Press, Chapter 4.

Further reading

Goodlad, S. (1995) *The Quest for Quality: Sixteen forms of heresy in higher education*, The Society for Research into Higher Education and Open University Press.

Johnson, G. and Scholes, K. (1989) *Exploring Corporate Strategy: Text and cases*, Prentice Hall, pp. 113–44.

Payne, C.M and Ballantyne, D. (1991) *Relationship Marketing*, Butterworth-Heinemann.

CHAPTER 5

Markets, quality and the health sector

Summary

The implementation of the internal market has created fundamental changes in healthcare management. The new market-
led environment has meant that all successful healthcare
organizations need to use marketing effectively. However, progress initally was slow. Quality management has also become
significant, with the most effective schemes being operated at
local level. The use of the marketing mix is variable, but
despite initial distrust there is now considerable development
in both marketing and quality.

Introduction

One of the largest employers in the UK, the National Health Service (NHS), has undergone a fundamental reorganization in the last decade. This chapter provides an overview of the internal market system in the NHS and its impact on management practices, specifically the issues related to market-led approaches and quality improvement.

Working for patients (Department of Health and Social Security (DHSS), 1989a), also known as the NHS Review, instituted the internal market in the health service which separated the functions of purchasing services from their delivery. This was a development from the Griffiths Inquiry in the early 1980s which had revealed a lack of management orientation and recommended the establishment of general management posts at all levels of the NHS (DHSS, 1984). It was felt that a more efficient NHS, modelled on business management practices, would facilitate savings which could be reinvested in the service.

The internal market has meant a new role for health authorities as purchasers of healthcare, the establishment of self-governing hospital trusts and the empowerment of fundholding general practitioners as the central focus of the new NHS (Glennester *et al.*, 1994). Managers and clinicians are gradually coming to terms with the increasing emphasis on performance outcomes and measures, patient satisfaction and purchasing and marketing functions (Laing and Cotton, 1995). The internal market has meant a radical change in the roles of the organizations involved. The providers of healthcare are concerned with ensuring their services are in demand from the purchasers. For purchasers, on the other hand, the emphasis is on value for money and delivery of services within strict budgets. The rationale behind the internal market is that competition between providers of healthcare for contracts from purchasers will improve the choice, quality and efficiency of healthcare. Contracting is therefore at the centre of the internal market with purchasers able to influence the level of services offered by providers in terms of cost-effectiveness and quality.

Marketing in the NHS

By the time of the NHS Review in 1989 it was estimated that no more than twenty of the one million NHS employees had a marketing background, and most of these were dealing with matters of income generation (Sargent, 1989). In spite of this, the literature includes several studies of the potential use of marketing in the NHS (Wood, 1984;

Farell, 1986). In contrast, the USA had adopted health services marketing on a widespread basis several years earlier (Fontaine, 1988), although the American tendency to preoccupation with the market share was not recommended (Sargent, 1989).

The argument that marketing is essential for any healthcare organization that wishes to stay in business in the new internal market of the NHS is a powerful one. Only the most efficient and effective organizations will ultimately survive in the new market-led environment where cost-effectiveness and high-quality services are the goals. The NHS Review was based on the premise that competition provides an incentive for improving service delivery in order to receive more funding and therefore expand facilities. The new healthcare market is intended to increase patient choice, and marketing is the means to establishing what the patients' needs are and how to meet them. One of the most important changes as a result of the Review has been the shift in emphasis from secondary to primary and community care. Fundholding general practitioners now have the power to choose the type and place of treatment for their patients from the services available.

Some elements of marketing existed in the NHS before the Review, including some quality assurance schemes, public relations, surveying and income generation. An introduction to quality assurance for health professionals is provided by Wright and Whittington (1992), including the social, economic and professional factors affecting its evolution. As Sheaff argues, the knowledge and monitoring of market needs and demands which the marketing process provides, particularly through market research, can overcome many of the problems encountered in the old NHS such as duplication and waste of resources, and will help to improve quality (Sheaff, 1991, pp 36–7). The resistance to marketing in the NHS came initially from managers and clinicians who misunderstood and mistrusted the aims of marketing. In common with many they viewed it as a purely commercial tool and confused it with promotion. Also, those hospitals which wished to become self-governing trusts were not required to include marketing expertise in their management skills to attain trust status. As Wheeler and Proctor (1993) showed, there has been little evidence that marketing principles have been systematically applied to improve the position of healthcare organizations in the marketplace.

Another reason for the slow development of the marketing function was the lack of knowledge of the information needed to undertake a strategic marketing programme on which its effectiveness depends (Grove, 1993). This information includes detailed market research to inform the internal planning and decision-making processes of management including assessing purchasers' requirements, market priorities, evaluating the competition and provider performance, and identifying their strengths, weaknesses, opportunities and threats (SWOTs). An example of a SWOT analysis applied to health visiting is provided by Kelly (1992), who examines how to market a new image of health visiting. Strengths are identified as including:

- the traditional role of health maintenance;
- health promotion;
- community work;
- support for parents and child protection.

Weaknesses include:

- the negative image of health visitors as fulfilling a policing role;
- a reactive role rather than proactive.

Opportunities exist in:

- challenges set by the new NHS reforms and emphasis on public health;
- moving towards the role as community health worker;
- the diversification in methods of working recommended by recent reviews of nursing practice.

Threats were described as:

- the purchaser/provider split in the NHS;
- a general lack of understanding of the health visitor's range of skills and knowledge;
- competition, lack of resources and policy changes.

The gradual, in some cases reluctant, acceptance of marketing in the NHS has developed from a new interpretation of the old definitions attached to marketing in the commercial and business world. From a profit-oriented approach the emphasis has turned, along with other not-for-profit organizations, to quality services and customer satisfaction. Marketing is a team effort involving the whole organization aimed at identifying the needs of customers and matching services to those needs. As Hayden (1992) has explained, 'Marketing is concerned with effectiveness, in terms of outcomes for the consumer'; it is a strategic tool to be used comprehensively throughout the organization as an aid to planning (Hayden, 1992, p. 5). Hayden also argues that marketing in the health service is important whether competition exists or not because it is more concerned with good management principles and service provision than with any competition. This definition of marketing is more appealing to those in the health service who dislike the concept of the NHS as a commercial enterprise merely attempting to attract the highest numbers of paying customers.

The development of quality improvement measures

Quality improvement programmes have been adopted by hospitals in the USA since the mid-1980s (Fischer and Reel, 1992; Orme, 1992) in order to raise the standard of healthcare while maintaining competitive prices. The fundamental precepts of quality improvement are

- identifying and meeting customer need;
- emphasizing joint responsibility of the organization;
- continuous improvement in all areas rather than meeting a set standard.

The combined influences of consumer demand for higher-quality services and more value for money with the competitive forces of the internal market have increased the need for quality-improvement measures in all health sectors. Until the implementation of the internal market the NHS had been outside the competitive environment and had little incentive to increase efficiency and customer satisfaction. The new environment requires a commitment to management reorganization with the focus on cost-effectiveness and quality of service delivery. Total quality management (TQM) is one of the methods used to try to achieve these aims. It comprises a set of values to guide the organization proactively through a programme of continual improvement in all areas. However, there have been many documented failures of TQM in healthcare (e.g. Gaucher and Coffey, 1993). Some writers have attributed failure to the differences between commercial organizations and public healthcare and the inability of adapting TQM to the not-for-profit sector. In the USA continual quality improvement (CQI) has had more success in healthcare organizations because it involves a systematic approach by staff to improve their own working practices, rather than the commercial TQM approach of adopting an organization-wide methodology and strategy based on customer requirements. In the NHS the concept of customer satisfaction is far more complex involving not only patients but also carers, purchasers, referrers and other groups. In many cases, for example, patients would not necessarily know whether they were receiving the best-quality care or not.

Following the Griffiths Inquiry and the government's programme of cost-cutting, the introduction of quality-improvement programmes became more widespread. Many problems were encountered including the identification and definition of quality in healthcare and confusion between TQM, quality assurance and quality circles. Many District Health Authorities (DHAs) neglected to monitor the development of quality-improvement programmes and there was often no specific budget allocated or staff with the relevant experience. While quality circles form only a part of TQM, many DHAs favoured these as a show-case and neglected both quality assurance and TQM which require fundamental cultural change in the organization (Debrah, 1994).

The most successful quality initiatives have been locally developed initiatives without the costly top-down radical reorganization approach of TQM (Ovretveit, 1994). At Ipswich Hospital, for example, a quality strategy has been developed which involves every aspect of the service and staff from all departments. A director of quality coordinates a programme led by a steering group with staff from all levels of the organization. While the internal market was a major influence on the initiative, the emphasis is on understanding the needs of individual patients, their carers, and the staff of the hospital. Months were spent establishing, refining and testing the main issues before an action plan was developed. The main elements of the internal market, contracting, monitoring and setting standards, were recognized, as well as the environment, including communication with patients and support for the more vulnerable or disadvantaged in the community. A patients' affairs manager was appointed to investigate and resolve complaints, identify bad practice and help with staff training in customer care. Surveys of patient satisfaction are conducted and consultations are held with local support groups and volunteers to ensure that the requirements of those with special needs are met by the hospital. Other changes in service practice include all staff wearing name badges, and the order of Accident & Emergency treatment decided by degree of urgency. In-depth quality monitoring reviews are carried out each year and details are sent to purchasers with other information on policy development, good practice and patient satisfaction feedback. In this way both consumers and purchasers have an input to the quality criteria and these are written into contracts by the trust rather than having them imposed from outside by the purchaser (Warren, 1994).

Proof of accreditation is another valuable weapon in the competitive market and accreditation schemes are increasing in the NHS, having long been in use in Australia, the USA and Canada. Accreditation is part of a process involving various strategies to ensure an improvement in healthcare quality by monitoring standards. It 'lets people know that an organization is seeking to follow good practice' (Hunter, 1995). Recent research into accreditation schemes in the NHS showed that interest in compliance with standards is increasing but that a number of different accreditation systems are being used, resulting in uneven coverage and a lack of consensus on good practice. There is a need for nationally accepted standards to ensure consistent quality of healthcare throughout the country. Compliance with standards could be assessed locally or by an inspectorate set up by the government (Scrivens, 1995). In the USA the Joint Commission on Accreditation of Healthcare Organizations has developed clinical performance indicators with emphasis on easy access to information for consumers. It has moved away from simply ensuring that hospitals conform to good practice towards monitoring outcomes rather than inputs in a programme of continuous quality improvement (*Accreditation Manual for Hospitals,* 1994).

In 1994 the Audit Commission's report *Trusting in the Future* recommended the implementation of service-level agreements (SLAs) for directorates and business units in the NHS. The importance of improving information and communication processes to facilitate the effective management of resources was also stressed. A recent survey has shown that the majority of NHS trusts plan to implement fully costed and priced SLAs by 1998. SLAs are viewed as essential in improving the quality and cost-effectiveness of healthcare services (Decker, 1995).

Strategic planning and the marketing mix

The development of a strategic business and marketing plan is necessary as a blueprint for the successful running of a healthcare organization and to implement the policies laid out in the mission statement (Nazareth, 1993). Issues covered by the plan should include the organization's objectives, problems and opportunities; local environment and customer profiles; the marketing strategy; target markets; specific services and events; and pricing. Developing a marketing plan enables senior management to analyse the organization in depth and provides them with a focus for the daily activities of the service and a framework for decision making. A major part of the plan comprises the interrelated tools of marketing, the marketing mix, which must be coordinated to facilitate implementation of the organization's objectives.

In addition to the local needs and conditions, the issues and circumstances involved in the macromarketing environment have an important influence on decision making. These issues include legislation and government policies, cultural traditions, competition, changing technologies and organizational patterns. An understanding of how these issues can affect local marketing plans is vital to the implementation of the marketing strategy and the marketing mix. In order to achieve an effective market-led approach to service delivery, and to reflect subsequent changes in customers' needs, managers must be continually aware of developments in the wider environment. Marketing must be seen as an ongoing process with continual review and reassessment based on reliable and accurate information.

The traditional elements of product, promotion, price and place make up the marketing mix for healthcare organizations. Priorities and partnerships are two concepts which should be added to these. Partnership is necessary between providers and purchasers to agree priorities, for example on waiting times for treatments in a particular locality and situation. Relationships already long established in the NHS between general practitioners and their providers and a reluctance to use the private sector have helped to ensure a stable market (Jebb, 1992). However, the development of permanent long-term relationships between purchasers and providers will ultimately be determined by government policy.

The involvement of clinicians in developing the marketing strategy and the commitment of all staff, not just management, to marketing policies is vital for a market-led service. The development of healthcare outcome criteria by linking processes with outcomes is another area where close partnership between all health professionals in a particular course of treatment is essential. The needs and priorities of patients must be recognized by both purchasers and providers in partnership in order to deliver the services required (Miles, 1993).

Product

Healthcare is the product supplied by the NHS, and since the Review this has been the subject of many changes and much discussion as to the most effective form it should take. One of the most contentious issues to arise from the purchaser/provider split in the NHS has been the overlap of roles between purchasers and providers and the distinction between the needs of patients and those of the purchasers. While provider (hospital) marketing is arguably more straightforward, purchasers have a more complex and basic need to formulate a marketing function. Purchasers (district health authorities and fundholding GPs) are now the force driving the NHS, assessing the population's health needs and contracting for the services required. Thus they must attract and maintain the attention and trust of their local communities (Chudley, 1994). It is the responsibility of purchasers to ensure that providers are supplying good-quality cost-effective services. The main marketing function of the providers is to monitor health service provision and also to assess the needs of purchasers and patients. It is important for provider units to distinguish between the needs of patients and purchasers. Providers are now in competition for contracts to supply healthcare and so depend to a large extent on their success in using marketing techniques and providing the right product for the market. An example in which smaller units in the NHS can compete is specializing in a particular market, such as the elderly, or concentrating on providing a high-quality service in a specialist area of healthcare like heart disease.

Market testing has been suggested by many, including the 1991 white paper *Competing for Quality,* as a means to improve quality and value for money in health service delivery. However, only a quarter of NHS services had been contracted out by 1995, mostly in the areas of catering, cleaning and transport services. Many managers are unsure of the value of market testing and are reluctant to use it, especially for clinical or core services (Decker, 1995). Reasons for this include the cost of the evaluation process as well as distrust of a beneficial outcome.

Promotion

Promotion could be called the public face of marketing and it is what many people wrongly perceive marketing to be. Promotion does have a vital role to play within the marketing process and includes advertising, publicity and other methods of sales promotion. Personal selling is an important part of promotion in the commercial world but has less relevance in marketing healthcare, where 'selling' and performing the service cannot be separated and salespeople as such are not employed. However, where personal selling is interpreted to mean the development of relationships with customers this can lead to benefits for both health provider and consumer. The objectives of promotion in the health service include:

- to increase the awareness among purchasers and the public of the services offered by the hospital/unit;
- to differentiate these services from those of the competition;
- to communicate the benefits of the services offered;
- to build and maintain the reputation of the unit;
- to persuade purchasers and patients to use those services.

As Cowell (1984) explains, 'ultimately the purpose of any promotional effort is to sell the service product through informing, persuading and reminding'.

Corporate identity has become increasingly important with the introduction of the internal market and the design of a logo helps to provide a recognizable identity and public profile. The corporate identity must be part of a wider marketing strategy to understand how the organization is perceived and how it should be promoted both to external purchasers, providers, the public, and internally to patients and staff.

While the basic need of both purchasers and providers is to assess health needs of the local population, the conflict arises out of different methods of presenting this information for change and the practice and principles involved (Whitcroft, 1995). There is a need for more consensus in managing the marketing and promotion of health services and in the provision of information for the public. Information represents the power to change traditional views and perceptions of the public as well as to manage the political environment.

Price

The internal market in the NHS means that provider units are in competition for contracts from purchasers of health services and their survival depends very much on providing cost-effective quality services. Pricing structures are based on the NHS rule that 'price equals cost', but the danger is that pricing will be set according to internal standards rather than based on patients' and purchasers' needs. A partnership is needed between clinicians, managers and purchasers to ensure that the right contracts are agreed to the benefit of patients.

Pricing is not an activity confined to the finance department alone. In conjunction with market research and the involvement of purchasers and clinicians a pricing strategy can be developed to reflect local patient and purchaser needs. As with the other elements of the marketing mix, pricing must be market-led. Differential pricing is one of the methods to achieve this while ensuring that difficulties over banding of services and complex invoicing systems are overcome (Miles, 1993).

The concern over the last decade has been with the provision of quality healthcare and cost containment, the problem being of maintaining an acceptable balance between the two. The relationship between quality and cost has been examined by other writers (Masso, 1989; Donabedian, 1984) who draw a number of conclusions:

- in many cases numerous rather than appropriate services are provided;
- there is a variation of performance between healthcare professionals;
- there is uneven distribution of quality healthcare;
- there are different views on what constitutes quality healthcare.

The evaluation and monitoring of healthcare outcomes to ensure cost-effectiveness is itself a cost outlay and measures to improve procedures may also involve more expenditure. However, while there is a cost/benefit exchange in all areas, including quality assurance measures, more information is needed to enable decision makers to balance outcomes against cost effectively.

Place

The concept of place, distribution, location and physical environment in the NHS is a vital component of the marketing mix. Issues of accessibility, availability, and communication comprise an essential element in the enormous network of services and units which form the modern NHS. In providing an efficient healthcare service the needs of the public for an easily accessible and fast response service must be balanced with the organization's need to provide a cost-effective service of benefit to a wide range of patients.

The location or delivery of services in the NHS depends on a decision-making process to designate services as core or non-core. Core services, such as ambulance, accident and emergency, must be provided locally to ensure speed of delivery. Services for the less urgent conditions may be non-core and provided at specialist centres round the country. Accessibility to services both locally and at a distance is a vital measure of quality assessment.

The overall environment, whether social, political or economic, exerts a major influence on the internal market in the NHS. The political environment is particularly important as government policy making and the NHS Executive play a large part in purchasing activity. Unlike the general commercial market where the influence of economic policies are felt, the government also exercises direct control over purchaser units in the NHS (Appleby *et al.*, 1994).

The consumer-driven market

With the emergence of primary healthcare as the main focus of the new internal market in healthcare the importance of consumer satisfaction has been highlighted as never before. The Griffiths Inquiry stressed the importance of monitoring patients' views through market research and recommended that the NHS use the information 'in formulating policy, and monitor performance against it' (DHSS, 1984, p. 9). The subsequent government review of primary healthcare and the NHS Review empha-sized the benefits of competition for service provision and the necessity of obtaining the views and opinions of consumers (DHSS, 1989a, b). The simultaneous growth of the health promotion movement and consumer health information generally has served to increase the role of the public in modern health service delivery.

Consumer orientation is the most fundamental aspect of marketing and particularly so in the not-for-profit public service sector. This is especially relevant in the case of health promotion where marketing per-sonnel must first understand and empathize with the perceptions and needs of the public in order to communicate the message effectively. When a Scottish health board wanted to initiate a programme of educa-tion on AIDS for teenagers research was undertaken to assess their per-ceptions and needs for information (Hastings and Scott, 1988). It was found that teenagers knew about the main causes of HIV and that the risks could be reduced by practising safer sex. However, their knowledge was theoretical and they had little experience of actually buying and using condoms. This led the health board to decide that teaching materials on AIDS and promoting skills in safer sex were necessary.

The value that healthcare organizations place on the views of their patients is reflected in the efforts made to discover and analyse them. Consumers' needs and opinions change rapidly and surveys of satisfaction need to be conducted regularly and changes implemented accordingly. Methods of obtaining the views and requirements of patients include:

- observation – direct and participant (staff opinion);
- analysis of correspondence, complaints and compliments;
- interviews – open-ended, critical incident, and structured;
- focus groups;
- questionnaires.

This information can be vital in the development and monitoring of services such as the efficiency of the appointment and referral system, accessibility and availability of staff, and the catering and transport systems. Particular areas with problems related to quality of service can be surveyed specifically by targeting those users concerned. From this information performance indicators may be set, against which service levels may be measured in future.

A research project in South Bedfordshire has provided a model for consumer audit and shown how the views of healthcare consumers can contribute to the policy decision making of purchasers and providers and improve service delivery. The audit took the form of in-depth interviews with a random sample of people in their own homes, focus groups, observation of service delivery, questionnaires and interviews with staff. Nine audits of specific service areas were conducted and resulted in a report providing new information which led directly to improved service delivery in specific areas. For example, day-surgery patients waiting on trolleys in corridors now have a waiting ward with improved facilities. It was also found that users generally required more information about services, processes and self-help. Purchasers have used the audit information to draw up service specifications and trained staff to prepare contracts. Managers have used the information to introduce change, while clinicians learnt from the individual experiences of patients. The research also revealed a number of issues to be resolved including the problems of dissemination of the information, accountability, and responsibility for implementation of recommendations. The problems of consumer audit on a district-wide basis as well as the difficulties of timing and choice of topics for audit must be carefully considered. Overall, the audit provided both opportunities and challenges for strategy development in consumer audit (Bradburn, 1994).

The Patient's Charter, first published in 1991, set out ten patients' rights and nine service standards and is a useful tool in the marketing of healthcare services. While standards such as waiting times for outpatient appointments, inpatient treatment and heart bypass surgery had been set, issues of clinical quality still had not been addressed by the second edition issued in 1995. *The Patient's Charter* is, however, a milestone in the development of a consumer-orientated health service, and is a basis for recognition of patients' rights and basic standards on which to build in the future.

Fundholding GPs have a real incentive to survey their patients' needs as well as the general health requirements of their local population in order to know and understand their market. Their view of the market is through health gain in terms of their own patient lists, whereas the other main purchasers, the district health authorities, have a wider interest in the needs of the whole district within the overall strategy of the NHS. There must also be a balance made in the marketing policy of GPs between the need to meet their payment targets and the specific requirements of individual patients.

Market segmentation or the grouping of consumers according to the similarity of their needs is another essential tool in the marketing process, and enables specific marketing strategies to be developed to suit each group. Sophisticated information technology now allows consumer groups to be more easily identified and these in turn are more able to communicate their needs and requirements. Segmentation is vital in the modern healthcare environment with scarce resources and over-stretched staff. The need to prioritize and target specific consumer groups is essential to allow equal opportunities to access healthcare services, for example, to housebound ethnic minorities, children with special needs, the elderly and patients with learning difficulties. Practitioners and managers must coordinate their skills to use demographic, epidemiological and resource information to determine where the greatest needs are. Policy strategies can then be developed to target and meet the requirements identified.

Training

Training in marketing management and procedures is necessary to teach unfamiliar technical skills and also, as Sheaff (1991, p. 45) argues, to increase confidence in staff and improve the rate of marketing activity. This may take the form of formal training courses combined with meetings and informal discussions as appropriate to different grades of staff.

Community health staff in Wales had been concerned with projecting their role and services to both purchasers and the public for some years. A programme of training in marketing skills was developed involving workshops with a marketing consultant, educational resource packs, training sessions and day courses for community nurse managers and staff. One of the main aims was to learn from commercial organizations like Marks & Spencer how to evolve a service known for its quality rather than its ability simply to sell products. Community health workers needed to identify key features of their service which distinguished them from other providers and be able to communicate their skills to the public and purchasers alike, particularly GPs. There was a recognition that community healthcare was now in a competitive business environment and that performance monitoring and target setting was necessary (Jackson, 1993).

Few healthcare professionals have had much formal training in quality improvement and audit although some in-house training courses are being developed. One example in Brighton has set out to overcome the distrust many clinicians have towards these initiatives. The organizers have produced a coursebook and facilitator's pack to accompany the course which covers the following areas:

- why quality matters – development and framework;
- organizing for quality;
- identifying and prioritizing quality problems;
- defining and analysing quality problems;
- quality measurement and data presentation;
- solutions to quality problems.

Follow-up sessions track the implementation in the workplace of skills learnt on the course and act as a forum for discussion and advice. The organizers claim a higher awareness level of quality improvement and the introduction of several new quality initiatives which have led to better patient care (Barnes, 1994).

Conclusion

In spite of an initial distrust, lack of knowledge and understanding of marketing and quality improvement, there is now considerable development in these areas in the NHS. The dual challenge of cost-effectiveness and a consumer-driven health service in a competitive environment has raised awareness of the importance of marketing and delivering a high-quality service. The growth of locally developed quality-improvement schemes and marketing initiatives should be matched by equal support and commitment from national level. There is considerable scope for more coordination between marketing and quality-improvement initiatives which could be given greater impetus by management. The importance of building on existing relationships and forging new ones between purchasers, providers and the consumer in order to establish healthcare priorities must be encouraged. To achieve these aims marketing and quality audit personnel in the NHS should cooperate and work more closely together.

Marketing has a major role to play in the new competitive NHS, specifically in relation to consumer orientation and the identification and targeting of patients' needs. Ensuring a responsive health service and providing a balance between cost containment and quality improvement will be the main objectives for marketing in the NHS into the twenty-first century.

Issues

1   The institution of the internal market which separated purchasing of services from their delivery and the consequent change of roles of organizations.
2   The slow development of the marketing function.
3   The significance of quality improvement measures.

Questions

1   To what extent is marketing now essential for any healthcare organization wishing to stay in business in the new internal market of the NHS?
2   Why was marketing resisted by certain groups in the NHS?
3   What is the role of strategic marketing for a function such as health visiting?
4   Which have been the most successful kinds of quality initiatives in the NHS, and why?
5   Assess the relevance of the marketing mix for healthcare organizations.
6   To what extent is pricing strategy simply an activity of finance departments?
7   What part is the concern for customer satisfaction playing in the development of a relationship-oriented approach to marketing in the NHS?
8   What is the role of training in developing marketing implementation in the health sector?

References

Joint Commission on Accreditation of Healthcare Organizations (1994) *Accreditation Manual for Hospitals*, Chicago, Illinois.

Appleby, J. *et al.* (1994) Monitoring managed competition. In Robinson, R. and Le Grande, J. (eds), *Evaluating the NHS Reforms*, Kings Fund Institute.

Barnes, J. (1994) Star quality. *Health Service Journal*, **104** (5427), 20–22.

Bradburn, J. (1994) Eye opener. *Health Service Journal*, 4 August, 20–21.

Chudley, P. (1994) How to build a healthy view of marketing. *Marketing*, 10 February, 31–2.

Cowell, D. W. (1984) *The Marketing of Services*, Butterworth-Heinemann.

Debrah, Y.A. (1994) Evolution and implementation of a quality improvement programme. *Total Quality Management*, **5** (3), 11–25.

Decker, D. (1995) Market testing – does it bring home the bacon? *Health Service Journal*, **105** (5436), 26–8.

Department of Health and Social Security (1984) *Inquiry into the Management of the NHS* (Griffiths Inquiry), HMSO.

Department of Health and Social Security (1989a) *Working for Patients*, Cm 555, HMSO.

Department of Health and Social Security (1989b) *Caring for People: Community care in the next decade and beyond*, Cm 849, HMSO.

Donabedian, A. (1984) Quality, cost and cost containment. *Nursing Outlook*, **32** (3), 142–5.

Farell, E. (1986) Marketing in the NHS. *Health Care Management Review*, **1**, 10–12.

Fischer, W.W. and Reel, L.B. (1992) Total quality management in a hospital library. *Bulletin of the Medical Library Association*, **80** (4), 347–52.

Fontaine, S.J. (1988) Health services marketing in a non-competitive environment. *Health Marketing Quarterly*, **5** (3/4), 75–88.

Gaucher, J.G. and Coffey, J.C. (1993) *Total Quality in Healthcare*, Jossey-Bass.

Glennester, H. *et al.* (1994) GP fundholding: wildcard or winning hand. In Robinson, R. and Le Grand, J., (eds), *Evaluating the NHS Reforms*, Kings Fund Institute.

Grove, R. (1993) Probably the best. *British Journal of Healthcare Computing and Information Management*, **10** (9), 20–21.

Hastings G.B. and Scott, A.C. (1988) The development of AIDS education material for adolescents. *Journal of the Institute of Health Education*, **26**, 164–71.

Hayden, V. (1992) How market-oriented is your service? *Journal of Management Medicine*, **6** (1), 5–9.

Hunter, H. (1995) Would you accredit it? *Health Service Journal*, **105** (5474), 10.

Jackson, C. (1993) Lessons in talking business. *Health Visitor,* **66** (10), 352–3.

Jebb, F. (1992) First wave lessons prove vital for hospital contracts. *Fundholding,* **1** (6), 18–19.

Kelly, A. (1992) Shaping and selling the health visiting image. *Health Visitor,* **65** (9), 310–12.

Laing, A. and Cotton, S. (1995) Towards an understanding of healthcare purchasing. *Journal of Marketing Management,* **11** (6), 583–600.

Masso, M. (1989). The quality assurance dilemma. *The Australian Journal of Advanced Nursing,* **7** (1), 12–22.

Miles, C. (1993) Market values. *Health Service Journal,* 12 August, 32–5.

Nazareth, A. (1993). Internal marketing. *British Journal of Healthcare Computing,* **10** (9), 22–3.

Ovretveit, J. (1994) All together now. *Health Service Journal,* **104** (5431), 24–6.

Orme, C.N. (1992) Customer information and the quality improvement process. *Hospital and Health Services Administration,* **37** (2), 197–211.

Sargent, J. (1989) How to take the NHS to market. *The Health Service Journal,* **99** (5169), 1158–9.

Scrivens, E. (1995) Measuring up. *Health Service Journal,* **105** (5447), 22–4.

Sheaff, R. (1991) *Marketing for Health Services,* Open University Press.

Warren, L. (1994) Getting used to quality. *British Journal of Healthcare Computing and Information Management,* **11** (9), 24–5.

Wheeler, N. and Proctor, T. (1993) Strategy analysis and the health service. *Journal of Marketing Management,* **9** (3), 287–300.

Whitcroft, M. (1995) Hard sell. *Health Service Journal,* 23 February, 30–1.

Wood, J. (1984) Can the NHS be marketed like detergent? *Health and Social Service Journal,* 17 May, 582–3.

Wright, C. and Whittington, D. (1992) *Quality Assurance. An introduction for health care professionals,* Longman.

Further reading

Gaucher, J.G. and Coffey, J.C. (1993) *Total Quality in Healthcare,* Jossey-Bass.

Sheaff, R. (1991) *Marketing for Health Services,* Open University Press.

Wright, C. and Whittington, D. (1992) *Quality Assurance. An introduction for health care professionals,* Longman.

CHAPTER 6

Leisure services marketing

Summary

Local authority leisure services have undergone fundamental reorganization, as a result of compulsory competitive tendering (CCT) and the restructuring of local government. The wide range of service provision has caused difficulties for setting objectives, and a more strategic approach to marketing has been found to be necessary in order to prioritize services. Quality-of-life marketing has provided a further means of approaching customers and developing a quality service in the CCT environment. Training of personnel has also become a key issue.

Introduction

As we discussed in Chapter 1, local government services are now subject to many of the same pressures of competition and cost-effectiveness as those in the private sector. Local authorities themselves have experienced a reduction of both financial and policy-making powers over the last decade. Leisure services in particular have been undergoing a period of fundamental reorganization and adjustment to the new commercial environment while attempting to provide a public service. The implementation of compulsory competitive tendering (CCT) following the Local Government Act 1988 meant the adoption of a business-led culture for local authority leisure services. At the same time, the responsibility for maintaining quality services lay with councils and leisure service managers 'emphasizing the need for clear policies and for contract specifications which accurately reflect those policies' (Audit Commission, 1989, p. 16).

In the late 1960s the rationalization of local authority sport and recreation services began with the Royal Commission under Lord Redcliffe-Maud. The Commission examined the structure of local government and recommended the streamlining of departments and committees (Ministry of Housing and Local Government, 1967). In 1968 the first department for arts and recreation was established in the new Teesside County Borough, merging five former separate authorities. Since the Local Government Act 1972 and the Local Government (Miscellaneous Provisions) Act 1976 leisure services for the community have evolved in England and Wales within a framework of larger coordinated departments, bringing together the previously disparate sport and recreation services and facilities (Torkildsen, 1992, pp. 192–3). Local authorities in England and Wales are required to provide leisure services in the three specified areas of libraries, youth and adult education, and allotments. The level and scale of provision of leisure facilities varies, therefore, between different authorities. In Scotland and Northern Ireland authorities have a wider duty to provide recreation facilities and services for the community.

Local authority constraints

Traditionally, leisure and recreation facilities and services have evolved as a result of a range of private, voluntary and statutory actions on both national and local levels. This led to a rich but diverse accumulation of facilities largely uncoordinated and inevitably leading to duplication and waste of resources. This is exacerbated by the fact that responsibility for local leisure services is spread between central and local government, for example in the areas of children's play, education and libraries, and between different levels of local government such as county councils and district councils. The various services may be the responsibility of one large department or separated out between several different departments.

Many local authority leisure departments lack a well-defined set of aims or objectives apart from vague notions of serving the whole community, which cannot easily be put into practice. This lack of aims and its effect on marketing practice will be looked at in more detail later in this chapter.

The inflexibility and traditionally slow-moving nature of local government decision making also makes for difficulties and constraints in the planning and management of local authority leisure and recreation services. Recent legislation such as the reorganization of local government and the implementation of local management of schools (LMS) and CCT require much time and effort to devote to restructuring, new contract specifications and resource allocation.

The creation of the new unitary authorities by the Local Government Commission has meant another huge upheaval for many leisure and recreation departments soon after the introduction of CCT. Some departments have disappeared altogether, notably in London boroughs, where over a third of leisure departments have closed; others have been amalgamated with health and housing to make community services departments and some have been joined with education, while others have been renamed as tourism – reflecting local needs to develop income generation. The optimistic outlook is to see the new unitary authorities as enabling and coordinating organizations which will facilitate a more proactive and cooperative approach to leisure provision by all relevant sectors.

Setting objectives

The 1970s and 1980s was a period of rapid expansion and development in leisure and recreation. Local authority spending in England and Wales rose from around £280 million in 1981–2 to £400 million in 1988–9 in real terms and there were 1700 indoor sports facilities by 1989 as well as outdoor facilities. In terms of marketing leisure this meant a large growth in the evolutionary development lifecycle of the services. Local authority culture encouraged the growth of outreach services and especially services to the various disadvantaged community groups. Inevitably, constraints on resources meant limited available finances and it became vital to relate service provision more closely to community needs.

A survey conducted of the marketing practices of 373 UK leisure service authorities (Kinnell and MacDougall, 1994) revealed responsibility for an enormous range of services and facilities from pitch and putt to Olympic sports stadia. This often disparate range of activities presents particular problems for marketing such a wide-ranging and complex product. The need to define a mission statement at local level which reflects national guidelines on provision and remains within strict financial limits is the central problem for leisure managers. The Audit Commission (1989) sets out the reasons for local authority involvement in sport as being

> for a variety of reasons . . . improvements in health, alleviating social deprivation and helping to promote excellence in sport at national and international level. Other reasons include improving the quality of life of the whole community and extending the range of choice of leisure activity; providing golf courses and outdoor pitches to preserve 'green belt' sites from development; helping urban regeneration and attracting tourists and thus helping the local economy.

It is necessary to balance these wide-ranging aims with those of local community needs, the political situation and levels of resources in order to develop a viable mission statement. The importance of an overall corporate policy framework of priorities or local authority strategic planning document is vital if leisure departments are to develop goals consistent with the overall aims of the authority.

In Birmingham, the aims and objectives of the city council have been clearly set out providing the context for specific departmental planning. The Policy Framework 1995/6 reviewed progress since the City Strategy report of 1992/3, and proposed priorities for the future of the city as a whole. Each council committee also prepared its own Service Statement summarizing its specific service priorities and stating the contribution each will make to achieving the city-wide goals. 'The Policy Statement and the Service Statements will together provide the policy context for specific action plans, for area strategies and for the City Council's performance management systems' (Birmingham City Council, 1995). The policy explains the context for council service provision, including the capping of local authority revenue, economic and legislative change, and sets out in detail its four main corporate priorities:

- improving the quality of life;
- securing Birmingham's future;
- tackling inequality, discrimination and disadvantage;
- involving local people in the decisions that affect them.

The Department of Leisure and Community Services developed a corporate communications plan to focus on and deliver the key messages which reflect the council's overall policy. The objectives were to improve the negotiating position of the department, correct existing negative impressions and to promote leisure services as essential services. The plan aimed to emphasize those services essential to quality of life such as its role in education and the development of the under-fives. Projects outlined included an under-fives' leisure and learning scheme, under-fives' swim and activity programmes, sport and schools strategy, fitness swimming and various library activities. Projects reflecting the need to secure Birmingham's future and protecting the environment included leaflets on discovering the countryside in Birmingham and a nature-conservation strategy combined with recycling schemes, energy saving and environmental arts projects. The department's role in developing tourism in Birmingham was promoted in many national sports events such as Euro '96, and major museum exhibitions. The need to tackle inequality and disadvantage was reflected, for example, in the depart-ment's adult education courses, ethnic language library services, women-only sessions, paralympics, and the libraries' disability-targeted publicity. Involving local people was seen as a role fulfilled in many departmental activities such as community arts projects, sport and school strategy, adult education, community libraries, user and visitor surveys and local consultation in the design and delivery of services.

In order to ensure the successful implementation of a programme like that of Birmingham it is essential that it be a carefully integrated and planned combination of activities which is based on the needs of indi-viduals and community groups. Constant evaluation and reviewing of the programmes (activities, facilities and services) are required to match changing demands and target markets and to balance social and financial objectives. A successful leisure programme is not merely a timetable of events. There is a need to understand the motivation and needs of individuals as well as organizations which participate in and provide leisure activities (Torkildsen, 1994).

Quality programming and community planning

The traditional approach to programme development was through social planning based on centralist policy making. Decision makers tended, therefore, to be detached from users and staff, resulting in poor commit-ment levels from staff, a lack of accountability, little understanding of the real needs of the community, and a dull and unoriginal approach to service development.

Successful programming depends on the involvement in the market-ing process of consumers in the development and improvement of services and facilities. This community development approach is based on the interaction of leisure management with individuals or small groups of users through the use of enablers or community developers. Long-term financial support and commitment are necessary if such outreach programmes are to be successful. Leisure managers need to be communicators with staff and the public in order to ensure a proactive and community-sensitive service.

Torkildsen (1992, pp. 312–16) has outlined a seven-step guideline to successful programme planning based on the community development approach and vital to an effective marketing strategy. A brief summary of the steps is as follows:

1   Interpret policy and establish aims and objectives – understanding the philosophy and purpose of the organization, producing a mission statement and policy guidelines with committee endorsement.
2   Assess resources and current and potential demand – profile current and prospective consumers; evaluate current resources and other agencies; collate all marketing information; identify market gaps.
3   Set objectives – put policies and needs into action, set targets, involve policymakers, staff and community.
4   Plan the programme – patterns of use and timetabling; decide programme areas and forms; consider needs of different user groups, priorities and balance, resources, flexibility, marketing strategy, staffing and communications.
5   Implement the programme – marketing strategy, promotion; a flexible approach; sensitive staffing policy, help to new groups, outreach; develop monitoring systems; anticipate problems; expand and experiment; pricing flexibility; communicate.
6   Evaluate – measure effectiveness and efficiency of input, process and outcomes using various criteria both quantitative and qualitative; effectiveness of marketing; responsiveness of staff and organization.
7   Obtain feedback and modify programme – an ongoing process; modify objectives and targets; obtain feedback from community; determine causes of failure, consider changes in staff training, responsibility and management.

In the past, little leisure programming or marketing included community involvement but tended to be reactive, based on an *ad hoc* policy of what had always been provided. This was a result of lack of planning and direction and little understanding of how to relate community needs and organizational objectives to programming.

Quality programming and marketing involves staff in all planning stages and measures consumer satisfaction continually. In this way improvements can be made all the time, increasing quality and cost-effectiveness of services and reducing unsatisfactory elements.

Quality-of-life marketing

The focus in recent years on customer care, consumer choice and customer-orientated services has led to an emphasis on quality of life and a new approach to marketing planning based on these principles (Sirgy and Lee, 1996). Writers including Cespedes (1993) and Ortmeyer (1993) have argued that traditional marketing practices which rely purely on increased financial gain are liable to be unethical and socially irresponsible. The aim of quality-of-life marketing is to improve the wellbeing of consumers or customers without having a negative effect on any other group. Kotler (1986) defined societal (or social) marketing in very similar terms:

> ... to determine the needs, wants, and interests of target markets and to deliver the desired satisfactions more effectively and efficiently than competitors in a way that preserves or enhances the consumer's and the society's wellbeing.

Sirgy and Lee (1996, pp. 20–21) have written that quality-of-life marketing is similar to, or an extension of, societal marketing in that it also attempts to meet the needs of consumers, the organization and society. The differences are that:

- quality-of-life marketing emphasizes consumers' wellbeing through long-term consumer satisfaction;
- quality-of-life marketing treats competitors as another public rather than a winning or losing situation; there should be cooperation between competitors to improve overall the wellbeing of consumers;
- quality-of-life marketing seeks to reduce any negative side-effects to consumers and other publics besides target consumers.

Leisure services marketing would seem to be naturally adaptable to the quality-of-life approach with little conflict of interests. The aims of most local authority leisure services would include the improvement in wellbeing of their community without negative effects on others.

Traditionally, target marketing involved identifying groups in the community most likely to use leisure facilities. The quality-of-life approach identifies activities which improve wellbeing, such as keeping fit, and then matches these to specific community groups. Leisure marketing should identify the areas of consumer wellbeing where the organization can develop services and facilities to improve the quality of life of target populations.

It is not enough to assume that leisure services enhance wellbeing; services have to demonstrate this by relating the benefits to aspects of quality of life, such as exercise to improved cardiovascular health. Leisure services should clearly demonstrate their objectives using the empirical evidence available.

One of the methods of reducing negative side-effects for the consumer is keeping costs down and providing services in the most cost-effective way possible. Local authorities already do this in many cases through subsidies. But, since the introduction of CCT, the emphasis has been very much on income generation. The quality of life approach is to develop long-term relationships with consumers by increasing customer loyalty, using economies of scale and scope and providing services at an affordable rate for all potential consumers. By increasing consumers' wellbeing and long-term satisfaction marketers can improve customer commitment to the services. In this way, providing services at low prices, profits are likely to increase as a result of increased demand. Other negative side-effects to consumers and the general community, such as safety worries, noise, increased traffic, parking problems and so on, should be minimized as far as possible to ensure quality of life for all.

In quality-of-life marketing competitors should not be seen as 'the enemy'. Rather, marketers should be challenged to provide services which improve consumers' wellbeing more effectively or should identify niche markets where consumers' wellbeing can be improved. Local authorities have an opportunity to cooperate with other leisure services providers in the area to supply a wide range of services and facilities to improve the quality of life of the whole community (Sirgy and Lee, 1996).

Implementing quality

Since central government cutbacks in resourcing for local government the importance of quality in service provision and management has increased. Financial constraints mean more emphasis on cost-effective running of services, improved adaptability and flexibility. Management styles must reflect these needs with efficient strategic planning, programming and monitoring measures.

Quality issues have become more significant in public service provision over recent years and particularly since the introduction of the Citizen's Charter initiative and the drive to implement BS 5750 (British Standards Institution, 1992). Some local authorities, like Clydesdale for example, were implementing BS 5750 as early as 1991. The impetus in Clydesdale came from senior managers with a seminar held for members of the council, and from a neighbouring authority, to explain the concepts and total quality management. Following this meeting the leisure service installed BS 5750 with the help of consultants. One of the main hurdles was that not only members' but also junior managers' attitudes had to be addressed through persuasion and gradual adjustment. In addition a detailed *Draft service plan* and a document entitled *Clydesdale leisure into the 90s* were produced to communicate the new structure and future plans to staff. This included clear plans of the new structure, and a statement of the department's training policy. Internal marketing was an important tool, and a marketing strategy outlined the market research, both quantitative and qualitative, information services and statistics, coordination of marketing resources, marketing mix, liaison, sponsorship, advertising, staff involvement and marketing plans required by the department. Leicester City Council Leisure Services Department produced a statement of aims and principles in 1991 to guide the development of leisure services in the 1990s. The main aims were to improve levels of participation and access especially for those suffering discrimination and to 'achieve effective and efficient service delivery through total quality management' (Leicester City Council, 1991). A quality strategy was developed and implemented to achieve these aims. This document listed outputs, outcomes and performance indicators under each of the headings: shared values, strategy, structures, systems, management style, staff, and skills. For example, under Strategy was included

- outputs, such as marketing and business plans and annual service plans;
- outcomes such as annual service targets met in each centre;
- performance indicators such as number of targets achieved.

The importance of quality is emphasized throughout, as under Systems:

- outputs – quality assurance;
- outcomes – customers receiving consistent standards of service every time;
- performance indicators – department achieves BS 5750 by April 1996.

By 1996 and the progress towards unitary status Leicester Leisure Services were updating these documents and initiating a pilot audit of the quality strategy. Managers were asked to evaluate their achievements through a self-assessment questionnaire. Annual service plans which were developed from the overall marketing plan ensure regular reviews of service delivery and updating of centre marketing plans. Although much time has been spent on preparing for unitary status a concerted effort has been made to make the service increasingly customer oriented. Whereas leisure services policy making was previously function-based they are now also area-based to reflect more accurately the actual needs of local communities. A work programme lists strategy documents, monitoring and budget reports, reviews, and presentations to be made to the leisure services committee over a three-year period.

Training

A commitment to quality leisure service provision entails an equal commitment to staff involvement and training. Both Clydesdale and Leicester gave staff training a high priority, and even with tighter resources Leicester Leisure Services had not cut back on training in 1996. The internal training programme was devised by the Director of Leisure Services on the premise that the most important resource is staff and that 'it is essential that the Department invests in effective training and retraining and that this training is organised to ensure that the Department's key objectives are achieved' (Leicester City Council, 1991, p. 9).

The aims of staff training are to improve overall effectiveness by ensuring staff have the necessary skills and also to improve the job satisfaction, career prospects and equal opportunities of all staff. It is important to see training as an investment not a cost, as the CELTS study found local authorities regarded it in 1990 (CELTS, 1990). It is therefore important to monitor training and conduct regular staff development programmes. In Birmingham the marketing department have produced a marketing handbook to enable staff at local levels to carry out marketing functions as part of their daily routines. Staff are also involved in the interpretation of marketing research studies at regular meetings.

The effects of CCT

In the early 1990s it was found that more than half of the leisure managers had no marketing plan. However, the effects of CCT were already being felt and over a third of managers reported that they had plans in preparation. The importance of developing partnerships between client and provider played a major part in the focus on a more structured marketing approach. Whereas the local authority may no longer be the direct provider of a service, it still maintains the ultimate responsibility for the range and quality of the service for the community. The local authority, therefore, still has control over some important areas of marketing, such as the organization and dissemination of information, and it is vital that effective communication is maintained on how these responsibilities are allocated (Sports Council, 1990).

Service development

Overall, the effect of CCT on leisure managers was to review marketing strategies and redefine the services offered and the consumers they wished to attract. Whereas some leisure managers received an increase in budgets to cover the costs of management information systems, for example, other services suffered as a result of being put out to tender. In some cases catering and cleaning services were reduced as staff were lost after other agencies took over the contracts (Kinnell and MacDougall, 1994, p. 122).

Research by the Centre for Leisure and Tourism Studies has found that after the introduction of CCT only 48 per cent of local authorities, and only 39 per cent of London boroughs, felt that they had kept total control over programming. The effect, for example, on leisure provision for women had been a big reduction in the number of posts with a responsibility for developing women's sport. There was a tendency to group all women and girls in a generic target group together with the elderly, youth, unemployed, people with disabilities and ethnic minorities. Contractors appeared to be mainly concerned with increasing overall numbers rather than the scope and range of services and facilities (Aitchison, 1994). The needs of women participators in sports and leisure services were also studied by Campbell (1996), who found that provision for over 50 per cent of the population was lacking.

This lack of provision for women's needs, for example, is counterproductive in many cases. In Sutton Leisure Services they found that women-only swimming sessions in off-peak times encouraged not only Muslim women but women from all backgrounds to participate because they preferred it to mixed 'more rowdy' sessions. This in turn has led to more income generation and a financial success for the service.

In Sutton the effects of CCT have been to make the Leisure Department more business oriented and with a devolved budget system each manager is under pressure to achieve results for their area. Effective marketing is an important part of the business plan for each project or objective. The contracts run in-house are very successful because managers have needed to increase income and had to go out and actively market centres – where previously they would tend to wait for customers to come to them.

Targeting

Targeting specific needs of particular groups in the community is a vital component of the marketing strategy and achieving a quality service for consumers. Although CCT has resulted in a more commercial approach by many leisure managers, local authorities still maintain control and a strong influence on the social and community priorities of the area. In the London Borough of Sutton the council is strongly committed to the dissemination and implementation of its core values. The Leisure Services Department marketing policy reflects closely the objectives and values of the council, which provided a helpful framework for planning and targeting particular community groups, such as refugees. In this way the council supports departmental programming and potential conflict is avoided. Consultations with users of local parks are regularly conducted to measure their satisfaction and identify problem areas like dog fouling. This is followed up by establishing Friends' organizations for each facility which, though time-consuming, are very valuable as a marketing tool in terms of feedback.

Externalization

Having survived and won the first round of CCT, many in-house Direct Service Organizations (DSOs) were disappointed at the lack of freedom and flexibility which could have resulted from the devolvement of responsibility. Management or employee buy-outs were considered by many to be a way of providing improved services, with more control, growth and flexibility. Partnership with the local authority means it retains control of overall standards of service, becoming an enabling authority with reduced costs and the power to negotiate capital investment with the new external organization. However, as DSOs have become more competitive, and the CCT market reduces, externalization is no easy option. The successful management buy-out companies need to focus on quality services to meet specific needs of the local community, although increasing financial constraints on local authorities have meant a tendency to select contractors at the lowest price (Leybourne, 1994).

The future – opportunities and obstacles

One way of increasing resources and improving quality is through marketing cooperative arrangements with other organizations, from both the public and the private sector. The number of partnerships and collaborations are growing in the increasingly competitive leisure market. One of the most beneficial connections has been between health and leisure. Promoting leisure as improving the population's health and thereby reducing absenteeism and health service costs while increasing personal satisfaction and general wellbeing has obvious benefits. The Institute of Leisure and Amenity Management (ILAM) has promoted initiatives such as the GP referral scheme and programmes to improve fitness and health. The growth in the number of health suites in leisure facilities bears witness to this. ILAM has collaborated with the Health Education Authority, the Sports Council and BBC Radio to encourage listeners to attend leisure facilities (Smith, 1994).

An early example of the GP referral scheme was described by Lockward and Goodwin in 1994. The Exercise by Prescription scheme was begun in Yorkshire following the appointment of an exercise specialist by the health promotion unit in York. Patients were referred for ten-week periods of exercise specially designed to fit the needs of each individual who were continually monitored. This was achieved at minimal cost to the health authority and benefited the leisure centres by increasing their off-peak attendance rates. Incentives in the form of reduced charges were offered and resulted in a high proportion of patients joining the centre on completion of their 'prescription' sessions (Lockward and Goodwin, 1994). Other collaborations to be exploited by leisure marketers include local voluntary groups, especially those aimed at the elderly. This is a growing population with more time and money to spend on leisure activities which would benefit from increased exercise and a healthier lifestyle. The striving for quality services is certainly at the top of local authority leisure services' agendas with Charter Marks and BS 5750 being popular goals. The changes imposed by CCT, unitary status and budgetary restrictions have had a detrimental effect in some cases, but overall the result has been to try harder for improved standards despite the difficulties. In this situation marketing personnel have an even more significant role to play in highlighting the benefits of participation in terms of improved health and quality of life for the community as a whole. It is to be hoped that in the course of restructuring this role is not overlooked.

Issues

1   The reorganization of leisure services within the new competitive environment of local authorities.
2   The lack of well-defined aims and objectives in many leisure services.
3   The emphasis on a quality of life approach to marketing planning.

Questions

1   What are the main features of the new business environment in which leisure services now operate?
2   What are the problems faced by leisure service managers in developing a marketing strategy for such a wide-ranging and complex product?
3   How should programme planning be developed?
4   Compare quality of life marketing with societal marketing approaches.
5   Why has quality management become such a significant part of public service provision in recent years?
6   From the examples offered in this chapter, what is the significance of staff training for the implementation of quality management programmes?
7   What has been the effect of CCT on service development?
8   What are the major opportunities for marketing management in leisure services?

References

Aitchison, C. (1994) Fairer provision. *Leisure Opportunities*, **123**, 32.

Audit Commission for Local Authorities in England and Wales (1989) *Sport for whom? Clarifying the local authority role in sport and recreation*, HMSO.

Birmingham City Council (1995) *Policy framework 1995/6*.

British Standards Institution (1992) *BSI Handbook 22. Quality Assurance*.

Campbell, K. (1996) Women's Realm, *Leisure Management*, **16** (5).

CELTS (Centre for Leisure and Tourism Studies) (1990) *Recreation management training needs*, Sports Council.

Cespedes, F.V. (1993) Ethical issues in distribution. In Smith, N.C. and Quelch, J.A. (eds), *Ethics in marketing*, Irwin, pp. 473–90.

Kinnell, M. and MacDougall, J. (1994) *Meeting the marketing challenge. Strategies for public libraries and leisure services*, Taylor Graham.

Kotler, P. (1986) *Principles of Marketing*, 3rd edn, Prentice Hall.

Leicester City Council, Leisure Services Department (1991) *Leisure in Leicester 2000*.

Leybourne, J. (1994) Option for change? *Leisure Management*, **14** (9), 28–31.

Lockward, F. and Goodwin, K. (1994) Gain without pain. *Health Service Journal*, **104** (5415), 29.

Ministry of Housing and Local Government (1967) *Management of local government. Volume I, Report of the Committee* and *Volume V, Local government administration in England and Wales*, HMSO.

Ortmeyer, G.K. (1993) Ethical issues in pricing. In Smith, N.C. and Quelch, J.A. (eds), *Ethics in marketing*, Irwin, pp. 389–404.

Sirgy, M.J. and Lee, D.-J. (1996) Setting socially responsible marketing objectives. *European Journal of Marketing*, **30** (5), 20–34.

Smith, A. (1994) Future possibilities. *Leisure Management*, **14** (7), 30–32.

Sports Council (1990) Competitive tendering and Sport for All. In *Sport for All facilities* (Fact File 1), London.

Torkildsen, G. (1992) *Leisure and recreation management*, 3rd edn, E & F N Spon.

Torkildsen, G. (1994) Setting programmes. *Leisure Opportunities*, **127**, September, 42–3.

Further reading

Audit Commission for Local Authorities in England and Wales (1989) *Sport for whom? Clarifying the local authority role in sport and recreation*, HMSO.

Kinnell, M. and MacDougall, J. (1994) *Meeting the Marketing Challenge. Strategies for public libraries and leisure services,* Taylor Graham.

Torkildsen, G. (1992) *Leisure and Recreation Management,* 3rd edn, E & F N Spon.

CHAPTER 7

Marketing public-sector information services

Summary

While public-sector information services are found in many contexts in the UK the public library service is the best recognized and established. There have been pressures on public libraries, following legislation to limit local authorities' funding powers and to encourage libraries to charge for some services. A major difficulty has been defining what public libraries should do, and whether they are leisure, educational or cultural institutions, or some combination of these. The current range of services is very wide, and often unfocused. Measuring quality has become a more significant activity, following implementation of the Audit Commission indicators. However, both quality management and strategic, planned marketing activities have been limited.

Introduction

By comparison with many other countries the UK is particularly well served by public-sector information services. It has an extensive network of public libraries, which statutorily have to be provided by every local authority designated as a library authority. These offer a range of services in addition to the core book-lending service which still forms the bulk of public library activity. In addition, the British Library functions as the national hub of library services through its role as the centre for the legal deposit of all items published in the UK. It also acts as a bibliographical service through its production of the *British National Bibliography,* and as one of the major research libraries in the country provides materials and information for use by businesses, scholars and other institutions at home and overseas. When the new British Library building at St Pancras is open, there will be opportunity for more of the general public to acess its vast resources.

Public-sector information services are also found in many other contexts. Local authorities, for example, often provide information services for citizens to inform them about services and council administration. Manchester City Council set up such a service to ensure that local services and council members communicated effectively with local people; a comprehensive directory for distribution throughout the city was one of its major outputs. Many local authorities are also now using the Internet to set up World Wide Web pages offering information on their locality and the leisure and business opportunities available. Voluntary organizations which supplement public libraries' information provision to the general public include Citizens Advice Bureaux, Youth Service information points and the Department of Trade and Industry-supported network of Business Links which provide business information and advice to small and medium-sized enterprises.

The context in which public sector information services are delivered is therefore complex, with many sources of information provision available to the general public. However, for the purposes of this chapter public libraries will be the focus, in order to assess the relevance of marketing for this well-established institution which began with the Public Libraries Act 1850 and has become one of the most familiar and visible of all public services.

Many of the voluntary-sector information services are important stakeholders to which public libraries need to relate and voluntary-sector organizations themselves also facilitate information flows within communities. Like many other service providers, public libraries depend on a complex supply chain and, at the same time, contribute to this chain in order to support the information work of other organizations. They rely on the national public-sector information infrastructure for their effective delivery of information (as well as on suppliers who include booksellers, library suppliers and commercial databases and on-line information services) and they also make their information services available for use by other information providers. Business Links, for example, have developed good relationships with their local public library services in order to access the often extensive range of directories and other materials which the public library has purchased for use by its community. Public libraries have not generally so far seen themselves as being in competition with Business Links; they are partners in information delivery to businesses. However, this pattern of a free, comprehensive and efficient service to all members of a local community which was confirmed in the Public Libraries and Museums Act 1964, still the most significant defining legislation for the service in England and Wales, is now being challenged by the competitive, entrepreneurial culture within which all public services now operate. (As with education, Scotland and Northern Ireland have separate legislation but the pattern of provision and the standards expected of services is similar across the UK.) The cooperative and collaborative culture which has characterized the development of public libraries is rapidly changing.

The pressures for public libraries came with the 1988 Green Paper, *Financing our Public Library Service* (Office of Arts and Libraries, 1988) and the subsequent Local Government and Housing Act 1989 which changed the basis upon which public library services were to be delivered. From being a largely free service at the point of delivery, public libraries were encouraged to charge for everything other than the 'core' service, defined as the lending of books and other printed materials. Joint ventures with the private sector were encouraged and attempts made to contract out some elements of the service (Kinnell Evans, 1991). Overall, government policy has moved public libraries much closer to a private-sector model of service delivery, with the potential for public library authorities to become service facilitators rather than providers, as with leisure services. This also means that they are increasingly seeing other information providers with whom they once had collaborative relationships (for example, in staff training) as competitors. This has happened in the case of schools library services, which as was discussed in Chapter 3, had been provided by public libraries on behalf of local education authorities. Now that these have become strategic business units operating on a commercial basis they are in competition with services in neighbouring authorities for the custom of schools.

Public library services: the evolution of a product

The nature of the product delivered by public library services and the objectives of a service with a duty to serve everyone in the community has been questioned as a result of this fundamental reconsideration of how libraries should best be organized and funded. In 1981 guidelines for developing clear public library aims and objectives were published (Heeks and Turner, 1981), but were not fully implemented by many library authorities. Even these came very late in the history of public libraries. Reports from the government departments responsible for public libraries have also offered guidance and have been regarded as useful, authoritative directives (Department of Education and Science, 1978; Office of Arts and Libraries, 1987, 1990). However, despite this wide range of advice from government and from within the library profession, there has continued to be widespread dissatisfaction that public libraries are not being managed appropriately in the straitened financial climate. It is felt that they need to focus on their key objectives and develop a more business-oriented outlook on those services which are additional to their major activity of book lending, reference services and other printed materials provision.

The greatest problem has been that public libraries have been reluctant to take up innovations from other sectors, particularly in the application of management skills. Even where they have developed new initiatives through participation in European and government-funded development projects, the imaginative use of information technology and the extension of core services to meet the needs of groups like the housebound, there has been a lack of resources to sustain these (Aslib, 1995, pp. 72–3). While lack of funding has been a key issue, so too has been the failure to exploit modern management techniques: especially marketing at the strategic rather than the tactical level.

Planning for a long-term reconfiguration of library services has not been undertaken. In a national study of the marketing strategies of public library services undertaken in 1991–2 (Kinnell and MacDougall, 1994) it was found that the range of services provided by public library authorities was remarkably broad. This was partly due to historic reasons in some authorities but also because of a widespread professional commitment to reaching out to the disadvantaged in society. There was also a lack of focus on what precisely was the role of the public library. The expansion of services during the 1970s and 1980s was possible because funding was relatively generous – for example, library spending per capita increased by 36 per cent from 1984–5 to 1988–9. It was also clear, though, that local political priorities as well as professional imperatives had played an important part in determining public library policies on the way money should be spent. The role of the elected members in developing local authority services, in this case libraries, has been an important feature of public service provision since the nineteenth century. Although now on the wane since the introduction by central government in the 1980s and 1990s of a range of legislation to curb local authority powers, this role meant that library services mushroomed in ways which supported local council objectives.

The concept of 'outreach', that is, moving services from a central point into the community, was particularly significant. In Lambeth during the late 1970s and early 1980s, one of the more extreme examples of this trend, services to children and young people were almost totally moved from library buildings into those venues where young people were likely to be found: crèches and nursery schools, youth clubs and playgrounds. Bookstocks in Lambeth libraries diminished so much that the library as a place to visit and borrow materials became less and less important, in line with the argument that librarians should be reaching out into their communities (Hill, 1973). While this trend was not so marked elsewhere, the emphasis changed from the library as a civic building with a centrally provided service to that of information and materials being made available wherever clients needed them in the community. As Table 7.1 shows, the range of services librarians were offering by 1991/2 reflected this trend to diversification and outreach.

Since this study, even more services have been added by many public libraries, especially in those libraries which now provide access to the Internet. Plans to link all of the UK's public libraries to the Internet, either through funding from the Millennium Commission or from other sources, could offer even further services to a wider range of the public (*Library Association Record*, 1996). On-line information provision and the loaning of CD-ROMs have already become increasingly significant.

Table 7.1 The range of services and facilities provided by public libraries in 1991/2

	No. of public library authorities	Total respondents (%)
Outreach services to elderly/housebound	130	94
Exhibitions	125	90
Mobile libraries	124	89
Room for meetings	114	82
Holiday activities	114	82
Business information services	104	75
Foreign literature collections	101	73
School library services	91	65
Hospital library services	80	58
Services to ethnic minorities	77	55
On-line bibliographic searching	75	54
Film shows/plays/music	67	48
Lectures	65	47
Prison library services	62	45
Viewdata	58	42
Television/teletext	57	41
Other services/facilities/events	39	28

Such a wide spread of services has created tensions between the education and leisure functions of libraries, which have resulted in problems at both local and national levels in defining the business libraries are in. Are they mainly purveyors of fiction – still the major element in borrowing figures – or are they providers of innovative services which are defining their role in new ways, as cultural and educational institutions with information provision at their core? There are problems in defining the primary product of public libraries precisely because they do serve everyone and are attempting to do so much. The Department of National Heritage set up a Review of public libraries in England and Wales to consider this issue, and specifically to consider potential changes to the 1964 Act. However, the then Minister's view of the 'core functions', which she restricted to a few key concepts, differed from the more complex and less easily measurable functions which emerged from the final Review report. Her key concepts were (*Hansard*, 1995):

1 Providing reading for pleasure.
2 Enlightening children and developing lifelong reading skills and habits in adults.
3 Encouraging lifelong learning and study.
4 Providing reference material including public information about local and national government and EU publications, current affairs, and business information.
5 Providing materials for the study of local history and the local environment.

The Review team, however, preferred to see the objectives of the library service in terms of the benefits perceived by customers: a marketing-led approach (Aslib, 1995, pp. 168–9):

1 *Continuing or perpetual benefits*
'These are aspects of the service which are regarded as necessary in any definition of the public library by all sectors of the community'
● enlightening children;
● popular reading;
● a community asset;
● an area for study;
● audio and video collections.
2 *Social benefits*
'A familiar relaxing place, which is safe, warm and well-lit . . . the library as a place at the heart of the community'.
● a familiar place;
● meeting friends.
3 *Sporadic or occasional benefits*
'The library as a reference point. . .'
● expert reference librarians;
● access to knowledge;

- local history;
- vital information;
- business information;
- local information.

Customers and potential customers, professional librarians and funders (government) have viewed the public library service differently, with varying if overlapping core objectives, a confusion which became very clear from this difference of view between the minister whose department comissioned the Review and the expert team who undertook it. This situation is very unlike that in some other countries where there is clearer consensus on the role of public libraries. A comparative study of quality management in Japanese and English public libraries, for example, has found that Japanese public libraries have a clear mission centred on books and materials lending, with the library a centre for lifelong learning, its agreed role throughout society. There, central government, professionals and library users see the library as basically an educational and cultural institution. Its role as an information provider is much less developed and hence less problematic (Kinnell and Oda, 1996).

A further major difficulty for UK library managers is meeting the wide-ranging needs for a high-quality public library service while continuing to address the political agendas of local authority members which reflect local priorities. All of this has to be achieved within the cash-limited budgets which have been imposed through central government capping controls on local authorities. Another key concern is that of maintaining the quality of services, services which have been copied widely internationally during the past decades, but which now need to refocus on their role for the next century.

Quality and performance

The pressure to move towards quality in all public sector services comes from five areas:

- competitive tendering;
- an emphasis on measuring performance;
- constraints on spending;
- a process of continual comparison with private sector practice;
- customer focus.

Competitive tendering

While compulsory competitive tendering (CCT) has not been imposed on public library services, many public libraries are managed within leisure directorates, with the inevitable impact of the CCT culture on their management practices.

An emphasis on measuring performance

There has been a need for library managers to reconsider the characteristics of the public library as a customer-focused service business and to reassess customer interactions which are so essential when measuring their quality of delivery (Schmenner, 1986). The Audit Commission, which assesses public service efficiency in England and Wales on behalf of government, in line with the Citizen's Charter legislation, has produced performance indicators that public libraries now have to use. These only go some way, though, to considering the value to the library's customers of what is offered. The measures are limited to (England and Sumsion, 1995):

1 The number of items issued by the authority's libraries:
   (a) books;
   (b) other items.
2 The number of public libraries:
   (a) open 45 hours per week or more;
   (b) open 30–44 hours per week;
   (c) open 10–29 hours per week;
   (d) mobile libraries.
3 The number of visits by members of the public to public libraries.
4 The amount spent per head of population on books and other materials.
5 The net expenditure per head of population on libraries.

Libraries also need customer-satisfaction surveys to add understanding of what their users require from a library service and, crucially in a context where the whole of the community is being targeted, but much more difficult to conduct, non-user surveys.

Constraints on spending

With the capping of local authority expenditure, public libraries have suffered budgetary constraints in recent years. One of the most obvious results of this has been the reduction in the numbers of hours libraries are open. In 1983–4 there were 79 libraries open over 60 hours per week (typically large city central libraries); by 1993–4 this had reduced to 45 (England and Sumsion, 1995).

A process of continual comparison with private sector practice

Libraries are now expected to assess their service delivery in relation to that of other materials and information providers, e.g. booksellers, database hosts, private-sector business information services. Despite the cautionary advice of Pollit and Harrison (1992) that 'managing public services is different', there has been considerable pressure for librarians to develop profit-making activities like bookselling, publishing, added-value business information services, commercially run video and CD-ROM loans.

Activity in local authorities has centred on quality assurance and accreditation, with librarians developing quality management techniques for their services. However, the progress of quality management in the sector has been limited, partly due to the public sector context which means that simply focusing on quality assurance as expressed by BS 5750/ISO 9000 is unhelpful (Walsh and Davis, 1993). There needs to be a more deeply considered understanding of what quality means to both customers and stakeholders. This includes the professional staff. Their view of a quality service might vary considerably from that of the public, many of whom have may have only a limited vision of what a public library can offer users in the new electronic era. It should be noted that this is not just a problem for public sector organizations. Certain other service sector businesses, including banks, finance and medical insurance organizations, have experienced similar difficulties in implementing quality systems (Drummond, 1992).

Marketing and the public library service

In attempting to create a market environment in public services, in which the needs of the customer become paramount, central government has created a new vocabulary for public sector employees. Competitive tendering has meant that many public services have found themselves in competition with the private sector to retain the work which was traditionally theirs (Barker, 1994). This has not yet happened to public libraries, although there have been some experiments to test its feasibility, notably in the London Borough of Brent. However, as we have seen, the competitive culture has permeated all this sector, and with it has come the recognition that services need to be involved in a range of marketing activities.

Marketing strategies

While a strategic, long-term view of library services needs to be developed, there is little evidence that this is happening. Uncertainty in the face of local government reorganization has created problems over the past two years (1994–6). Before that many public library services were subject to internal reorganizations to cope with the taking out of layers of management, a move driven by funding pressures. Leicestershire Libraries and Information Service has undergone this type of restructuring and was faced in 1996 with preparation for local government reorganization, with Leicester City, Rutland and a rump Leicestershire taking over its previous services. Strategy has therefore focused on ensuring the survival of the core services and minimizing the damage which the most radical reorganization of local government since 1974 is inflicting (Library and Information Plan for Leicestershire Working Party on Local Government Reorganization, 1996).

Local political influences are also a strong feature in strategy making. In Birmingham it was noted by the Director of the Library Service that:

> We would look at the Council's priority target groups and assess what the specific contribution of library services could be in meeting their needs ... the role of the chief officer of a service department is to see how the Council's objectives can be best achieved. You're working in a political environment and their priorities have to be for completely practical reasons at the top of your work list (Kinnell and MacDougall, 1994, p. 50).

There was no separate marketing strategy in evidence in Birmingham. Service policies and priorities for the year ahead were outlined, with promotional activities noted as a separate item, but it was difficult to identify specific marketing functions in their Committee Strategy Report. Marketing was felt to be better implemented if it was integrated with other strategic issues:

> Most of what's contained within our strategy is about saying our service is much more ... there are a number of proactive things that we need to be doing, and those proactive things are not just put in place in order to benefit groups within the community although that's their primary purpose. They will also have the spin-off effect of raising the profile of the library service and expectations of what it can deliver (Kinnell and MacDougall, 1994, p. 53).

Clydesdale, in Scotland, was an interesting and exceptional example of a library service which had taken a rather different approach. Clydesdale libraries were controlled from within a Leisure Services Directorate and this had considerably influenced their operations. The Directorate was created in 1989 as a result of the introduction of CCT. As well as a detailed Draft Service Plan, a document entitled *Clydesdale*

Leisure into the 90s had been published, to communicate to staff the new structure, future plans and training policy. Internal marketing was treated seriously. A separate *Marketing Strategy* had been produced, with clear objectives and an outline of market research to be undertaken.

Marketing planning

At the level of tactical planning for marketing operations, public library services have also tended to lag behind other public sector services, such as leisure or health. As with strategic planning, there have been several exceptional examples of effective marketing activity in libraries, but there is a lack of coherent planning – and a preference for more *ad hoc* programmes, as three senior managers explained:

'A statement of marketing strategy and a plan would assist in the improvement of marketing, but absence of both does not prevent marketing activities.'
'It is part of the general culture.'
'As the service is swamped by the present level of demand, marketing is not a priority' (Kinnell and MacDougall, 1994, p. 66).

The concept of 'de-marketing' to manage demand more effectively was neither widely understood nor practised. However, it is important to recognize that this experience of poor take-up of planned marketing activity is shared by the for-profit sector. In one study it was found that only between 10 and 20 per cent of companies undertook comprehensive planning (Greenley, 1985) and in another only around 50 per cent undertook annual marketing planning in the context of longer-term strategic plans (Doyle, 1988).

One example of the successful development of marketing planning in public libraries is that of Manchester City Libraries' Commercial Library, one of the main public library services for business in the UK, as described by Gallimore (1992) and in the Channel 4 series, *The Marketing Mix*. Demand for its services were high, with around 35 000 telephone enquiries answered in a typical year, as well as visitors to the library. However, many of these came from beyond the Manchester area, and there was a need therefore to concentrate efforts more on the individuals and organizations within the City of Manchester in order to attract more of those who did not use the service. The marketing effort needed to be low-key, so that the response was limited to what the library could handle, and to persuade more people to visit the library so that they could help themselves to information. The intention was not to increase telephone enquiries but to limit them to Manchester council taxpayers. The more local calls that got through, the fewer enquiries from outside the City would be answered.

It was important, first, in developing a marketing plan for the library to define its main business – which was to 'make a positive contribution to the local economy and to the needs of the people in Manchester by providing and promoting the use of information about business and commerce' (Gallimore, 1992). Its customers were seen as the individuals and organizations in the City of Manchester and, since the service was funded wholly by the City Council, the primary market should be limited to this area. The fact that significant numbers of users came from beyond the City was important to the marketing strategy and planning. From user surveys it was possible to identify targets which had not yet been reached: ethnic groups, small firms and trade unionists. There was no one competitor able to offer the range and depth of resources of the commercial library, and other information services such as the Small Firms Service covered only niche markets. There were several clear advantages to users of the Manchester Commercial Library because of its central location, free service and wide-ranging facilities. A market analysis was undertaken to assess the primary market and market segments: companies, the people who worked for them, individuals, local and national government departments, journalists, consultants, marketing managers, other information and advice agencies, students, lecturers and researchers. The marketing plan which emerged as a consequence of this analysis focused on a promotional strategy which included reorganizing and refurbishment; better guiding and instructions to users; contact with local media; literature distributed to local venues and organizations in Chinese, Urdu, Gujarati and Bengali, as well as English; targeting of trade unionists; the appointment of a small firms liaison officer who 'cold-called' local firms to introduce the library's services; promotional talks to business clubs. Evaluation and feedback was based on continuing analysis of telephone enquiries and visits to the library (these on an occasional sample basis), but it was found difficult to measure the impact of specific promotional activity. Any increase in use of the service by those groups targeted had to be set against the existing high use of the Commercial Library. A detailed evaluation was possible with regard to small firms, with records kept of all those visited and a sample telephone survey as follow-up.

This example of the potential for impact of a large city central library can be seen elsewhere in innovative developments in marketing. Croydon Central Library, with its emphasis on IT, has become a centre for information use throughout a wide area. Sutton Central Library, in Surrey, has made a similar impact through its emphasis on the library as a focal community resource. It was one of the first to see the importance of the library providing a range of complementary facilities such as a coffee shop, bookshop and loans of popular music. In both of these library services, the concept of the library was developed through assessment of local needs and the design of appropriate services. As with Manchester City Libraries, though, the product is increasingly information, and not simply the book or other media. As Cronin (1984) noted, librarians are now 'moving into the age of de-institutionalized information retailing'; their service planning has to reflect changes in information delivery , especially the increasing significance of multi-media.

Services to children and young people have similarly shown how effective marketing planning can transform services by identifying more clearly the needs of customers and providing appropriate services (Kinnell, 1996). In 1983, Renfrew Public Libraries identified the need for a service that supported young people in a relatively deprived, high-unemployment area, with a specialist teenage library. The library service received an urban aid grant and was able to provide a space quite separate from both adults and childen, with a specialist librarian who selected materials and trained other staff in dealing with this often quite difficult client group. Consequently, it was found that these teen-agers' understanding of information issues which would help them find employment and gain entry to further education was much improved, thus meeting a major objective of the library service (Neill and Johnson, 1991). Another example of innovation in meeting the information and leisure needs of young people, developed through analysis of their lifestyles and environment was that of Bradford's Xchange, a specialist service for teenagers centred on multicultural needs (Wilkes, 1986).

Service product development

As we have seen, much of the impetus for a more market and quality-driven approach to managing public library services has come from an increased emphasis on how well services are performing. Library service products comprise a mix of tangible and intangible benefits which are difficult to measure, although measurement is now being expected of managers, through the Audit Commission indicators. Benefits are closely connected in customers' minds with aspects of the service such as standard and range of provision, the helpfulness of staff, the quality of the surroundings and service delivery. Cowell (1984) has analysed these in terms of:

- the consumer benefit concept;
- the service concept;
- the service offer;
- the service delivery system.

For library managers this means that quality has to be measured not only in terms of how many items are borrowed, or how many visits are paid to the library, or even how many hours a week the library is avail-able for use. The quality of the experience of using the library also has to be measured – a more complex and less readily quantifiable concept.

User and non-user studies therefore have to be pursued by library services in order to understand what the community thinks of them. They can then develop services to meet the community's needs, in line with organizational objectives, the priorities set by the elected members and funding constraints.

A further example of service development is that of Cheshire Libraries. In 1993, the Information and Leisure Services Committee recommended that user surveys should be undertaken, to test preferred patterns of opening hours. Proposed changes which could be achieved within resourcing constraints would then be considered by them (England and Sumsion, 1995). Cheshire has a long record of library user research and their 1994 survey was an excellent example of clear conclusions being drawn from well-constructed research, which were then carried forward into further action. The survey, which was undertaken by the Council's Research and Intelligence Unit was conducted over a full week in larger libraries and over two weeks in smaller libraries, to ensure a large enough representative sample. Questions were asked about why people were visiting the library, whether or not they found what they wanted, the helpfulness of staff, the range of stock, opening hours, the reservation service, and general satisfaction with the service. From those 31 libraries surveyed up to 1995, 14 400 completed questionnaires were returned. The main results were:

- 89 per cent of those looking for a specific item found it;
- 96 per cent of those seeking information found the answer;
- 27 per cent of visitors had asked staff for help; of these 91 per cent found them very helpful, and 9 per cent helpful;
- views on the range of stock varied, with children's books scoring best;
- 57 per cent were very satisfied overall with the service with 39 per cent satisfied;
- only 6 per cent thought opening hours were inconvenient, but there were varying views on ideal opening hours for particular libraries.

Because attitudes to opening hours were localized, a more detailed analysis of the responses was needed, upon which the committee could then act; and on suggested improvements to the service there were clear issues about the range of book stock being provided. These would also require action.

Conclusion

All public library services now need to develop marketing approaches in the way that many of the larger library authorities routinely do, as a means of ensuring the quality of their delivery to their communities. The review of the public library service undertaken for the Department of National Heritage underlined this relationship between performance and marketing, with concern expressed at the inward-looking attitudes of many public library managers who failed to recognize both competition for their services and the potential for innovation. The Review team recommended a public and school library inspectorate (OFLIB) to appraise library authorities' plans and performance in order to raise the levels of service delivery. This recommendation has not been taken up by government, and instead individual library services are expected to use the Audit Commission indicators to guide them in their performance evaluation and to support their marketing planning. Most important of all is the need for public library services to probe long-held assumptions about their role and to establish clear objectives. They can then undertake well-targeted marketing activities which will include extensive and sustained market research to test customers' perceptions and identify the potential for reaching further groups in the community.

Undoubtedly, the reorganization of local authorities which means that many large library services are being split into smaller units will cause a reappraisal of how marketing should best be developed for an area, in order to sustain the relationships with library users which have been built up over many decades. It has been suggested that regional cooperation is a way forward. This already exists to some extent through the operation of Library and Information Plans which have been developed to provide a more strategic focus on information provision for regions. However, these have made little impact on delivery at grassroots level. As the Department of Heritage Review recommended, there is now scope for a more regional approach to support the wider implementation of marketing (Aslib, 1995, p. 97):

- Potentially, cooperative 'marketing' is a benefit for communities working together.
- They could also share facilities and systems with other communities, develop better quality control and possibly develop alternative funding sources.

Issues

1 The complex interactions between the varying kinds of public information provider.
2 The need for fundamental reappraisal of the roles of public library services.
3 The reluctance of public library managers to apply management principles from other sectors.

Questions

1 What are the main pressures facing public libraries?
2 What is the nature of the product offered by public libraries?
3 Why is the primary product so diverse?
4 How is the impetus to quality affecting public library management?
5 Consider the performance measures currently being used by managers – are they adequate?
6 To what extent are marketing strategies constrained by local political concerns?
7 Why has the tactical implementation of marketing in public libraries lagged behind that of other public sector services?
8 What are the priorities for public library services in developing a marketing orientation?

Marketing public-sector information services **121**

References

Aslib (1995) *Review of the Public Library Service in England and Wales for the Department of National Heritage. Final Report.* Aslib.

Barker, L. (1994) *Competing for Quality,* Longman.

Cowell, D.W. (1984) *The Marketing of Services,* Butterworth-Heinemann, p. 99.

Cronin, B. (1984) The marketing of public library services in the UK – practical applications. In Yorke, D.A. (ed.), The marketing of local authority lesiure services. *European Journal of Marketing,* **18**, 45–55.

Department of Education and Science (1978) *The Libraries' Choice,* HMSO, Library Information Series 10.

Doyle, P. (1988) Marketing and the British chief executive. *Journal of Marketing Management,* **3** (2).

Drummond, H. (1992) *The Quality Movement,* Kogan Page.

England, L. and Sumsion, J. (1995) *Perspectives of Public Library Use: A compendium of survey information,* Book Marketing Ltd and Library and Information Statistics Unit, 6, p. 107.

Gallimore, A. (1992) Marketing a public sector business library: developing a strategy. In Cronin, B. (ed.), *The Marketing of Library and Information Services 2,* Aslib, pp. 126–43.

Greenley, G.E. (1985) Marketing plan utilization. *Quarterly Review of Marketing,* **10** (4), 12–19.

Hansard (1995) Parliamentary Answer, 268, column 852–4, 18 December, HMSO.

Heeks, P. and Turner, P. (eds) (1981) *Public Library Aims and Objectives,* Public Library Research Group.

Hill, J. (1973) *Children are People: The librarian in the community,* Hamish Hamilton.

Kinnell, M. (1996) Meeting their needs: marketing and library services. In Elkin, J. and Londsale, R. (eds), *Focus on the Child: Libraries, literacy and learning,* Library Association Publishing, pp. 159–73.

Kinnell, M. and MacDougall, J. (1994) *Meeting the Marketing Challenge: Strategies for public libraries and leisure services,* Taylor Graham.

Kinnell, M. and Oda, M. (1996) Coals to Tokyo: quality management in UK and Japanese public libraries. *Public Library Journal,* **11** (5), September/October, 131–3.

Kinnell Evans, M. (1991) *All Change? Public library management strategies for the 1990s,* Taylor Graham, Chapter 1.

Library Association Record (1996) Millennium bid progresses, **98** (12), 603.

Library and Information Plan for Leicestershire Working Party on Local Government Reorganization (1996) *Key Issues in the Delivery of Library, Information and Advice Services Following Local Government Re-organization in Leicestershire,* Leicestershire County Council.

Neill, L. and Johnson, I.M. (1991) Information for unemployed teenagers. *International Review of Children's Literature and Librarianship*, **6** (2), 95–117.

Office of Arts and Libraries (1987) *A Costing System for Public Libraries*, HMSO, Library Information Series 17.

Office of Arts and Libraries (1988) *Financing Our Public Library Service: Four subjects for debate*, HMSO, Cmnd 324.

Office of Arts and Libraries (1990) *Keys to Success: Performance indicators for public libraries*, HMSO, Library Information Series 18.

Pollit, C. and Harrison, S. (eds) (1992) *Handbook of Public Services Management*, Blackwell.

Schmenner, R.W. (1986) How can service businesses survive and prosper? *Sloan Management Review*, Spring, 21–32.

Walsh, K. and Davis, H. (1993) *Competition and Service: The impact of the Local Government Act, 1988*, HMSO.

Wilkes, B. (1986) Library services for city children: a case study of Bradford, England. *International Review of Children's Literature and Librarianship*, **1** (2), 12–26.

Further reading

Aslib (1995) *Review of the Public Library Service in England and Wales for the Department of National Heritage. Final Report.* Aslib.

Kinnell, M. and MacDougall, J. (1994) *Meeting the Marketing Challenge: Strategies for public libraries and leisure services*, Taylor Graham.

Pollit, C. and Harrison, S. (eds) (1992) *Handbook of Public Services Management*, Blackwell.

CHAPTER 8

Social services

Summary

Social welfare continues to be one of the major items of government expenditure, so that there has been considerable effort to introduce tighter controls and a more businesslike approach to managing state welfare provision. Government has introduced a 'quasi-market' to replace some state provision with private or independent providers; and both nationally and locally social and welfare professionals now have to adopt marketing practices to deliver a more effective service. Involving clients in service delivery has become more important: communication is now being better targeted at the different client groups. As with the health sector, purchaser/provider relationships have been introduced which have created difficulties, and ethical issues have to be considered when marketing principles are applied in such a sensitive sector.

Introduction

The social security budget for the United Kingdom in 1996 was almost £90 billion, the largest single item of public expenditure and comprising one third of all public spending (Central Statistical Office, 1995). This is in spite of government attempts since the 1970s to limit public spending particularly in the areas of social security. Since 1979 successive Conservative governments have introduced a series of reforms to eradicate inefficiency and break down the so-called 'cycle of dependence' whereby traditional family-based forms of support were displaced by the compulsory provision of welfare services (Castles and Pierson, 1996, p. 235). The Housing Act 1980 was followed by a series of changes to social welfare entitlement laws and pensions through the Social Security Act 1986, the Housing Act (1988), and the National Health and Community Care Act 1990. The overall aims of this legislation were to transfer the responsibility of social provision from the state to the individual and employers, thus reducing central government costs and encouraging private insurance and pension schemes.

Whereas social welfare legislation has raised less media comment than that devoted to the wholesale changes in education and health over the past few years, the effects on unemployment and the labour market have been significant. The introduction in 1996 of the Job Seeker's Allowance in place of unemployment and other benefits has meant much more stringent tests of willingness and ability to work, and increasing resources devoted to detecting cases of fraud. These aims were given further emphasis in the four strategies for reducing public expenditure issued by the Department of Social Security in 1995 (DSS Press Release, 95/087):

- to focus benefits on need;
- to help people off benefit and into work;
- to encourage self-provision;
- to fight fraud.

The quasi-market

Although these measures have had limited success in terms of reducing spending and poverty, the pressure on social services has been gradually increasing with the imposition of quasi-markets while government controls continue. The traditional state provision of social welfare is being replaced with private or independent providers competing in quasi-markets. At the same time, the state is becoming a purchaser of services under continually restricted centrally controlled budgets and the threat of new purchasers in the form of voluntary organizations. As Aldridge (1996) argues, social service professionals need to promote themselves and their services in an increasingly competitive environment to gain their share of public resources. Problems of a low profile and lack of public recognition have to be overcome and a picture of a proactive, consumer-oriented and cost-effective professional service developed.

Developing a marketing approach

In recent years social service and welfare professionals have been forced to adopt a more business-like approach to their everyday activities. In order to do this they also have to adopt marketing practices. Unlike many other public service sectors like health, education, leisure and public libraries, social services have not generally regarded marketing as beneficial to management activities apart from some public relations and publicity programmes. Whereas much has been published generally on the not-for-profit sector, relatively little has been published on marketing in the social services professional press and the profession has a comparatively low appreciation of marketing values. Marketing is still seen by many as business oriented with a profit-centred approach and having little relevance to social welfare work.

As Lauffer (1986) has asserted, many social services providers work, wrongly he believes, from the assumption that their services are in the best interests of the public and that there is a need. Therefore, because there is a need, it is assumed that finance will be always available from government and other organizations to provide those services. In recent years it has become apparent, both in the USA and the UK that this is no longer the case and that not-for-profit services cannot assume high funding levels purely on grounds of providing a worthwhile service (Hansler, 1986). At the same time, competition from voluntary organizations and private contractors means increased overlap of service provision and further pressure on fewer resources. These trends indicate the necessity of a marketing-oriented approach to service delivery, the development of strategic marketing planning and a more effective public profile. Since the advent of the Citizen's Charter the growth of consumerism has emphasized the need for, among other things, improved communication, greater choice and more accountability and overall responsiveness from the public sector generally. In terms of social services marketing there are specific problems to be overcome which include the dual constituency, the purchaser/provider split and ethical considerations.

The dual constituency and the marketing mix

In order to develop a marketing approach for social services a number of factors must be taken into consideration which distinguishes the public from the private sector. The dual constituency of donors (both public and private) and clients for whom services are provided forms one important factor. Effective marketing must recognize at the outset the needs of both groups as well as the efficiency of the organization itself. The donor group which includes central and local government as well as voluntary and charitable organizations will have various needs including accountability, impact and responsiveness of services. Political issues and affiliations and the new quasi-market of the purchaser/provider split also play a large part in the marketing function and will be looked at in more detail in the next section. The needs of the client group are equally varied but based on the overall effectiveness of services. An examination of client needs should be based on the definition of clients needing specific services (target markets), the types of actual services required and the identification of particular areas in which the organization can effectively and efficiently provide services.

The dual purposes of resource attraction and resource allocation are central to the marketing task (Segal, 1991). The basic marketing mix of product, pricing (value for money), distribution, and promotion must be planned to accommodate both activities at every stage.

The product

The service product is particularly difficult to market because of its characteristics of intangibility, inseparability from the personnel providing the service, variability and perishability as well as the inherent involvement of the client receiving the service (Kotler and Andreasen, 1996, pp. 367–86). For example, in the case of inseparability of service from provider, if the social worker gives the impression of having too heavy a workload to deal with a client's further problems and appears unwilling to discuss them, a negative reaction is experienced by the client. The client may then go on to make complaints to the funding body which may ultimately reduce funding or other support. Customer orientation for social services staff is an obvious but necessary programme with staff empowered to deal on the spot with problems as they arise rather than referring them to higher authorities or incurring irritating procedural delays. The client satisfaction and service loyalty thus gained can do much to ensure equally long-term allegiance from donors.

Value for money

The price or value of the social service product depends to a great extent on the quality of the product provided. This includes a variety of elements related to the intangibility of the service. Although the value of the services provided cannot be measured in concrete terms in advance many features will provide keys to the value for the client to assess. These include the atmosphere or environment in which the service is provided, the level of hygiene, the state of the building (maintenance and decoration) and the attitude of staff themselves. The level of involvement by staff in an individual case exemplified by a follow-up telephone call to check on satisfaction or otherwise will also go a long way to ensuring that the client's expectations of value for money are satisfied.

Distribution and variability

Distribution and variability of the service product are particularly important factors in marketing social welfare services. Clients in need of social services come from a widely disparate area geographically, culturally and socially. Likewise, those responsible for voting funds to finance social services will often have equally diverse origins. High-quality service provision is necessary to ensure a widely dispersed service maintains a product which is consistently good value for money. Staff training and constant evaluation of continuing education courses are a method of ensuring a uniformly high standard of service delivery. Monitoring of client satisfaction through surveys and focus group studies as well as careful investigation of complaints and suggestions from clients are also essential to guarantee a high-quality service for all clients.

Promotion

In the promotion of services offered by social welfare organizations it is especially important that the balance between appealing to the donor and client constituencies is carefully maintained. People are often uninterested in or even opposed to welfare services for a variety of reasons, including political and social attitudes, apathy and lack of knowledge. Social services must therefore spend considerable effort in persuading both clients and donors that their services are beneficial to society as a whole and to them in particular (Segal, 1991). A common view of clients is that acceptance of social services is demeaning and others may react with aggressive resistance to any approach. Media coverage of a small number of badly handled cases have increased fears among many potential clients and made donors more wary of involvement whether it be in a voluntary or a financial capacity.

The involvement of the client in the provision of services could be used more effectively in promotion of services if, as Kotler and Andreasen (1996, pp. 382–3) suggest, marketing strategies facilitated 'helping consumers consume'. Clients who misuse or do not benefit from the service as they should are getting a lower-quality service and are more likely to be dissatisfied. Kotler and Andreasen suggest several methods of overcoming this situation, involving changing either the marketer or the consumer. The most obvious approach is for the marketing team to tailor the service as far as possible to the client's ability to understand and accept the service. This could mean making the initial approach to social services as easy and accessible as possible. The involvement of clients is essential to be able to design systems to suit each type of approach – whether it is from an unemployed school leaver or an elderly disabled person. Separate leaflets, posters, information tapes or more accessible enquiry points may be required for each type of client.

In the late 1980s the Department of Health and Social Security hired a design consultancy to improve its range of social security literature which was complex, inconsistent, and inaccessible (Arundel, 1987). A new communications strategy was developed and information literature was produced in five stages. Overview leaflets gave brief details, leading on to promotional leaflets targeted at particular claimants, and more technical guides with detailed information. Benefits were described according to the specific market group such as the sick and disabled, people bringing up children and so on. Forms with simple questionnaires to establish eligibility were then supplied. Attention was given particularly to plain language, a consistent simple design and structure, colour and typography, and user-friendliness.

Another approach is to teach the client to use the service in more effective ways. This can be done through more community contacts such as meetings with representative groups and talks at day centres, youth clubs and schools. Client expectations should be studied and social services organizations consider whether they are able to meet them. At the same time, consumers may be helped to make more discriminating choices and to evaluate services on offer, such as the range of public or private nursing homes in the area. Guidelines on standards to expect and on making an informed choice could be made available to potential clients. Various ways of ensuring long-term client and donor loyalty can be established through careful attention to building strong relationships with consumers and donors as a partnership.

The purchaser/provider split

The aims of the new community care and social welfare policy are based on matching services to client needs by shifting the burden from provider-led to needs-led services, from the public sector to a mixed economy of care, and from institutional to domiciliary care (Wistow *et al.*, 1994). The introduction of an internal market between the purchasers and providers of services is seen as the method of achieving these aims. By reducing the influence of the providers of services and introducing competition it is believed that services will more directly reflect the specific needs of clients and be more responsive to them. The two key components of the new policy are to ensure sensitivity and flexibility of service provision and to increase choice through a range of services (Department of Health, 1989, para 1.10).

The case for assuming that providers are necessarily always self-interested and that reducing their powers and increasing competition will automatically increase choice and responsiveness in community care is analysed by Lewis *et al.* (1996) who find some of the evidence equivocal. Other writers have also reported concern over the lack of improvement for clients and their carers and the increase in insecurity and costs (Wistow and Robinson, 1993). The efforts required to establish the purchaser/provider split have been enormous and disruptive, demanding considerable investment of time and financial resources, while simultaneously social services are attempting to continue providing a service.

Establishing separate purchaser and provider roles within integrated social services has been problematic especially in the case of care managers whose tasks included providing both counselling and purchasing services. These problems were recognized by the last government, which advised a pragmatic approach to overlapping roles (Price Waterhouse and the Department of Health, 1991). On the whole, however, care managers were seen as purchasers and in some cases this has meant a concentration on purely administrative tasks at the expense of sensitive interaction between managers and clients (Lewis *et al.*, 1996).

Purchaser/provider relationships

The relationship between purchasers and providers has also proved to be difficult in many cases with artificial barriers suddenly being erected between fellow-professionals. Difficulties have arisen whether local authorities have chosen to adopt a purchaser/provider split quickly or to use a gradualist approach. An example of this is a multi-agency team dealing with mentally disabled people where the health service members were designated providers and the social service members as purchasers, although they were both performing the same tasks (Lewis *et al.*, 1996). Relationships such as these will inevitably suffer – at least in the short term – when it is seen as a 'them and us situation'. Other factors often adversely affecting relationships include the enormous upheaval and confusion engendered by huge numbers of staff being transferred or redesignated in a short space of time, with little guidance or advice to help them. Failure to devolve budgets to purchasers or to provide a range of services to choose from led to unsatisfied clients and low morale in staff.

The whole culture of social welfare services has been turned upside down with the introduction of the purchaser/provider split. For decades social workers have avoided involvement with the financial side of service delivery and have evolved a culture of service and social values which tended to eschew the business-like practices of the marketplace. Since 1991 social services have had to learn to adopt some of these practices, of which marketing management is one of the main components. As Lewis *et al.* (1996, p. 9) reported there was little evidence by the mid-1990s of a commitment at that stage to strategic planning, needs identification or market mapping. Reduced funding and a lack of sufficient guidance from central or local government had slowed the pace of implementation. In the USA it was found that the effects of contracting for social services bore little relation to government policy documents or to marketing theories (Gronbjerg, 1991). Increased administration and bureaucracy have tended to obscure the feeling of empowerment for purchasers and to increase some providers' resentment at relinquishing their needs-assessment roles.

There is little evidence that the purchaser/provider split has succeeded in creating more competition in all areas. Whereas there has been a considerable increase overall in private nursing homes (there have also been many closures and bankruptcies), in the domiciliary care sector there has been very little growth (Wistow *et al.*, 1994). Therefore one of the main requirements of the quasi-market, multiple purchasers and multiple providers, is not consistently being fulfilled. Quality of service provision in meeting the requirements of clients is limited to the range of choices available.

Ethical issues

Modern social pressures and accountability require that marketing practices be conducted ethically, in particular in all activities concerning the public service sector. Marketing practices raise ethical issues in all areas and particularly so in the provision of social services. Whereas many social welfare organizations use marketing techniques, albeit unknowingly, to increase community support and acceptance, many social workers find the concept of formally adopting a marketing strategy for resource allocation and attraction unacceptable. This would appear to be because the idea of 'selling' an ideal or a service goes against the traditional belief that good work has its own rewards and will be automatically supported and resourced. A widespread lack of understanding of the underlying principles of marketing is often to blame. With the introduction of the quasi-market, however, it is becoming even more apparent that social services departments need to integrate marketing principles into the day-to-day organization of services in order to raise their profile and compete successfully with other providers.

Several writers have referred to the importance of introducing an ethical approach to marketing which takes account not only of customer satisfaction but also the means by which this is achieved (Fraedrich *et al.*, 1991; Martin, 1985). This ethical or deontological approach to marketing tries to ensure that the success of a product in meeting a need is not achieved at the expense of environmental damage, health or safety or other negative effects. In social services terms this could mean the effective marketing of a new meals on wheels service without reducing the numbers of clients served, reducing the opportunities for social contact, or delivering the meals at unsuitable times for example.

Other ethical issues revolve around the expense needed to implement an effective marketing strategy into a social services department. The benefits can only be demonstrated by reference to the literature and to examples provided in this book on the many successful cases in other areas of the not-for-profit sector where marketing has proved a valuable tool in service development and delivery. The danger that marketing practices can play on the fears and anxieties of potential clients is a dilemma faced by many in social services departments. The privacy and sensitivity of clients must be considered at all times when dealing with such issues as unemployment, homelessness, poverty and deprivation (Segal, 1991). Much can be achieved in overcoming objections to marketing on ethical grounds by improving relationships between clients and service providers based on mutual exchange and the fulfilment of expectations.

One of the major developments in market growth in recent years has been the increase in demand for long-term residential care and the appropriate provision of services to meet this need. As the elderly population increases in numbers, marketing strategies will be necessary to provide information to aid decision making. Encouraging the demand for residential care has ethical and moral considerations. Negative aspects include the possible creation of need where it may not have previously existed, the increased isolation of the elderly, and the neglect of poor and sick elderly people in preference to the affluent and active who can afford high-quality private care. However, responsible marketing can be said to promote a more positive image of the elderly, provide more suitable and specialized facilities, and lower costs by increasing demand and accessibility (Kaye and Reisman, 1993).

The encouragement in recent years of the role of the private sector in residential care has focused attention on the need for a partnership between the private sector, health authorities, social services and voluntary bodies as well as patients themselves. The fear has been that economic rather than welfare considerations will be given priority in marketing private nursing homes. The benefits of economies of scale developments, such as increasing the numbers of residents and thereby reducing unit costs, can easily be appreciated, but the quality of life for the individuals concerned may not be so high. In these terms market forces are difficult to correlate with services for vulnerable people. Partnerships of various kinds can be developed to provide services which try to balance the needs of both sides. Groups of residential homes can offer care on a small and intimate scale if they share purchasing costs, certain facilities, and in other areas such as joint training schemes involving social services departments and voluntary organizations. Local authorities must work with the private sector to share valuable experience and pool resources to ensure quality services for those needing them (Bibby, 1990).

Relationship marketing and a pluralistic approach

The issue of conflicting interests between service providers, purchasers and clients is especially prominent at a time of enormous organizational changes and restructuring. The tensions and conflicts that have arisen over recent years in addition to much negative media coverage mean it is essential that social services make clear both internally and externally that their priorities are clients' needs. In the marketing of social services the need to harmonize the interests of purchasers and providers must be integrated with the main aim of satisfying clients' needs at all times. Relationship marketing would seem to be the most appropriate approach.

As we have discussed in Chapter 2, relationship marketing consists of 'building bridges' between the stakeholder groups – the service providers, purchasers, managers and the clients. The development and maintenance of high-quality client relationships is at the core of the marketing approach with long-term client loyalty as its aim. In the provision of social services the involvement of clients with the services provided is taken for granted but in fact is often not achieved. The activities necessary in the provision of social services must be based on the needs and wants of the clients targeted rather than on their perceived needs and wants.

A satisfactory mutual exchange between service provider and client and between provider and purchaser must be based on equal treatment and fairness for all partners. Commitment between these partners is essential in relationship marketing comprising as it does the individual's identification with the organization through stability, sacrifice and loyalty (Modway *et al.*, 1979). Stability is necessary to balance the conflicting interests of purchasers, providers and clients by establishing mutual trust and a common belief in the organization's aims and objectives. Sacrifice entails the willingness to be flexible in dealings with partners to the benefit of the other, thus ensuring long-term relationships in marketing. Loyalty is essential for marketing in that it involves the long-term commitment of clients to the service. An ethical approach to achieving these aims is based on the premise that all activities undertaken uphold high moral standards based on honesty and equity.

The increasing emphasis in recent years has been on providing the best possible service with limited resources. The moral and ethical challenge for social workers is to balance the needs of clients with the restrictions and accountability pressures of local authority budgets. It is necessary to adopt a pluralistic approach to monitoring and evaluating not only efficiency but also accessibility and responsiveness to the clients' needs (Powell and Goddard, 1996, pp. 94–5).

Evaluation and monitoring quality outcomes

For any organization to achieve its objectives it is essential to have information on how successfully it is meeting these objectives and, in the case of not-for-profit services, to know that the clients' needs are satisfactorily met. Kotler and Andreasen (1996, p. 599) describe the development of a continual systematic monitoring control programme, or tactical control system, to allow 'day-to-day fine tuning of the strategic plan to correct for undesirable performance'. This includes monitoring of cost-effectiveness and customer satisfaction. In the not-for-profit service organization customer satisfaction must be given a higher priority.

In the new quasi-markets of social services there must be attention to cost-effectiveness, budgets and resource allocation and attraction, but this must be monitored in close conjunction with clients' needs and satisfaction with services. In the reorganization necessary for the split between purchasers and providers it is easy to become overwhelmed by the administrative tasks at the expense of attention to details of service delivery. Whereas a great deal of attention is paid to the necessary practice of cost-efficiency measures and budgeting, relatively little time has been spent on accessibility and responsiveness for the client. Evaluation procedures must be conducted taking account of both cost and satisfaction levels to provide a balanced view of service effectiveness. A model put forward by Powell and Goddard (1996) argues for a reconciliation of the sometimes conflicting interests of resource management and clients' needs. There is a need for a partnership based on continuing dialogue, a pluralistic approach which incorporates both measures of service delivery into the monitoring process. Client participation in the assessment and evaluation processes can have a valuable impact on service planning and delivery.

A marketing survey of a meals-on-wheels service in Leicestershire looked at the service from the perspective of the users themselves (Tilston *et al.*, 1992). The authors noted that other studies had examined nutritional aspects and logistical problems but consumer needs and requirements had been neglected. Leicestershire Social Services provided over 1500 meals per day at the time of the survey and regarded the study as a vital marketing tool to identify consumer characteristics and needs and to evaluate service delivery and satisfaction levels. A high response rate of 75 per cent to the self-completed questionnaires resulted in valuable information on clients' age, sex, living arrangements and number of meals received. Satisfaction was measured in terms of meal arrival times, delays, temperature, variety and reheating. The popularity of possible new services were studied such as the provision of ready-to-cook meals delivered weekly or monthly, evening deliveries and cold packed meals. Other important marketing data revealed by the survey included the fact that widowers were the least well-nourished, a third of recipients had no surviving children, and that it was necessary to reassess short-term recipients to encourage them to regain their independence and not to rely unnecessarily on the service if they no longer needed it. The social contacts made during delivery of the meals and the security of a daily check on their wellbeing was a significant factor; the staff were regarded with affection and esteem.

The need to monitor the outcomes of community care reform in order to evaluate service quality and client orientation is also emphasized by Henwood *et al.* (1996, p. 50). They suggest a framework of measures to assess the effectiveness of community care changes in improving choice and quality of services. The four main criteria comprise

- the definition of desired outcomes by clients and their carers based on their views and those of involved professionals;
- the specification of service systems needed to deliver such outcomes and any changes required in existing services;
- the promotion of access to services appropriate to the needs of individual clients and carers, including assessment, care packaging, information and the removal of socio-economic, geographical and physical barriers to access;

- the development of operational policies and the allocation of resources necessary to enable access to services geared to the promotion of high-quality individual outcomes.

Monitoring exercises have in the past concentrated on the implementation of systems and processes rather than the quality-of-life aspects that the reforms were intended to improve. Using such a framework managers and marketers could negotiate for funding and target services to meet clients' needs more effectively.

Conclusion

In recent years social services departments have had to undergo unprecedented reorganization involving the adoption of a market-led approach to service delivery which in many cases was contrary to the ideals and experience of social workers. The purchaser/provider split has led to problems redefining the roles of social workers as well as areas of service provision. The incorporation of competition and business practices generally are having fundamental repercussions on the management of social services.

Although slower to adopt a marketing approach than other areas of public services like health and higher education, social services are beginning to accept the importance of applying marketing principles in increasing service effectiveness and efficiency. A marketing approach in some areas has already been developed such as in the promotion of services and in client-satisfaction surveys. The increasing emphasis on consumerism in public sector management has meant more emphasis on the responsiveness of services. The use of surveys and other market research has facilitated more informed decision making and improved relationships with clients.

Public-sector services require more openness and accountability than organizations in the commercial world and marketing should be used as a tool to improve access to services as well as cost-effectiveness within limited budgets. The trend towards the enabling authority where local authorities will be responsible for ensuring that services are adequately provided but not actually supply the services themselves will emphasize further the importance of consumer choice, responsiveness and politically aware marketing (Walsh, 1994).

Social services managers have encountered difficulties managing the often-conflicting demands involved in the creation of the quasi-market while maintaining service delivery. An ethical approach to management and marketing practice would ensure a consumer-oriented service which is responsive to needs, while maintaining its efficiency and effectiveness. The adoption of marketing principles and practices will, however, entail the development of a new outlook and applied definitions of marketing to match the specific needs of social services providers.

Issues

1   The imposition of a market, together with the continuation of government controls.
2   Overlap of service provision, competition, and the need for strategic marketing.
3   The introduction of the purchaser/provider split and consequent culture shift in social services.

Questions

1   Why do social services professionals now need to promote their services?
2   What has been the impact of the Citizen's Charter initiative on this and other public service sectors?
3   Why is the service product so difficult to market in the social services sector?
4   What are the particular issues that have to be considered in promoting social services?
5   How effective do you consider the purchaser/ provider split to be in introducing competitiveness?
6   What are the ethical issues in relation to social services marketing, and how important are they?
7   Why is relationship marketing relevant to this sector?
8   How does evaluation and quality monitoring support the new market-led ethos in social services provision?

References

Aldridge, M. (1996) Dragged to market: being a profession in the post-modern world. *British Journal of Social Work*, **26** (2), 177–94.

Arundel, S. (1987) Designing for the dole. *New Society*, **82** (1293), 22-3.

Bibby, P. (1990) What price quality? *Community Care*, 14 June, 25–6.

Castles, F.G. and Pierson, C. (1996) A new convergence? Recent policy developments in the United Kingdom, Australia and New Zealand. *Policy and Politics*, **24** (3), 233–45.

Central Statistical Office (1995) *Social Trends: 25*, HMSO.

Department of Health (1989) *Caring for people. Community care in the next decade and beyond*, Cm 849, HMSO.

Fraedrich, J.P. *et al.* (1991) An empirical investigation into the ethical philosophies of managers. In T. Childers *et al.* (eds) *Marketing Theory and Applications*, p. 463. American Marketing Association Winter Education Conference.

Gronbjerg, K.A. (1991) Managing grants and contracts. The case of four nonprofit social service organisations. *Non-Profit and Voluntary Sector Quarterly*, **20**, 5–24.

Hansler, D.F. (1986) Marketing volunteers can help your cause. *Fund Raising Management*, **17** (6), 38–43.

Henwood, M., Wistow, G., and Robinson, J. (1996) Halfway there? Policy, politics and outcomes in community care. *Social Policy and Administration*, **30** (1), 39–53.

Kaye L.W. and Reisman, S.I. (1993) Elder consumer preferences of marketing strategies in the human services. *Health Marketing Quarterly*, **10** (3/4), 195–210.

Kotler, P. and Andreasen, A.R. (1996) *Strategic marketing for non-profit Organizations*, 5th edn, Prentice Hall.

Lauffer, A. (1986) To market, to market: a nuts and bolts approach to strategic planning in human service organisations. *Administration in Social Work*, **10** (4), 31–9.

Lewis, J. *et al.* (1996). The purchaser/provider split in social care: is it working? *Social Policy and Administration*, **30** (1), 1–19.

Martin, T.R. (1985) Ethics in marketing problems and prospects. In G.R. Laczniak and P.E. Murphy (eds), *Marketing Ethics: guideline for managers*, pp. 1–7. Lexington Books.

Modway, R, Porter, L, and Steers, R. (1979) The measurement of organizational commitment. *Journal of Vocational Behaviour*, **14**, 224–47.

Powell, J. and Goddard, A. (1996) Cost and stakeholder views: a combined approach to evaluating services. *British Journal of Social Work*, **26**, 93–108.

Price Waterhouse and the Department of Health (1991) *Implementing community care. Purchaser, commissioner and provider roles*, Department of Health.

Segal, U.A. (1991) Marketing and social welfare: matched goals and dual constituencies. *Administration in Social Work*, **15** (4), 19–34.

Tilston, C.H. *et al.* (1992) The meals-on-wheels service in Leicester: a marketing study. *British Food Journal*, **94** (2), 29–36.

Walsh, K. (1994) Marketing and public sector management. *European Journal of Marketing*, **28** (3), 63–71.

Wistow, G. *et al.* (1994) *Social Care in a Mixed Economy*, Open University Press.

Wistow, G. and Robinson, J. (1993) *All Change. No Change? Community care six months on. A second report of developments in the health and social care divide*, Kings Fund Centre.

Further reading

Aldridge, M. (1996) Dragged to market: being a profession in the post-modern world. *British Journal of Social Work*, **26** (2), 177–94.

Gronbjerg, K.A. (1991) Managing grants and contracts. The case of four nonprofit social service organizations. *Non-Profit and Voluntary Sector Quarterly*, **20**, 5–24.

Walsh, K. (1994) Marketing and public sector management. *European Journal of Marketing*, **28** (3), 63–71.

CHAPTER 9

Charities and voluntary organizations

Summary

The voluntary sector is operating in a highly competitive environment with state bodies, local authorities and the private sector competing for public attention. Socio-economic as well as cultural changes affect the way charities market their causes. The change in the role of marketing in this sector and the growth of consumerism have led to an increase in professionalism in marketing practice. The use of sophisticated marketing techniques, the development of donor relationships, and the emphasis on image by many charities has raised public awareness of many causes.

Introduction

The definition of 'charity' and 'voluntary organization' refers to a wide range of organizations which are independent of government control, employ both paid staff and volunteers and receive various types of support from public funds. A board of unpaid trustees controls the activities of the organization which seeks to improve the lives of those it was set up to help. For the purposes of this study those non-state voluntary bodies and registered charities such as private schools, professional associations, churches, trade unions or political parties are not included in this chapter.

Since the introduction of the welfare state in the 1940s the number of charities and voluntary organizations has increased enormously, while many have a much longer history. The Charity Commission, which registers charities in England and Wales, had around 182 000 charities registered in 1996 with a combined annual income of £16 billion. Approximately 27 000 of these were subsidiaries or constituents of other charities and therefore 154 500 main charities were registered. This sector is growing at a rapid rate with 582 charities added to the register in October 1996 alone. Three-quarters of all charities have an annual income of less than £10 000 a year while only the top 8 per cent receive over 92 per cent of the total money given to charity each year.

With an annual income of £16 billion there would seem to be no lack of financial support for charities. However, as the figures above show, the competition for funds among the smaller organizations in particular is fierce and becoming stronger. In the 1990s, charities have to operate in a tough, commercial and competitive world and need to adopt efficient management and marketing practices in order to survive. From the meek and mild approaches of the 1950s, charities now have to compete for funds with ever more powerful and sophisticated communications techniques. At the same time, the vast range of organizations competing for a share of public charitable funding is growing in extent and diversity. If charities are to benefit the causes they set out to help, marketing could be the way to achieve those aims to save a dying child or rescue an endangered species. Some charities have still failed to realize the importance of marketing, assuming that to have a good cause guarantees immediate support. However, the public have so many good causes attracting their attention that there must be something specific to retain that attention and gain support. Charities need to have a high profile and market their cause to achieve recognition and make an impact on the public consciousness.

Socio-economic influences

The marketing of charities and voluntary organizations is particularly influenced by and vulnerable to changes in the economic climate. Whereas other types of not-for-profit organizations such as local authority services may rely largely on statutory funding of one kind or another, charities are reliant largely on the goodwill of the public and commercial organizations. In times of recession donations may be reduced or cease according to the financial status of donors, whether private or corporate. The Charities Aid Foundation mediates the process of funding from grant-making trusts and corporate bodies like British Petroleum, ICI, and the Hanson Trust, which donate millions of pounds annually to British charities. However, these generally comprise only a small number of the larger, high-profile charities and the competition for funds between the smaller organizations remains fierce. Many voluntary organizations receive financial support from the state in the form of grants and concessions through the European Union and central and local government. State funding, however, can impose constraints on the organization's autonomy (Saxon-Harrold, 1990). The introduction of the National Lottery into Britain in 1995 had a big impact on charities with many of the smaller organizations complaining that while some large charities did benefit, they suffered as a result of people spending spare cash on the lottery rather than giving to them.

Political influences

The influence of political developments are as significant to the voluntary sector as financial changes and are often related, whether at local or national level. While charities have to be careful to operate within their charitable status many organizations have to lobby on particular issues to influence political policy making and subsequent legislation. Charities like Shelter and the Child Poverty Action Group need to argue their case strongly both to achieve long-term change and to attract more public donations. Government policy on statutory funding of charities, on methods of giving such as deeds of covenant, investment funds, and tax changes must be carefully monitored and taken into account by marketers in the voluntary sector. Major changes in the control of charities and voluntary organizations such as the transfer of responsibility from the Home Office to the Department of National Heritage and the recommendations of the Commission on the Future of the Voluntary Sector have a fundamental effect on the development of marketing strategies and planning. Managers in the voluntary sector have to consider these political changes when developing marketing strategies.

Cultural and demographic change

Changes in cultural attitudes and demographic factors also play an important role in the way charities are perceived. The increase and variety of ethnic backgrounds must be taken into account by charities when marketing their causes. Cultural differences necessitate a sensitive approach in attracting support from groups with different religious and moral viewpoints. Environmental conservation groups can use the public's perception of the use of the countryside, road building and preservation of country walks to their advantage when marketing their cause. The rise in the number of elderly people and the support they need is a major cause for concern in local and national government. As a result, organizations like Age Concern and Help the Aged are able to increase their profile as well as taking on an even more important role (McIntosh and McIntosh, 1984, p. 15).

Other important changes in the socio-economic environment include the increase in women working full-time. This affects the voluntary sector in their ability to recruit volunteers to run services and assist in fund-raising activities. Together with increasing levels of poverty and demand for social services this poses a serious challenge for charity managers and marketers.

The role of marketing in this environment is to focus organizations on their objectives, determine the needs of the organization, and to identify the people (the donors) who can help achieve those objectives. This must be achieved through effective research, planning, communication and evaluation.

The changing role of marketing in the voluntary sector

In recent years, with so much competition for funds, donors have become more discriminating and need to know more about the cause they support and the way in which funds are administered. Accountability is an essential part of financial marketing. Earlier studies have shown that the main reason for not giving to charities was the belief that too much money was spent on administration and generally that potential donors did not know how the funds were spent (Schlackman Report, 1978). In 1976 Lord Goodman reported that the 'community is entitled to be sure that their resources are being put to the best possible use ...' (Goodman, 1976). In the 1990s it is essential that organizations dealing with public money are open to inspection and are accountable for their efficiency in raising funds and how cost-effectively the money is used. Ethically, it is essential that charities are seen to perform honestly and that all monies are accounted for in annual accounts to the Charity Commission and/or in annual reports to regular donors. As Taylor (1996, p. 58) notes in her study of voluntary sector accountability, voluntary organizations also 'play an important role in developing an informed and active citizenship, which not only holds to account but demands to be taken into account'.

Consumerism and community care

The growth of consumerism and campaigning organizations in the voluntary sector over the last twenty years has had a profound impact in that there are more opportunities for donor involvement and more choice for users or clients (Leat, 1990). Marketing techniques such as promotion and public relations can take full advantage of these characteristics to attract both donors and users. In many cases voluntary organizations provide a forum for their users to be consulted, to share their experiences and develop a greater understanding of their position in society and their own needs (Taylor, 1996).

One of the most significant changes to affect the voluntary sector in recent years has been the introduction of new community care policies (Department of Health, 1989) as we discussed in Chapter 8. This has meant that many voluntary organizations are now having to operate in a business-like market competing for contracts to deliver public services instead of receiving grants, causing a change of culture and style in the management and marketing methods used by voluntary bodies in providing their traditional services. Compulsory competitive tendering and the purchaser/provider split in the public sector also have far-reaching implications for the voluntary sector. Instead of their previous role as complementary provider of services with local authorities they are now taking over as alternative service providers and frequently, as in the case of residential care, as the main provider (Deakin, 1996).

The growth of professionalism

These changes in the voluntary sector reveal even more emphatically the need for a professional approach to marketing and increasingly sophisticated techniques for fund raising. The larger charities adopted the professional approach several years ago with well-trained staff able to deliver a marketing service as effective as any commercial company. New marketing techniques adopted by charities in recent years include direct response television appeals inviting viewers to make donations by telephone, affinity credit cards, cause-related marketing, and marketing on the World Wide Web. In 1994, when the Yorkshire Building Society wanted to launch a new different service for young savers, the marketing account was won by a team from the National Society for the Prevention of Cruelty to Children (NSPCC). A new account for children was launched under the NSPCC's established brand 'Happy Kids' which already included a range of clothing and greeting cards. This gave the building society a good start and provided the NSPCC with £1 for every account opened plus 10 per cent of the gross interest paid on each account (Fendley and Hewitt, 1994).

Affinity credit cards

As the credit card market became saturated a new method was needed to market them and affinity cards were introduced. Affinity credit cards have developed as a result of agreements between charities and banks or building societies linking a credit card with one or more charities. Every time a new customer receives their credit card and each time it is used the charity gains a proportion of the money generated. The cards work in the same way as any credit card except that they are linked to a particular cause and bear its logo and name. In this way the consumer can support the cause they are most interested in with no loss of income to themselves and both the card issuer and the charity benefit through increased card turnover and improved donations respectively. The charity can also use the bank's mailing lists and regular statements to communicate with donors at no extra cost. The reluctance of the voluntary sector to adopt professional business-like marketing techniques and some of the difficulties encountered in reconciling the conflicts between donors' and beneficiaries' needs can be overcome using affinity marketing. The first charity affinity card in the UK was introduced by the Bank of Scotland in 1987 with the NSPCC (Worthington and Horne, 1993).

Cause-related marketing

Cause-related marketing is another use of links between the voluntary sector and commercial business. In 1986 the American Express company first used this term to describe a campaign to raise funds for the restoration of the Statue of Liberty by donating a penny for each transaction made using the card (Shargorodski, 1992). Partnerships such as those between Cadbury and Save the Children and British Telecom and the Samaritans are highly valued by the companies and charities alike and are another example of the increased professionalism of charity marketing. Nevertheless, a balance must be struck by the charity between excessive marketing zeal and appearing too slick, and presenting the cause in an effective way geared to the company's interests and strengths (Fendley and Hewitt, 1994).

From the company's point of view the benefits of cause-related marketing include increased sales, a higher public profile, improved image and a larger customer base. The charity receives more funds but also increased publicity and improved awareness of its aims. Careful planning is necessary to avoid problems. These include (Varadarajan, 1989):

- ensuring the commitment of the company to the cause and not just to the potential profits;
- the choice of low-risk high-profile charities at the expense of smaller equally worthy groups;
- companies simply replacing corporate giving with cause-related marketing;
- traditional supporters of a charity being deterred by a commercial approach;
- public perception that the company is exploiting the charity;
- consumers feeling they have fully discharged their charitable duty by participating.

In order to avoid these pitfalls charity marketers must carefully profile and target companies whose products or services can be identified with the cause and whose management style and image in terms of ethical behaviour can be closely matched to the charity.

The World Wide Web

Charity marketing on the Internet or World Wide Web (WWW) is growing very fast with many organizations having their own home page or web site providing information, advice and methods of donation. Help the Aged, for example, has a home page offering a wide range of information including:

- The older population – answers to the most common questions asked;
- Older people's lives – a section on the experiences of older people;
- Help the Aged in action – work as campaigners and advocates for old people;
- How we can help you? – a range of services for senior citizens and their carers;
- How you can help us?

Several ways of donating to the charity are listed in a simple, straightforward manner, suggesting covenants, payroll giving, and legacies. Information and a plea for volunteers includes a list of ways to help, while their mail-order catalogue is described and offered in large-print form. Corporate support is also sought with a separate section aimed to attract companies who wish to enhance 'the positive side of their profile' with corporate events, branding and sponsorship. To each of these categories is added a name and contact address and/or telephone number. There is also information on mailing lists with a choice of type of information to be received by email and a questionnaire on the use of the site (Help the Aged, 1996).

The Voluntary Organizations Internet Service (VOIS) provides information on and for the voluntary sector including advice on how to market web sites or home pages. This was compiled in response to a customer-satisfaction survey which highlighted the need of organizations for support in marketing sites (VOIS, 1996). This provides basic advice on the importance of linking the site to other affiliated sites around the world, promoting the URL, the importance of graphics, updating, and user-friendliness.

Using the World Wide Web is an extremely cost-effective method of promoting organizations as well as fund raising and communicating with both users or clients and donors (UK Fundraising, 1996). As the use of the WWW proliferates, more savings will be made on traditional and expensive communication methods by media and mailings. Organizations can be their own news media with the ability to represent their own point of view, react immediately to events, and information can be updated centrally on a daily basis. A web site has massive marketing potential for charities and voluntary organizations where hundreds of pages of information can be made available without the need for an index. By pointing and clicking on to either words or images the reader can go further into a site in a much more flexible and faster way than with books or leaflets. Other developments include automatic on-line giving facilities launched by the German Charities Institute for 53 German charities in October 1996 (German Charities Institute, 1996).

The donor relationship

Charities and voluntary organizations have two equally important market groups comprising a dual constituency similar to that of social services providers: the clients for whom the charity exists to benefit and the donors without whom the charity would not exist. The importance of maintaining a strong relationship with donors over a long period of time is a central requirement of charity marketing. The difficulties and expense of recruiting new donors have led to increased emphasis on the importance of building stronger relationships with existing donors and supporters. Job titles such as 'relationship fund-raiser' reflect the importance attached to this new approach by some voluntary organizations (Burnett, 1993).

The involvement of donors is a primary function of relationship marketing in the voluntary sector. They must feel a sense of 'ownership' of the organization's objectives and aims and this involves both educa-tion and communication processes. This means adapting traditional marketing techniques to fit the needs of the organization. This must be based firmly on the particular relationship that exists between the donors and the organization they support. This relationship must be maintained, improved and continued to the benefit of both donor and charity.

Problems can arise, however, from conflicts of interest between those in the organization trying to meet the needs of the beneficiaries and those building relationships with donors. The exchange process between all the constituent parts of a large organization is complex with trustees, professional carers, administrators, marketers and volunteers to be considered. It can be difficult to match the demands of all parts of the organization with the marketing objectives. The involvement and understanding of the whole organization in planning and building donor relationships is essential.

The personal approach

The personal approach using communication by telephone and meet-ings, rather than by mail only, is essential in relationship marketing. As Burnett (1993, p. 46) asserts, it is basically a matter of common sense and in fact many fund raisers have been successfully practising relation-ship marketing for years without realizing it. Relationships with donors must be built on trust and individual attention rather than on mass mailings which achieve a small response. Potential donors do not appreciate the hard sell approach of marketing, but will respond posi-tively to a personalized approach which takes account of details of their own experience and previous support. This can be done by segmenting the market into smaller, more identifiable groups of donors with similar backgrounds, responding appropriately to donor contacts with thank-you letters, welcome packs and information files.

In Canada the World Wildlife Fund (WWF), having suffered a drop in contributions in the late 1980s and early 1990s, realized the importance of treating donors like customers who gave not just out of charity but because they really believed in the cause and wanted to see definite results (Orr, 1994). They aimed to provide the donors with more than just the satisfaction of giving to the cause by keeping them informed of the organization's actions and how their money was used. In this way donors feel they are involved in the way their money is spent. Donors were treated like members, with a welcome pack and a 'We're listening' guarantee which allows them to have a say in which causes should be supported and to choose whether or not to accept all mailings. These options include

- a monthly automatic bank withdrawal;
- receiving all regular mailings;
- receiving only mail about Canadian issues;
- receiving mail only about international issues;
- receiving only one letter per year;
- receiving gift catalogues from WWF and/or from other organizations.

WWF Canada was one of the first organizations to give donors the option of having their names given to other organizations. Through being honest with donors, WWF explained the benefits to the charity of not choosing this option because exchanging lists with other charities constituted their most cost-effective way of finding new donors. In this way the natural distrust of marketing techniques by many donors will be displaced by a feeling of empowerment and involvement. Also, donors who choose to be contacted less frequently often give more at less cost to the charity.

The personalized approach can be taken a step further with the one-to-one relationship of sponsoring a child's education in Africa, for example, where personal letters are exchanged to check progress, or an endangered species in a wildlife trust where donors' names are posted on the barriers and special visiting terms are received. Individual donors' names may be placed on the doors of rooms in a hostel for abused children to emphasize a personal relationship between donor and recipient. To achieve these aims a high level of understanding of donors' characteristics and interests is necessary.

The scope for market segmentation

The increasing use by charities and voluntary organizations of a more systematic approach to marketing has meant more attention to market segmentation. Charities need to develop a profile of those groups of people most likely to support the cause, facilitating a marketing strategy which can be targeted at specific groups with common characteristics. These characteristics typically fall into demographic and geographic, lifestyle, and psychographic variables (McIntosh and McIntosh, 1984). Demographic variables include:

- age
- sex

- family
- income
- occupation
- race and nationality
- social position.

Some charities attract donors of specific ages. For example, the Red Cross traditionally attracts people in the middle to elderly age range while Greenpeace has tended to appeal more to a younger population. AIDS charities also attract the younger age groups. Women traditionally comprise the highest number of supporters of charities while the stage of the family cycle can have implications for marketing depending on the age and number of children, single status, etc. The amount and type of income plays an important part in the segmentation of donors according to whether they are on a fixed income like pensioners or earn a high income. A particular segment will determine the level of donation suggested: pensioners may be more interested in learning about legacies while high earners may wish to know about tax advantages and covenant arrangements. Occupation can be relevant in market segmentation, especially if a campaign is aimed at particular organizations or sponsorship deals where the charity will need to know more about the employees. Race and nationality has some influence on targeting certain groups as in the case of charities aimed at helping immigrants or those needing to learn English as a second language.

The most commonly used device for segmentation is social position or grade. These are:

- Grade A – upper middle class, top professionals and executives
- Grade B – middle class, professional and business
- Grade C1 – lower middle class, white collar
- Grade C2 – skilled working class, blue collar
- Grade D – semi-skilled and unskilled working class
- Grade E – lowest levels of subsistence.

It is important to know which groups the charity is targeting as they are often shown to read similar newspapers and have similar interests. Combined with geographic and psychographic variables charity managers can use these categories to assist in marketing strategy and planning policies.

Geographic variables are significant for charities aiming at particular age ranges or cultural groups. For example, it is easy to identify areas of the country with large elderly populations (like East Sussex) or Asian populations (such as Leicester) in order to target particular campaigns at these groups. Lifestyle and psychographic variables may be used to identify potential donors' particular lifestyles, free-time activities, reading habits, religion, frequency and type of donation, opinions and attitudes.

Problems of segmentation

Whereas charities are becoming increasingly sophisticated users of marketing practices there are many problems in simply adopting techniques such as segmentation of the market for the not-for-profit sector and charities in particular. The most obvious problem already highlighted is that of the dual constituency of donors and beneficiaries. A study by Schlegelmilch and Tynan (1989) of UK charities has shown that segmentation of the market according to the above popular categories has limited relevance and concludes that particular types of charities are not necessarily associated with particular types of donor categories. The 494 respondents expressed a preference from eight different types of charities (welfare, youth, animal, arts and education, international aid, environment, missionary work and health). Three groups of segmentation variables were used – demographic, lifestyle (spare-time activities) and psychographic (opinion and attitudes). The preferred charities were those connected with medicine and health, welfare and international aid. On a demographic basis only the fact that more women than men gave to healthcare charities was significant. The analysis of lifestyle activities showed little of significance apart from the fact that those giving to welfare charities were less likely to take part in creative activities. Segmentation based on psychographic variables was also found to be unhelpful in identifying donors who preferred certain causes. The researchers, while acknowledging the importance of market segmentation to identify likely large donors, do conclude that preferences for particular types of charities are not associated with particular market segments. Thus, people who give to one charity do not necessarily differ from those who give to another. The implications for charities and voluntary organizations are significant in that they need to market their cause to the same potential donors as other charities rather than being able to identify a niche market. Also, charities who have the most effective position or profile in the market will attract most donors while the smaller organizations will have to struggle to compete with the larger ones.

The importance of image

With the gradual adoption by charities and voluntary organizations of modern marketing practices the attention given to image, identity and positioning has become paramount. Charities no longer wish to be viewed as old-fashioned institutions doing good works. Powerful images and strong lines of communication are necessary in order to compete with the modern commercial advertising techniques used by the private sector. Stark images such as the RSPCA's poster of a pile of dead dogs, used in the late 1980s, are designed to shock, have an immediate effect and remain in the public mind longer. In an increasingly competitive and sophisticated market a strong image and message is necessary to attract potential donors.

Targeting

The question of image is also important when targeting specific markets. The Multiple Sclerosis Society (MSS) ran a marketing campaign featuring photographs of beautiful young bodies each with a part of the body torn out providing a stark reminder of the effects of the disease. It was specifically targeted at young adults to reflect the typical victims of MS, and at women who traditionally control the rate of family contribution to charity. The results included a 35 per cent increase in income over the first three years of the campaign and a much-improved rate of awareness of MS and the Society (Thomas, 1989).

Charity positioning

Many charities have redesigned their logos, image and corporate identity, and even changed their name to reflect their position in modern society and to attract new donors. Dr Barnardos has become simply Barnardos and the Spastics Society has become Scope in order to mark a change of emphasis in their aims and development and also to help create a new, positive attitude towards their causes. The Spastics Society felt that their name gave a negative image of disability to some people and was beginning to work against the organization. The NSPCC appointed the Conran Design Group to develop a new image for the charity which would reflect their serious purpose, provide an easily recognizable identity and attract funding. In this way, as with the branding of commercial products, a strong image becomes associated in the public mind with a particular organization and its values.

Marketing a new charity for a cause with a traditionally 'difficult' image presents a real challenge to managers. Breast cancer was one area seen very much as a taboo subject until recent years. It was regarded as purely a woman's problem and not a cause that men would relate to easily. The charity BreakThrough, launched in 1991, set out to break down many of the barriers by aiming to raise funds for a new specialized research centre, in spite of competing with dozens of other cancer charities. The directors aimed to market the charity to corporate donors as well as individuals. With a powerful publicity campaign, including the support of the *Daily Express* whose columnist Jean Rook had recently died of breast cancer, large UK companies were targeted in spite of being dominated entirely by male managers. Although some did not want their product to be associated with such an image, others like PowerGen and National Power did provide substantial funding and sponsorship. These companies regarded involvement as a way of showing the public that they were caring as opposed to faceless organizations. In this way marketing is also helping to break down taboos and raise the profile of much-needed research (Latham, 1991).

Promoting a positive image

One of the disadvantages of building a strong image designed to shock the public's awareness is the danger of encouraging prejudice and negative views of those the campaigns are designed to help. Eye-catching advertisements showing disabled people as pathetic, helpless and pitiful do not contribute to a positive image. While charities may receive increased funding and support, those they are trying to help may be damaged in the process. However successful from a marketing point of view – as, for example, in the case of the MSS tear campaign – those suffering from MS may regard such a campaign as counterproductive. Employers interviewing for a job may be less likely to appoint someone with MS if they have just seen one of the posters showing someone with no backbone. Sensationalism is successful in selling charity causes to the public but at some cost to those suffering from conditions like schizophrenia, when disturbing pictures of victims are portrayed. If marketing campaigns become too emotionally charged they can be counterproductive if the public are disgusted or repelled by the images projected. A balance needs to be reached where strong ideas can be transmitted without portraying unnecessarily negative images. Other advertising campaigns have compared sufferers with heroic achievements such as a person with MS struggling through a crowded street with a polar explorer in the Arctic. The importance of frequent consultation and collaboration with those portrayed in advertising campaigns is essential if marketers are to reflect a true image and promote positive attitudes (Levy, 1990).

Conclusion

Charities are operating in a fiercely competitive environment with increased emphasis on consumerism and significant socio-economic, political and cultural changes. Managers in the voluntary sector must be equipped to raise the profile of their cause and attract more donations in an ever tighter market. Organizations need to focus on their mission and develop a marketing strategy that emphasizes the need for increased donor involvement and choice.

The need for all voluntary organizations to be openly and publicly accountable has a significant effect on the marketing of charities which must be able to show that they are using donations effectively and efficiently to retain the confidence and loyalty of both donors and beneficiaries. The increased professionalism of marketing practice in the voluntary sector, especially in the larger charities, has meant the introduction of more business-like techniques such as affinity credit cards, cause-related marketing, and use of the World Wide Web computer network.

Building strong relationships with donors through a more personalized approach to communication and a sensitive adaptation of segmentation methods have become necessary to improve fund raising levels. Several large charities have already repositioned themselves in the market using modern media and/or shocking images to attract new donors and update their public profile. Promoting a positive modern image of the cause and its beneficiaries is essential to raise public awareness and increase support.

Issues

1 The influence of the economic climate on charities and voluntary organizations.
2 The changing role of marketing for this sector.
3 The impact of IT on marketing practices.

Questions

1 Why is competition for funds now so much more intense than in the past?
2 To what extent is the political environment a factor in developing marketing strategy in this sector?
3 How can marketers make use of consumerism to attract both users and donors?
4 Why is cause-related marketing so significant?
5 What potential does the Internet hold for the marketing of charities?
6 How important is relationship marketing for charities and voluntary sector organizations, and what are its key elements?
7 How is market segmentation used by charities?
8 What are the problems faced by charities in promoting difficult messages and how do they resolve them?

References

Burnett, K. (1993) The challenge of relationships. *Fund Raising Management*, July, 44-54.

Deakin, N. (1996) The devils in the detail: some reflections on contracting for social care by voluntary organisations. *Social Policy and Administration*, **30** (1), 20–38.

Department of Health (1989) *Caring for People: Community care in the next decade and beyond*, Cm 849, HMSO.

Fendley, A. and Hewitt, M. (1994) When charity begins with a pitch. *Marketing*, 23 June, 14–15.

German Charities Institute (1996) http://www.fundraising.co.uk.

Goodman, Lord (1976) *Charity Law and Voluntary Organizations. Report of the Goodman Committee*, Bedford Square Press.

Help the Aged Home Page (1996) http://www.vois.org.uk/hta/.

Latham, V. (1991) Breaking the taboo. *Marketing*, 3 October, 21.

Leat, D. (1990) Voluntary organizations and accountability: theory and practice. In Anheier, H.K. and Seibel, W. (eds), *The Third Sector: Comparative studies of nonprofit organisations*, Walter de Gruyter, pp. 141–53.

Levy, L. (1990) A positive image: bitter-sweet charity. *Marketing*, 15 March, 43–5.

McIntosh, D. and McIntosh, A. (1984) *Marketing: A handbook for charities*, Directory of Social Change.

Orr, A. (1994) Treat donors right! *Target Marketing*, July, 19–20.

Saxon-Harrold, S.K.E. (1990) Competition, resources and strategy in the British nonprofit sector. In Anheier, H.K. and Seibel, W. (eds), *The Third Sector: Comparative studies of nonprofit organisations*, Walter de Gruyter, pp. 123–39.

Schlackman Report (1978) *Survey of Attitudes towards Overseas Development*, HMSO.

Schlegelmilch, B. and Tynan, A. (1989) The scope for market segmentation within the charity market: an empirical analysis. *Managerial and Decision Economics*, **10**, 127–34.

Shargorodski, L. (1992) *Association Management*, August, 170.

Taylor, M. (1996) Between public and private: accountability in voluntary organizations. *Policy and Politics*, **24** (1), 57–72.

Thomas, H. (1989) Still grateful but not humble. *Accountancy,* **104** (1156), 65–6.

UK Fundraising (1996) http://www.fundraising.co.uk.

Varadarajan, P. R. (1989) Cause related marketing. *Incentive*, February, 30–4.

VOIS (Voluntary Organizations Internet Service) (1996) http://www. vois.org.uk.

Worthington, S. and Horne, S. (1993) Charity affinity credit cards –
marketing synergy for both card issuers and charities? *Journal of
Marketing Management*, **9** (3), 301–13.

Further reading

Burnett, K. (1993) The challenge of relationships. *Fund Raising
Management*, July, 44–54.
Leat, D. (1990) Voluntary organizations and accountability: theory and
practice. In Anheier, H.K. and Seibel, W. (eds), *The Third Sector:
Comparative studies of nonprofit organisations*, Walter de Gruyter,
pp. 141–53.
Worthington, S. and Horne, S. (1993) Charity affinity credit cards –
marketing synergy for both card issuers and charities? *Journal of
Marketing Management*, **9** (3), 301–13.

CHAPTER 10

Churches in
the marketplace

Summary

While religious organizations have been urged to take up marketing, there have been criticisms of its values and application in the management of churches, especially in the recruitment of new members. The concept of relationship marketing may be more acceptable, through its focus on continuity and on the quality of relationships. There are two levels of church organization for the Church of England where marketing can be applied: the local and the national. The emphasis on the parish and its links with the local community means that marketing is mainly, but not exclusively, being developed at the local level.

Introduction

Several authors have argued that churches need to engage in formal marketing activities in order to cope with the rapid changes in religious observance and in society at large (Kotler, 1979; Hoge 1979; Dunlap, Gaynor and Roundtree, 1983; McDaniel, 1986, Barna, 1988; Stevens and Loudon, 1992). While it is acknowledged that churches belong to that group of organizations who 'cannot change many elements of their basic offering at all because these elements very much define who they are' (Kotler and Andreasen, 1987), it has been increasingly seen that religious organizations can make use of marketing techniques to support activities like fund raising and increasing their membership. However, there have inevitably been problems associated with possibly the most worldly of all management activities – marketing – being practised by religious organizations. One of the best-argued criticisms of the use of marketing by Christian churches is by Kenneson (1993), who contended that while everyday life in the USA has been 'thoroughly shaped and governed by management and market relationships' these have tended to transform everything into manageable objects and marketable commodities which run counter to religious observance. He considered that marketing approaches, rather than helping churches to solve their problems of membership and funding, had misnamed the challenges and issues facing contemporary churches:

> The management fix offered by the church marketers, focused as it must be on matters of church life that are measurable and controllable, cannot address the real problems facing churches in America, not the least of which is their deep confusion about the church's identity and purpose.

Measuring performance in terms of instrumental values and marketing to improve performance has been seen as a difficulty in other services, such as education and health services. For churches, though, there is seen to be even more of a danger that overemphasis on management principles by those charged with the duty, literally, to *minister* to a congregation can detract from their spiritual role in meeting individual and social needs.

Perhaps more than for any other kind of organization, therefore, the concept of relationship marketing may offer a way forward for churches in the application of management principles. Relationship marketing can meet the needs of those who view more hard-edged marketing approaches with suspicion. As part of their mission, churches are engaged in developing lifelong relationships with individuals through membership, and also with establishing and sustaining links with a range of other organizations. Their 'customers', i.e. members, are a key target, but so too are all of the many other stakeholders whom they seek to influence, which may include other religious faiths, local authorities, schools, charities, government and its agencies: in other words, society as a whole. There is also the need for churches to engage in relationships simply because of their role as a large employing organization with buildings to maintain, services to provide and a staff to manage. As well as marketing activities which are directed at their fund raising role, their need to develop and sustain membership and to impact on society, there are therefore complex relationships with suppliers and other stakeholders. It has been suggested that there are six contingencies which affect the development of a relationship between organizations (Oliver, 1990). These can be seen to have equal relevance for churches:

1   *Asymmetry*   Churches are generally in the position of influencers rather than having real power with organizations such as local authorities or central government. Their subservient role means that they have to seek long-term links which minimize the potential impact of policy decisions on them.
2   *Stability*   The churches' historic need to ensure stability for themselves and their role in society means that they seek ways of handling environmental uncertainty through the development of relationships.
3   *Legitimacy*   Organizations may seek relationships with churches to enhance their reputation, a factor which churches need to understand when developing relationships with both commercial organizations and other not-for-profit organizations.
4   *Necessity*   Even for churches there are legal and regulatory necessities which compel them to develop relationships with legal firms, auditors, local authority planning departments, etc.
5   *Reciprocity*   Many relationships develop because of the pursuit of common goals. Both parties recognize that the advantages of such a relationship outweigh any disadvantage of the cost of managing the relationship or some loss of independent action. Churches may, for example, see the benefit of joining with other organizations in lobby-ing on a specific social issue or in developing long-term links with suppliers.
6   *Efficiency*   Costs may be minimized by joining forces with another organization, for example in the use of church facilities.

In this chapter, the role of marketing will be explored with reference to the wide scope of relationship development, as well as those specific marketing tools, especially promotional techniques, which churches are using. While reference will be made to a range of religious organizations, the focus will mainly be on the Church of England in order to examine the significance of the marketing environment for choices of marketing approach.

The marketing environment

Social context

All the institutions in Western society have undergone profound changes in recent years. The churches are no exception, although paradoxically they are also some of the last bastions of tradition and the establishment in a culture where changing fashions and style have become more important to organizations. For many businesses, marketing has largely been about identifying trends in buying behaviour and positioning the organization's products in the marketplace so that customers perceive the overwhelming benefits of a specific product compared with the competition: style and design features are crucial to success. For the churches, though, retaining the core values which have lasted for centuries and maintaining traditions despite changing fashions has become a key issue.

A common perception is that the decline in church membership means the churches are dying because of their failure to keep up with the times. The capacity of the churches to cope with problems which include the erosion of their moral authority, theological doubts and diversity, financial pressures, and the difficulties of maintaining plant and personnel is also questioned. The steady secularization of society can be seen in the increase in civil marriages, from 2.6 per cent in 1844 to 34.1 per cent in 1967 (Currie, Gilbert and Horsley, 1977; Medhurst and Moyser, 1988) followed by increases in cohabitation without marriage since then. However, despite these threats to the role of religion as a means of legitimizing relationships, threats which are just one part of the turbulence of contemporary society, the churches are remarkably resilient – both in the UK and across the world. As Perman (1977) noted, 'there is a great power of resilience and inertia in them and identifying where this lies is a more fruitful exercise than going over the familiar ground of declining membership'. Christian faith and faith in a deity remain strong within society; Christians see more in their churches than mere social convenience. A further factor is the power of churches to survive against all odds, including – or perhaps one should argue especially – during persecution. In Russia, attendance at the Orthodox churches remained strong throughout Communist rule, and in other countries where religious affiliations are proscribed Christian churches continue to flourish.

> All this has led some Christians to wonder whether a dose of persecution might not be a bad thing for Christianity here (Perman, 1977, p. 217).

However, for all its failings, the Christian tradition in Britain has remained remarkably constant, and has maintained a close relationship with the fabric of the establishment, with cross-fertilization of religious and secular ideas and contacts coming from a range of sources. The Crown's links with the established churches of England and Scotland, the presence of Anglican bishops in the House of Lords, and the role of the church in state education has made for a unique tradition quite unlike that in other countries where more polarization of religious and political views has been evident. Consensus between Church and State on many issues has been made possible because of their long history of cohabitation.

An important element of the social context is continuity. For most of its recorded history the Christian church has been present in Britain, and for a thousand years the faith has been organized in geographical areas of dioceses and parishes which have become significant social units. The parish has been the smallest unit of local administration for most of that time, with the parish, parish priest and parish church constituting a fundamental part of the concept of Christianity in Britain.

The political and economic context

There are therefore two levels of church organization which are important when considering the relevance of marketing: the national level where political involvement is a key issue, and the local, where for many people their church still exists to enable them to perform certain rites of passage: baptism, marriage and burial, as well as fulfilling a pastoral role in the community. In the mass politics which dominate society today, and during a period when individualism has been favoured, the church has stood out at the national and local level for the importance of community and the sharing of resources. This was a key concern in the major report by the Archbishops' Commission on Rural Areas (ACORA) Report (1990), *Faith in the Countryside*. ACORA investigated not only the Anglican church's role within the countryside but also the political issues which government had to face in planning for the future balance between urban and rural development:

> Central to the discussion is the question of what type of society we expect to find in the countryside of the future. The trend is towards a professional, wealthier group; but our judgement is that if this is the market trend, it is insufficient. Policies which provide local work, local homes and local communications for those who are less well-off, but who wish to remain in the country, are crucial if rural living is to retain ... balance and cohesion (Archbishops' Commission on Rural Areas, 1990).

In its recommendations, ACORA covered housing and transport policy, the impact of modern technology on the environment, training, agriculture, care in the community, management: the whole range of issues concerning government.

Church organization

This dual role of local ministry and national influencer in the political sphere is reflected in how the Anglican church is organized. Essentially it is a parish-based religion. The diocesan bishop reaches beyond the local confines but in practical terms it is the local vicar or parish priest who takes precedence (Davies, 1991). The parish still retains its powers, and while the diocesan bishop has a management and pastoral role in relation to his clergy, the priest's autonomy within the parish is very strong. The pyramidal organizational structure rests on the Parochial Church Council (PCC) at the base, with deanery synods representing groups of parishes. These consist of all the local clergy plus lay elected lay representatives of each PCC. Deanery synods elect clergy and laity to the diocesan synod and these then elect delegates to the General Synod of the Church, which since 1970 has had legislative powers in ecclesiastical matters delegated to it.

The significance of this hierarchical organizational structure for marketing is that communications between parishes and the General Synod are limited; in practice, the Church of England relies largely on parishes and on its large cathedrals to manage their own affairs. The national picture is dominated by the views expressed in Synod and by bishops and archbishops retaining a high public political profile through the media: a former Archbishop of Canterbury even had his envoy taken as a political hostage in the Lebanon.

Competition

The Church of England, as the Established Church, could be argued to have a monopoly position in national life. It has withstood pressures to relinquish this status largely in order to maintain its unique influence on the establishment. Competition for its influence and for membership has come from many quarters, but most recently the increasing secularization of society has posed the greatest threat, a phenomenon shared by other Western churches. A 1988 American poll found that 49 per cent of adults surveyed felt that religion was losing influence on American life, while only 36 per cent felt that it was increasing in influence, a reversal of a finding from two years previously (Wrenn, 1993a). Declining membership has affected all churches: however, for the Church of England, with its responsibility for so many large historic buildings, the impact of falling collections has been more profound. The impact of competition from other Christian denominations has varied over time, but first became evident in 1851 when Horace Mann's religious census showed that Anglicans were no longer a majority of actively religious citizens (Davies, 1991). Methodism and the rise of other dissenting churches as a consequence of industrialization has remained a strong competitive influence and the ecumenical movement has developed as a response.

A role for marketing?

Marketing is being seen as having a role to play in supporting churches to maintain their membership and finances at a time when both are dwindling. However, it is also argued that the quality of Christian faith in those growing churches in the USA, where the most evident use of marketing is practised, has not been adequately proven (Kenneson, 1993). Despite these concerns, though, marketing and the practice of sound management are considered by many to have a great deal to offer the Church at a time of crisis in its financial management.

The problem of financing the Church of England has become 'paramount' (Archbishops' Commission on Rural Areas, 1990), with clergy stipends being funded much less than in the past by the Church Commissioners and more being expected of parish giving. It was found that few parishes were acknowledging their debt to income from historic resources or were accepting the need to fund the shortfall themselves to ensure their priest was paid a reasonable salary. The diocesan quota (a sum paid by the parish to help support its clergy, based on its church electoral roll) was seen as a 'tax' rather than a contribution to the ministry. The upkeep of church buildings is also seen as a huge burden by many parishes. Financial performance is therefore now a key element in diocesan and parish planning. An emphasis on planning for the delivery of pastoral care has also become more significant, with the ACORA report recognizing that dioceses should draw up a statement of aims with parishes as part of corporate pastoral planning. This was not termed 'product development', but shares many of the aspects of product design management which marketers would recognize.

The product

Using the term 'product' to describe the complex intangible benefits offered by the Church lays marketers open to criticism. However, there are ways in which marketing can offer insights into how churches are viewed by both their members and by society at large, and how they can develop their 'product offering' in ways which are consonant with their spiritual role. In this sense, marketing for churches is no different from marketing in other complex and sensitive professional contexts such as health or education. Jennings and Saunders (1993) quote a letter to a newspaper which defined the problem thus:

> ... the national churches of both Scotland and England display many of the sclerotic symptoms that mark nationalized indisutries: an all-embracing rhetoric of monopoly and service to the whole nation disguises an actual failure to discern the market and to prepare and deliver goods and services required by the customer in, or out of the pew.

There is a problem with defining the product, which is unique, and of changing people's perceptions of the church.

> The dilemma is the recognition that the church is product orientated in its servicing of existing customers, rather than attracting new customers, and that new customers can only be attracted when the church begins this paradigmatic shift in its attitude towards both mission and objectives (Jennings and Saunders, 1993).

> Some attempts have been made to develop the product, especially through the modernization of services through the introduction of the *Alternative Service Book*. But even this liturgical revision has been criticized, on the one hand as being 'a somewhat conservative volume' (Medhurst and Moyser, 1988, p. 56) and by the traditionalists on the other as being a step too far from the English of Cranmer.

Ministry at the local level

The complexity of the Church's role in society causes particular problems. It takes an active part in contemporary life through involvement at local, national and even global levels. In the inner cities, in particular, the churches have become involved in their neighbourhoods and estates and the importance of relating to the groups, networks and associations to be found there has meant the development of new forms of church organization and worship. This has included moving towards neighbourhood churches or worship centres, and house groups. It was found that churches could not rely just on maintaining and preserving membership and leadership through traditional ways of teaching, worship and organization. Committee structures, agendas and long-term planning were often being approached in ways which made it much less likely that local people would participate. Parish meetings rather than formal PCCs were felt to be a better way of involving local people, and commitment to what is local could be better achieved through changing the patterns of worship, music, presentation of the Gospel and theology.

> The Church of England in the urban priority areas must avoid reflecting an inherited middle-class culture, and draw on the gifts to be found in its neighbourhood (Archbishop of Canterbury's Commission on Urban Priority Areas, 1985).

So far, this view of the product offered by the Church of England at the local level can be compared with the American experience of churches, which similarly found during the 1980s and early 1990s that there was a need to look at concepts of customer satisfaction in relation to their product offerings. Satisfying the customer meant ensuring that the congregation was satisfied by the minister's abilities as a 'preacher, counsellor, administrator, enabler, teacher, leader, nurturer, etc.'. Above all, it meant that members should want to continue their active participation in the Church through the impact on their lives, not just on their feelings about church services and the church's organization. 'Members are satisfied because you have made *them* better: better at sensing a Divine presence in their lives, better at relating to their family and better at relating to other members.' Church administration should simply add value to this central role of the church (Wrenn, 1993b).

However, different groups of parishioners perceive their church in different ways. This partly derives from the varied age-ranges targeted by churches, but it also relates to the very different motivations of people for joining a church and attending regularly. It was argued in a study of American protestantism during the 1960s, for example, that church membership was often linked not to religiosity but to status, and could be a prerequisite for obtaining credit, or a job. Other influences on how individuals perceive their church come from parental influences: most new church members are received at baptism as babies or young children, and retaining membership has also been shown to derive from parents' behaviour (Currie, Gilbert and Horsley, 1977, pp. 19, 80).

The Isle of Wight experience

Given the importance of the church at the local level, it has become important for local intitiatives – especially in data gathering about church membership and attendance – to be better coordinated. A detailed case study of the Isle of Wight, which arose from a book on the rural church (Francis, 1985), provided useful marketing information through a research exercise which could be replicated elsewhere

(Francis and Lankshear, 1991/2). A lengthy questionnaire was sent to sixty-one Anglican churches on the island, asking them to provide a profile of their activities over two Sundays and the intervening weekdays. Contacts with the numbers of people within age categories were also counted. Information about church activities throughout the year was gathered, including the number of baptisms, confirmations, Sunday school membership, Easter and Christmas communicants, choirs, house groups, etc. The result was a rich picture of Anglicanism on the Isle of Wight outside the holiday season.

At the time of the survey there were 124 600 people on the island with sixty-one churches in regular use and thirty-four full-time parish clergy: a church for every 2000 people and a paid minister for every 3700 people. There were also three non-stipendiary ministers, twenty-three further clergy who had permission to officiate at services, one school chaplain and twenty-seven lay readers. Church membership was stronger than on the mainland, 5.5 per cent of the population compared with 4.1 per cent for the Church of England as a whole, and 39 per cent of infants were baptized before the age of two years, compared with 32 per cent nationally.

The age profile was interesting, with more children being contacted through the Church than adults. Children's work was well developed: nine of the churches had a parent and toddlers' group; thirty-eight ran groups for children from 2 to 13 years old and seventeen churches ran youth clubs. However, the proportion of 14 to 17 year-olds in membership was only 1.4 per cent. Uniformed groups (Cubs, Brownies, Guides and Scouts) also brought young people into contact with the Church on a regular or casual basis. Choirs and bell ringing were significant for developing links with young people: choirs 'often provided a key point of contact' and eleven churches on the island had teams of ringers involving young people from 9 to 21 years old.

This survey provided a useful base-line for data collection and was used to help inform decisions at parish, deanery, archdeaconry and diocesan levels. It was suggested that further in-depth surveys be undertaken at ten-year intervals, in other words a census of Church activity and performance in relation to membership and contact levels which would support local planning of worship, activities and outreach.

Ministry at the national level

The Church of England continues to play a major role in deliberations on moral, ethical and political issues, with General Synod debating many of the large questions of the day. In recent years Synod has considered questions of sexuality, abortion, animal welfare, and economic and social deprivation, as well as significant doctrinal issues such as the Ordination of Women which have also impacted on social attitudes to the Church. The two reports, *Faith in the City* (Archbishop of Canterbury's Commission on Urban Priority Areas, 1985) and *Faith in the Countryside* (Archbishops' Commission on Rural Areas, 1990), were directed to a much wider audience than the Church. The moral authority with which the Church still speaks on social issues means that politicians have at least to acknowledge and take into consideration the Church's deliberations, especially when these are founded on considerable research and data gathering. Controversial pronouncements such as those from the former Bishop of Durham on questions of doctrine also manage to attract media coverage and to maintain the Church's prominence despite the increasingly secular nature of society.

The role of all the churches, but especially the Anglican Church, on all the great state occasions provides important continuities in national life. The Remembrance Day service at the Cenotaph, royal weddings, state funerals, coronations, have all placed the Church in a key role as a foundation of the establishment, but also as a medium through which national consciousness can be articulated.

The church as building

In addition to churches' roles in ministry at local and national levels, the most significant tangibilizing of their product is in their buildings, which are a national as well as local asset. Churches comprise some of the most significant of heritage sites. The local church, as well as historic cathedrals like Canterbury, Durham or York, are the visible signs of the continuity which the Church of England offers the nation. Upkeep of church buildings is therefore one of the greatest preoccupations of all parishes, with fund raising activities often dedicated almost solely to this.

> Sometimes parish life seems to be an endless round of church fêtes, garden parties, whist drives, luncheons and coffee mornings. Almost all these things have as their *raison d'être* fund raising for the church, and in most cases the funds raised will be used to help repair the fabric of the church (Davies, 1991, p. 182).

A difficulty for many parishes is simply the time and money they have to spend on dealing with their buildings, to the detriment of the other aspects of ministry. Resources are spent on renovation, refurbishment, cleaning, heating and decoration. There is also the view, though, that the building focuses the whole parish on its visible manifestation to an area, and that for many people the church as building gives it meaning as a social space for the community. Cooperative voluntary effort to support the church building is an important part of shared church membership or affiliation to the church. Even non-members are likely to see their parish church as an important asset to the community. One of the tensions which can arise for clergy is in the conflict between how church buildings need to be changed and modified to fit them for modern worship and community use, and the heritage function of churches as architectural spaces and community assets. Small grants are available from English Heritage to help with restoration work, but their interest is more on the restoration aspects of work, rather than fitting the building for use. Churches need to understand how English Heritage can be used to support some aspects of their work and build appropriate relationships (Davies, 1991, p.184).

The example of Southwell Minster, which is given in Chapter 12, demonstrates the need for clergy and parishioners to identify those elements of their product offering which are heritage based and which rely on other factors, including the pastoral aspects of ministry, choir and music, patterns of worship, social activities. There, the building provided an important focus not only for local support but also for diocesan-wide activity. Selecting the appropriate targets for fund raising had to be preceded by a clear definition of the product.

Marketing management

The management of marketing for the Church of England is complex for a variety of reasons. The need for a national as well as local approach to marketing the Church is evident, given the wide-ranging 'product'. It is both a national institution which continues to enjoy much respect and affection and a local presence with varying impacts on different communities. Its buildings are also some of the most precious of the nation's architectural assets.

At the local level, the time devoted to specific management activities is limited because of time pressures on clergy. The single most time-consuming activity is visiting – in itself a 'marketing activity', but also a key part of ministry. This takes on average just over seven hours per week. Parish administration takes around six hours, with preparation for and attendance at services each taking up four to five hours. The variety of tasks undertaken by clergy is immense, but religious observance and the sacerdotal aspects of ministry, as one would expect, take up the largest percentage of time: around 41 per cent in all (Davies, 1991, p. 75). Management of marketing on a regular basis in most parishes will therefore be integrated with decision making on parish affairs and not seen as a separate function.

For the larger cathedrals, marketing activities may be linked to wider campaigning activities, as with the Southwell example, where a firm of consultants were employed to offer advice on the development of fund-raising.

Marketing mix decisions

The product

Developing an understanding of how a church can relate better to its community begins with research into the community's profile and how effectively the church is reaching out to existing members as well as recruiting new ones, like the Isle of Wight example. Parish audits have been developed to help local churches understand their situation and to plan; these also help the deanery and diocese to develop better strategies to support local churches (Archbishop of Canterbury's Commission on Urban Priority Areas, 1985, pp. 367–72). However, defining the quality of ministry is more problematic. The issue of faithfulness is involved, as well as that of churches' effectiveness in recruitment and maintaining interest. A problem for marketers is the assumption that 'if a church is successful (measured in terms of quantity and quality), then it is probably faithful' (Kenneson, 1993). Developing ministry to support faithfulness has to be a prime concern of both clergy and lay people within the Church. As well as those activities which have already been discussed, those visible and outward signs of effectiveness such as services which meet the needs of the community, prayer and other religious observances will be regarded as an essential part of ministry.

Place

The church building is often regarded as synonymous with the Church, but increasingly, especially in inner cities, churches are operating without the support of a large central location. In some areas, small neighbourhood-based worship centres are being developed in house groups which reach out to the whole community. However, for many rural communities local parish churches remain significant social centres and a focus for social interactions as much as for religious observance. Women's groups, children's and youth groups, crèches and play-groups may all benefit from use of church facilities as well as participating in religious services. The clergy's role in visiting and pastoral outreach has to be balanced with their role as ministers within the church building.

Promotion

An integral part of the Church's role is to evangelize. The Church of England is presently engaged on its Decade of Evangelism, with the goal of reaching out to more of the community, locally, at diocesan level and nationally. However, the Church is all its members, not just the clergy, and promotion of its message involves each member of a congregation, with much of the emphasis lying with interpersonal relationships at the local level. Training for evangelism is therefore an important issue, one which has to be addressed. Styles of promotion which may be effective in the USA may not be acceptable in many churches in the UK – although styles of evangelism vary between different denominations of the Christian church. Roman Catholics, Methodists, Baptists, Seventh Day Adventists and Salvationists each have particular approaches to the spreading of their message and even within the Anglican Church there are many traditions, from conservative Anglo-Catholicism to charismatic evangelicalism. Promotion has to be tailored not only to the community being targeted but also to the cultural tradition of a particular church – even within a single denomination. This is what gives the Church of England its peculiar distinctiveness. Despite its national status, promotion is based on the parish, its activities and what is acceptable to the local community.

Parish magazines, newsletters and visits are traditional methods, but other methods which have been used in the USA may have some merit, despite their overt marketing emphasis. Direct mailing, which tends to be very focused, can achieve maximum impact on a specific target group, can be private and confidential, costs very little and can have measurable results. Churches which have used professionally produced brochures that address perceived needs and welcome people to the church have seen increases in church attendance (Considine, 1994). The use of billboard slogans outside city churches has become well established in the UK: using advertising techniques such as those developed by the Churches' Advertising Network which has run radio and poster advertisments since the 1990 Broadcasting Act lifted the ban on religious advertisements is simply a logical extension of this practice. The Pentecostal Evangelical Alliance has also used television to advertise, rather more controversially, with a two-minute slot on Channel 4 for the 'Jesus in me' (JIM) campaign, which was based on the British Gas 'Where's Sid?' advertisement.

At the national level, the churches also communicate through religious broadcasts which cover all the major religions, but still focus largely on Christianity. Worship programmes of church services, national events and meditations are still regularly broadcast on a wide variety of radio stations and on television. BBC Radio 4 continues to have a *Thought for the Day* slot at the prime morning listening time of 7.50 am and the Sunday *Songs of Praise* slot is also placed in prime-time position.

As McDonnell (1993) has noted, the media also promotes religion – including the Anglican church – in other more subtle ways through its depiction of religion in soap operas, dramas, and documentary presentations as well as through news broadcasts on church affairs and items about church dignatories. Managing the impact of these images is difficult, and can only be balanced by the experiences provided to their communities by local churches, especially clergy.

Conclusion

Despite the difficulties associated with the use of marketing for churches, there are considerable benefits to be won from approaching marketing in a more systematic way. Developing relationships between churches, their communities and the wide range of stakeholders with whom they are in contact may be enhanced by a pragmatic acceptance that marketing techniques may properly be used. Not all the marketing mix is appropriate: emphasis on developing the product offering in such a way that it meets the needs of society, while remaining true to its enduring message and values will be the focus. Promotion which enhances the message has to be built on these values, as the Southwell 2000 campaign discussed in Chapter 12 describes.

Issues

1   While marketing is needed by churches, it can detract from their spiritual role.
2   The paradox of complexity/change and continuity in the social context.
3   The dual local and national roles of the church.

Questions

1   What are the main arguments for and against marketing for churches?
2   Why is relationship marketing an appropriate response to critics of marketing for religious organizations?
3   What are the main features of the social/political/economic context for churches?
4   How important is the competition for church attendance to marketers?
5   How is the 'product' of the church defined?
6   From the examples offered in this chapter, what elements of marketing have been used most successfully?
7   How should marketing management be organized by church marketers, taking into account the wide-ranging roles of the church?
8   To what extent is the marketing mix an effective set of tools for church marketing?

References

Archbishop of Canterbury's Commission on Urban Priority Areas (1985) *Faith in the City: A call for action by church and nation*, Church House Publishing, Chapter 4.

Archbishops' Commission on Rural Areas (1990) *Faith in the Countryside*, Church Publishers, p. 310.

Barna, G. (1988) *Marketing the Church*, Nav Press.

Considine, J.J. (1994) Direct mail: can it work for religious organizations? *Journal of Direct Marketing*, **8** (4), 59–65.

Currie, R., Gilbert, A. and Horsley, L. (1977) *Churches and Churchgoers: Patterns of church growth in the British Isles since 1700*, Clarendon Press, p. 100.

Davies, D. (1991) *Church and Religion in Rural England*, T. & T. Clark, Chapter 2.

Dunlap, B.J., Gaynor, P. and Roundtree, W.D. (1983) The viability of marketing in a religious setting: an empirical analysis. *Proceedings of the Southern Marketing Association*, 45–8.

Francis, L.J. (1985) *Rural Anglicanism*, Collins.

Francis, L.J. and Lankshear, D. (1991/2) Faith in the Isle of Wight: a profile of rural Anglicanism. *Contact*, **105**, 28–33.

Hoge, D.R. (1979) Why are churches declining? *Theology Today*, April, 92–5.

Jennings, D. and Saunders, J. (1993) Can the church look out of the widow? Marketing the Church in England today. In *Proceedings of the 1993 Annual Conference. Emerging issues in marketing*, Marketing Education Group, pp. 527–33.

Kenneson, P.D. (1993) Selling [out] the church in the marketplace of desire. *Modern Theology*, **9** (4) October, 319–48.

Kotler, P. (1979) Strategies for introducing marketing into nonprofit organizations. *Journal of Marketing*, **43**, January, 37–44.

Kotler, P. and Andreasen, A.R. (1987) *Strategic Marketing for Nonprofit Organizations*, 3rd edn, Prentice Hall, p. 62.

McDaniel, S.W. (1986) Marketing communication techniques in a church setting: views on appropriateness. *Journal of Professional Services Marketing*, **1** (4), 39–54.

McDonnell, J. (1993) Religion, education and the communication of values, In Arthur, C. (ed.), *Religion and the Media*, University of Wales Press, pp. 89–99.

Medhurst, K. and Moyser, G. (1988) *Church and Politics in a Secular Age*, Clarendon Press.

Oliver, C. (1990) Determinants of interorganizational relationships: integration and future directions. *Academy of Management Review*, **15** (2), 241–65.

Perman. D.C. (1977) *Change and the Churches: An anatomy of religion in Britain*, Bodley Head, p. 216.

Stevens, R.E. and Loudon, D.L. (1992) *Marketing for Churches and Ministries*, Haworth Press.

Wrenn, B. (1993a) The role of marketing for religious organizations. *Journal of Professional Services Marketing*, **8** (2), 237–49.

Wrenn, B. (1993b) What business can teach religious organizations about customer service. *Journal of Professional Services Marketing*, **8** (2), 251–68.

Further reading

Archbishops' Commission on Rural Areas (1990) *Faith in the Countryside*, Church Publishers.

Kenneson, P.D. (1993) Selling [out] the church in the marketplace of desire. *Modern Theology* **9** (4) October, 319–48.

McDaniel, S.W. (1986) Marketing communication techniques in a church setting: views on appropriateness. *Journal of Professional Services Marketing*, **1** (4), 39–54.

CHAPTER 11

Quality concerns in marketing management: conclusions

Summary

Customers' needs and expectations have become a major concern of not-for-profit managers, but developing a strategic vision of marketing has not been much in evidence. In surveying the quality aspects of marketing management, elements discussed in Chapter 2 will be revisited, through summaries of the issues presented by the different sectors. Building bridges, quality and marketing, and marketing management are the focus for discussion.

Introduction

In this book we have identified the context for marketing across a range of diverse sectors in the not-for-profit field. Marketing has become increasingly important, for a variety of reasons:

1 Legislation has increasingly impacted on public-sector services, which now need to focus their services more clearly on customers.
2 Quality of services has become of concern as part of the need for accountability to both customers and funders.
3 Competitiveness has become intense in public-sector services, with the introduction of marketplace economics and the availabilty of more options than previously for customers.
4 Consumer expectations have risen, in line with a more consumer-conscious society.

Customers' needs as well as expectations have therefore become a major focus of concern for managers. With this has come the acceptance that while the quality of single transactions are important in building confidence between the organization and its customers, the real significance of marketing for not-for-profit organizations lies with building and sustaining long-term relationships. This realization has developed quite slowly, and has emerged with the growing confidence of not-for-profit organizations in applying marketing techniques to their operations. Some of the earliest uses of marketing in not-for-profits were concerned with social marketing, or changing people's ideas about social causes, campaigns, or practices. This was developed in the 1980s with texts by Manoff (1985) and Kotler and Roberto (1989). From this time, too, as Kotler and Andreasen (1996) have discussed, the literature abounded with examples from the health, education, religious and social sectors. Library and information services practitioners had begun to consider marketing concepts from the late 1970s, at about the same time as leisure and arts professionals and for them, too, a range of sector-specific studies was produced. The emphasis in many of these, however, was on the adaptation of marketing in the profit sector to suit the needs of not-for-profit organizations. Many of the concerns related to survival, increasing immediate funding opportunities, and on efficiency in developing specific services. Developing a strategic and long-term vision of marketing with emphasis on sustaining excellence over a considerable period was much less in evidence. Indeed, much of the criticism levelled at marketing by professionals in public services was precisely because it was perceived as a 'quick fix' which ignored their need to provide a quality professional service for clients in the long and not just the short term.

However, as the examples from the organizations discussed in this book have shown, the concerns are much more complex than some of the early texts on marketing for not-for-profits indicated. Ethical considerations have become more important in discussions about the quality of services and in the uses of marketing. Marketing has had difficulty in becoming accepted, partly for this reason, but also because it was felt to be largely unnecessary: demonstrably necessary public services simply did not need selling; marketing was a waste of public money; and marketing activities were seen as intrusive and manipulative (Kotler and Andreasen, 1996, pp. 22–3). The development of interest in relationship marketing has largely developed as a reaction to criticisms that the marketing mix relied too heavily on techniques which exhibited these tendencies. Earlier marketing theories were perceived as product rather than service driven and insensitive to the concerns of professionals to deliver services which met their professional standards as well as satisfying customers' expectations.

In surveying the quality concerns in marketing management which have emerged in this book, we shall therefore return to the analysis of relationship marketing. Each sector will be considered with reference to the themes which were discussed in Chapter 2.

Building bridges

Ensuring continuing links between the organization and both its customers and stakeholders has become particularly important in the public sector. Diminishing funding and the threats posed by new ways of working through competitive tendering, the purchaser/provider split and internal markets have created the need for new kinds of relationships as well as extending the numbers of relationships that organizations now have to sustain.

Since 1988, schools have found themselves in the situation of being both customer for their local education authority's (LEA) services and suppliers of services to their own customers: pupils, parents, employers, colleges and universities. The complexity is heightened by their need still to relate to the LEA as the statutory authority for supplying some services, for example to statemented, i.e. special needs, pupils. The LEA is also a key stakeholder in that it has to plan for education services across the local authority, to ensure that all pupils receive the education to which they are entitled. Schools are now competing with each other and with further education colleges, to recruit and retain pupils. This in many cases has changed what once were key, collaborative local relationships. Marketing to customers is therefore only one aspect of the development of relationship marketing which schools need to consider in their planning. In addition, their network of key relationships has developed considerably in recent years.

Universities and colleges have faced similarly turbulent environmental conditions affecting how they need to relate to customers and stakeholders. Their relationships have been particularly influenced by considerable funding problems and the need to recruit more students for a decreasing unit of resource, but with a ceiling placed by government on undergraduate recruitment. International student recruitment has therefore appeared to be a lucrative and attractive option. There has been the need to continue to offer the high-quality product for which international students and their sponsors are willing to pay high fees, while balancing this with a more assertive approach to marketing. Retaining long-term relationships with overseas markets has been jeopardized by some institutions, though, particularly those who have engaged in franchising and overextending their operations. As funding restriction have bitten, ensuring that staff – one of the key stakeholder groups – remain committed to the complex objectives of universities has become more difficult.

The new market-led environment in the health sector has created similar problems to those experienced by schools, but more dramatically and with greater impact financially. The NHS Review of 1989, which instituted the internal market separating purchasing from the delivery of health care, created competition between services which had previously collaborated and made GPs formal customers of hospitals for the first time. The end-user, i.e. the patient, was also a customer, but the focus on managing a whole range of other relationships has dominated much of management thinking. Radical changes to the ways in which organizations relate to each other have resulted. There has been a considerable shift in emphasis from secondary to primary and community care, with fundholding GPs now in a more powerful position to choose what kind of treatment they wish to have for their patients. While the new Labour government may change some aspects of this market, particularly the competition which has developed as a consequence between GPs within a region, the likelihood is that health professionals will continue to have to sustain more complex relationships with other health providers.

The implementation of compulsory competitive tendering (CCT) has meant that local authority leisure services have had to become business units, with a clearly defined relationship to their customers, the users of the services. However, local authorities have retained the responsibility to ensure quality and so the new business units also had to relate to local councils as customers for their services. In addition, there are other internal stakeholders to whom leisure services need to relate. Many leisure services are administered within large leisure directorates which include a range of other services: arts, community services, library and information services. Collaboration and also competition characterize the kinds of relationships between the different service programmes and their staff within the CCT culture.

Library services cannot stand alone in delivering information to their communities and have therefore built up long-standing collaboration with other information providers. However, the impact of the competitive entrepreneurial culture established since CCT and local management of schools were introduced has meant that previous partners are now perceived as competitors.

As with health services, the traditional state provision through one provider has been replaced with a variety of provision. Purchasers and providers are now established, with artificial barriers erected between professionals. This has meant that social services departments in local authorities now have to recognize former partners in service provision as competitors for funding, and reconfigure their relationships with them.

While charities have always needed to support a wide range of relationships, including those with their donors, client groups, other voluntary organizations and government, since the introduction of the National Lottery in 1995, they have faced even fiercer competition for funds. This has meant greater emphasis on building long-term relationships with donors and with commercial organizations through methods such as cause-related marketing.

More than perhaps any other not-for-profit organization, churches have developed their marketing through the practice of relationship marketing, if not the adoption of its principles. The emphasis on long-term commitment on the part of both churches and their customers has meant that churches seek stable and continuing links with other organizations and have had centuries to perfect their ability to penetrate the social fabric.

In building bridges with their customers and stakeholders an important distinction between for-profit and not-for-profit organizations lies in the complexity of those publics to whom they market themselves. Kotler and Andreasen (1996, pp. 79–85) identify input publics, internal publics, intermediary publics and consuming publics as being significant. The problem for many of the organizations we have considered is that the publics to whom they now relate have shifted category, and are now of much greater significance to their operations than in the past. Many who were part of the intermediary category are now 'consuming publics' – and are customers/clients for services. Recognizing this and adopting appropriate marketing techniques has become a major problem as a consequence of the radically altered macro-environment in which not-for-profit organizations are operating. Multiple sets of customers have required differentiated marketing, with communications targeted more carefully at the various groups.

Quality and marketing

Quality management has become a key focus for not-for-profit services in the newly competitive, entrepreneurial environment of the public sector. As much of quality is to do with customer service and customer satisfaction, and is based on long- rather than short-term valuing of an organization both from within the organization and externally, it has considerable relevance to not-for-profit marketers. The emphasis on league tables and evaluating performance by means of performance indicators has become important to all public services. This has caused interest in benchmarking techniques and in continuous measurement of services to ensure sustained performance (Bullivant, 1994). In each of the sectors we investigated, organizational performance was now being questioned not only by customers but also by their key stakeholders, and this was causing a refocusing of management activity to include greater use of market research techniques such as customer-satisfaction surveys and behavioural analysis. Understanding customers and their motivations was essential in order to develop marketing communications (Foxall and Goldsmith, 1994). There was a considerable, related interest in quality management, although its implementation was variable.

In schools, quality has become a key issue, with schools competing partly on examination performance but also on less tangible aspects of their services. Parents and children require not only excellence in examinations from a school but also a caring and supportive environment. Good schools are defined not only by the indicators which government is enforcing; effectiveness is also determined partly by the shared values and ethos of staff and pupils. The role of head teacher leadership is crucial in developing a shared culture that includes all a school's elements, not simply the delivery of the curriculum.

Quality has similarly become a key issue for universities and colleges, but 'whose quality?' has also been a major question. Government, through the funding councils, has largely determined the performance criteria, but with such a lack of precision that universities continue to see their role as much wider than the performance league tables of degree results, 'A' level entry grades, research funding, etc. (Barnett, 1992). When international customers' views were examined, it was found that the quality desired from the product was very complex, and included sensitive personal contact between staff and students, language support and accommodation, as well as the overall quality of the degree programmes. The various stakeholders of universities hold different views on quality and of the objectives of higher education, and different communications are therefore needed for each group.

Quality improvement has been introduced into the NHS, but total quality management has not been effectively implemented. A major difficulty has been the failure to recognize that the complexity of introducing quality has meant the need fundamentally to change the culture of an organization. One impetus to quality has been accreditation, to support compliance to certain standards, but monitoring the implementation of quality and relating this to patients' perceptions of quality assurance has not always been successful (Debrah, 1994).

Emphasis on the customers' perception that leisure services could enhance quality of life has been one focus for quality. In other services, accreditation through formal quality systems – ISO 9000/BS 5750 – has also been the motivation to introduce a quality approach to service delivery. In both instances, the main purpose has been to improve participation rates in leisure services, with the emphasis on a partnership between the organization and its customers. For many local authorities, a quality strategy has been developed to help them achieve improved levels of access from a wider range of the community, with increased emphasis on outcomes for customers in terms of receiving consistent standards of service at each transaction.

While there is less interest in implementing quality systems in public library services than in leisure services, the link between marketing and quality has begun to be well established. However, work on developing a more strategic focus to marketing activities is still lacking in many library authorities. Performance indicators have been imposed by the Audit Commission, and these have been an important influence on systematizing the collection of data and the development of charters which promise levels of service for customers. They are limited, though, in their consideration of what library customers should expect from a public library service. The role of professionals in determining what quality means is also important, and local circumstances have to be taken into account in determining the range and depth of materials offered to a community. The needs of individual library users and the library as a community information resource have had to be balanced. While there has been extensive use of customer-satisfaction surveys in libraries, there has been insufficient progress in linking these to definitions of the key objectives of public libraries.

The issue of conflicting interests, defining service objectives and ensuring quality has been a particularly sensitive one in social services, where equal treatment and fairness for all the partners in the service provider/purchaser relationship is essential. Balancing the needs of clients with the restrictions of budgets has meant that monitoring of service quality also includes evaluating accessibility and responsiveness, as well as efficiency. It has been only too easy for services to be overwhelmed by the management burdens of reorganization and to ignore the details of service delivery. There is a need to reconcile resource management with clients' needs. Monitoring the outcomes of care in the community reforms as a way of evaluating service quality has meant that clients and their carers have needed to be involved in order to identify quality-of-life aspects, rather than just the systems and processes of management which had previously been the focus for quality management.

The increase in choices of charitable giving has forced charities and voluntary organizations to focus on the quality aspects of their operations in order to sustain donations and meet the needs of their clients more effectively. A more professional approach to marketing has been the result, with marketing emerging as a key tool in delivering effective communications. Cause-related marketing has been particularly important for achieving a higher public profile, improved image and a larger customer base. Relating effectively to donors is a central requirement, and this has also been given particular prominence; the success with which a charity retains its donors over a long period is a significant performance indicator. It was particularly notable that many of the major charities appeared to have reconciled the quality of their operations in relating to donors with the effectiveness of delivery of services to their clients.

Like charities, churches exist through establishing and maintaining long-standing relationships, and a major quality indicator is therefore the success with which they achieve and retain membership. While marketing and quality have not been seen by religious organizations as relevant to them until relatively recently, statistics of membership have frequently been used by the media as indicators of the declining relevance of the churches to national life. Using marketing as a means not only of halting this decline but also of refuting this perception has therefore become more pressing. Identifying the less tangible aspects of churches' contribution to local and national life have been one focus: churches are significant community resources through their pastoral and social care, and provide important buildings. Customer satisfaction with the churches has been another focus, with the role of the minister seen as particularly significant. The concept of quality also includes how effectively the churches encourage faithfulness in their congregations, with marketing communications having a useful role to play.

The variable uses of quality approaches to marketing their services across the sectors is very evident. Benchmarking (comparing service processes from one organization to another in order to identify best practice) was being implemented informally in many of the sectors. The health sector has developed this the most, with a Benchmarking Reference Centre based in Wales (Bullivant and Naylor, 1992), and there is considerable scope for further cross-sectoral work, which could benefit each of the not-for-profit sectors. Library and information services have begun to undertake benchmarking studies within their sector, but there is still wariness of attempting comparisons of key processes with other organizations. Some of the marketing practices which we have identified in charities, for example, would be of relevance to public library services, and indeed to churches.

For all the sectors, building loyalty among both customers and stake-holders, or frequency marketing, was essential to quality in delivering services and in retaining support. Delighting the customer (Lynch, 1993) and ensuring repeat 'buying' of the service was just as important to charities as to library services: churches, too, were identifying those aspects of their work which could be developed to increase attendances and membership.

Marketing management

While the four P's have been criticized as too restrictive when consider-ing marketing management issues, it is helpful to use them as means of assessing the range of marketing activities being undertaken and to see them as tools in successful relationship marketing. Marketing mix decisions are important to organizations, so that there continues to be value in using the four P's as a checklist of activity in the not-for-profit sector.

Product

Defining the product for not-for-profit services is complex. It is important not just to rely on customers' expectations for developing service/products as customers' expectations are frequently too low, or ill-informed. Manufacturers will similarly not rely solely on their customers to define new products. Market research into customers' desires in both the for-profit and not-for-profit sectors needs to be informed by profes-sional judgement about the quality and levels of product/service for specific needs. The not-for-profit sector also has a particular concern for ethical considerations.

This complexity was very evident in schools, where the nature of the product was being interpreted by pupils, their parents, teachers, local education authorities and government, together with colleges, univer-sities and the local community. Examination results were only one of the indicators which determined the quality of the product and helped to define it: schools' ethos was also significant and this was made up of a range of elements, from the caring attributes of schools to their pupils' behaviour in and out of school, the range and quality of extra-curricular activities and schools' history and traditions.

In universities, too, the product is defined variously by customers and the numerous stakeholders. Producing well-qualified graduates is the most visible product, but research training, research outputs which include staff publications and contributions to scholarship, industry and the professions and the provision of 'life chances' for a wide range of groups in the community (Barnett, 1992) are also significant. Government, the major funder, is increasingly the most important influencer of product design and development, with modes of teaching delivery and research activity determined by funding mechanisms.

The health care which is delivered by the NHS forms the product, but has been subject to many changes, arising especially from the purchaser/provider split. Competition between providers to supply good-quality health care has meant an increased emphasis on cost-effectiveness and also targeting their products within specific markets, such as care for the elderly. The involvement of clinicians has been seen as vital in determining quality; as well as ensuring that patients' needs are central to the purchaser/provider relationship.

Traditionally, leisure services were developed by local authorities through social planning and centrally directed policies. Now, the emphasis has switched to considering the lifestyles of customers and involving communities in decision making in order to determine priorities within the wide-ranging policy objectives of local councils. 'Quality-of-life' marketing has been prominent, with marketers emphasizing customers' wellbeing as a goal of leisure service provision. Activities which improve customers' health and wellbeing have therefore been developed.

The product of public libraries has been difficult to capture, because of the wide-ranging aims of libraries to act as educational, leisure, social and cultural institutions. Whereas leisure services have found a focus through identifying customers' need for physical and psychological wellbeing, libraries have attempted to cover every need across their materials and information provision. Taking up innovation from other sectors has largely not been successful, and there is a reluctance to use management techniques such as quality and marketing in defining the service. One major difficulty is that libraries serve everyone in the community; segmentation has been developed, for example by age and occupation (business information services), but with declining resources there needs to be clearer understanding of the limitations of what should be provided. Freedom of access versus charging for services has become a central issue. Ethical considerations about the role of libraries as essential information providers in a democratic society are set against commercial considerations as services seek more funding.

The involvement of clients in receiving the service and of personnel in delivering it also make it particularly difficult to separate the social services product from its customers and stakeholders. As with all services, intangibility and inseparability make definition difficult (Kotler and Andreasen, 1996, pp. 371–4), but tangibilizing has become increasingly important as a means of demonstrating both to clients and funders that funding is being used effectively – and fairly. Timeliness and responsiveness are important to both groups.

In order to develop their relationship with the market and develop products which meet their needs, charities have undertaken systematic segmentation of the market to promote to specific groups with common characteristics. Specific ages have been attracted to different kinds of charitable 'product' and occupation and income levels are also important variables in presenting products to donors.

The complex benefits offered by churches make it particularly difficult to describe their product, but, as with charities, there are ways in which segmenting their targets can offer insights into how they can best tangibilize specific aspects, such as church services and pastoral visiting. Like charities, the Anglican Church offers its product both locally and nationally, and the differences between the product for a national audience and for a local community also has to be understood.

Price

In all the sectors, funding considerations are a major impetus for marketing development. Pricing the elements of services in a not-for-profit context has frequently been uncomfortable for managers, but has now become a major element in decision making. Conflicts are endemic: maximizing use of a service may run counter to the need to recover as many costs as possible (Kotler and Andreasen, 1996, p. 446). Many of the services we have considered also have to take account of their funders' (especially government) policies which determine how they cost and price their products. Of all the elements in the marketing mix, pricing has caused the most unease among not-for-profit organizations in the public sector.

Following the Education Reform Act 1988, in order to ensure sufficient funding each school now has to operate as a strategic business unit, attracting and retaining pupils and maximizing other aspects of its provision. Schools are also customers for other education services and budget decisions take account of what they are willing to pay for services that once were provided centrally for them. The role of schools within the wider community as a collaborator with other schools to provide education to an area has been jeopardized by their need to take sometimes quite narrow cost-based decisions.

Pricing is a similarly value-laden issue for universities and colleges. While tuition for undergraduates is at present supported through local authority and government funding, other elements of the product, especially international students' tuition, is charged at 'full-cost' to the institution. Identifying these costs, and developing long-term relationships which enable customers to negotiate with the institution on fee levels has become an important element in marketing.

With the introduction of the internal market, provider units are competing for contracts from purchasers and cost-effectiveness of delivery is therefore essential for survival. But pricing has sometimes not taken account of patients' needs. As with universities, health services need to identify the true cost of services, rather than assuming that price equals cost; differential pricing has been seen as one method to achieve a market-led approach to services (Miles, 1993).

Pricing of leisure services has to ensure that services meet the policy objective of wide access by the community, while attracting a level of income that supports quality of delivery. The needs of individuals and pricing decisions targeted at particular segments have to be set against community needs (Kinnell and MacDougall, 1994). The effect of CCT has been to make leisure services more business oriented, but at the same time they remain a community service which local authorities facilitate. Income generation has to be based therefore on achieving wide-ranging targets: encouraging access and also ensuring income generation.

The extent to which public libraries can charge for their services is statutorily limited at present, and for many professionals charging for any information remains an ethical problem. The reality is that library services have to recover costs for materials other than books, and for added-value information services to businesses in order to be able to provide sufficient range and depth of service to the community. As with leisure services, though, there is an inherent conflict between income generation and the maximizing of use.

Pricing social services is similarly complex. The value placed on a service by clients is often influenced by tangibles such as the state of the building and the attitude of staff, as much as on the efficiency of the service in delivering effective support or advice. The purchaser/ provider split was intended to introduce more competition and encourage a greater responsiveness to clients by providing services, to a price, which better met their needs. However, increases in costs have sometimes resulted, and there has been dissatisfaction at the introduction of market-driven pricing policies which have interfered with service delivery (Wistow and Robinson, 1993).

In determining their fund-raising needs, charities have to cost the requirements of their clients and also of their operations, as in any business. How they pass on those costs for services they offer will, however, be determined by their core objectives. A charity such as Oxfam is in the business of distributing its services without cost to the end-user, and relies on donations to break even. Cost recovery will feature more in other organizations who develop pricing in line with their objectives and the needs of their clients. As in other not-for-profit sectors, pricing is a sensitive issue for charities and voluntary organizations. Managers have to take account of the organization's clients as well as the expectations of donors.

Pricing has not been a major consideration for churches, but is now receiving greater attention because of their need for funding.

Campaigns have been mounted which are similar to those designed by charities, with fund raising by a variety of methods. The upkeep of church buildings has been a particular impetus. Segmenting the market for fund-raising is essential, in order to identify which elements of the church's product attract specific targets.

Pricing issues have become increasingly relevant but have been less thoroughly investigated than in the for-profit sector. Comparisons across the not-for-profit sector indicate that there are similar concerns for organizations, but that models of pricing which have been developed need to take account of the complex variables of client needs, funders' concerns, stakeholders' agendas and organizational objectives.

Place

Distribution channels varied across each of the not-for-profit sectors, with decisions on the placing of services presenting similar problems to for-profit organizations. This has proved uncomfortable for many professionals. Changes in the mode of some public-sector services have meant less emphasis on area-wide delivery of services and more on the survival of individual business units. For other services, the cost of local provision has had to be set against quality of delivery which may best be met by regionalization.

In schools, there is now much more concern to maximize recruitment in the local catchment area than to be a collaborator with other schools. Local education authorities have found their role in balancing needs across local communities diminish, as competition between schools has been encouraged.

While universities have always had a national as well as local community role in delivering education, they too have been forced to develop greater competitiveness locally. Conversely, access to higher education has also developed through distance learning; the use of IT has enabled distributed universities to evolve, and franchised international links have become significant to some institutions.

Accessibility, availability and communication are highly significant to the NHS. Patients need an easily accessible service which responds quickly to needs. Balancing this with cost of delivery has become an issue in the provision of some services, e.g. Accident & Emergency and maternity services: patients want their services to be locally based, but centres of excellence can often only be developed at regional level. A similar balance has to be struck in the provision of leisure facilities, which need to be sufficiently local for customer access but which also need an optimum population level to sustain a range of quality services. This has also been a key issue for public libraries, which have seen a decline in the opening hours of large central libraries at the same time as questions have been raised about their core objectives.

Social services clients come from a wide area, so that the service has to be dispersed through local offices and through direct personal contact with clients. Like health services, providers need to balance access issues with the cost of provision.

Relationships with charities' clients and donors is maintained through a variety of channels. Direct mail has become particularly important for communications with donors, but local support groups and regional offices of charities are an important means of developing links with what could otherwise seem to be faceless bureaucracies.

Local provision has been the bedrock of Church ministry and despite the use of media channels the local or parish church continues to be the primary means of delivering religion to communities. While the national dimension is also significant, the role of the minister in delivering religion to a congregation remains the most important element in services.

Placing services where customers want them may conflict with other elements in the mix. To support relationship marketing, decisions on distribution channels should ideally take account primarily of customers' access needs, but cost and quality of the service also have to be considered.

Promotion

Communicating with customers is a crucial element in successful marketing and promotion therefore played a prominent part in the application of the marketing mix. For many not-for-profit organizations, promotion is equated with marketing and in the sectors represented in this book promotion was a key factor in successful marketing.

Now that schools are focusing more firmly on marketing, and especially on communicating more effectively with their customers, building links with the community has become increasingly important to them. Promotion means more than the production of new literature. Development plans which provide measurable statements of purpose and organizational targets have been helpful in developing schools' products and communicating their goals to both customers and stakeholders. A quality approach to educating pupils through every facet of a school's activities is in itself a promotional tool.

Promoting their programmes has also become a key marketing activity for universities, with varying messages dependent on the culture of the institution. Mass media have been used by the new universities, and more subtle messages presented by older institutions. The targets include new students, their parents and also alumni, whose funding support is also significant. As with schools, the quality of universities' product is also an important promotional message.

Promotion has become important to health services in order to increase awareness by purchasers and the public of services, to differentiate services, and to communicate service benefits. Separating promotion from the actual delivery of services is often difficult, as the effectiveness with which a service is performed is in itself a promotional activity. Corporate identity has also become an important means of promoting services.

For leisure services, promotion is an integral part of the product, as they have to demonstrate contributions to customers' wellbeing through their services. Developing long-term relationships with customers and thereby enhancing customers' loyalty ensures word-of-mouth promotion is effective.

While quality concerns have become increasingly important to public libraries, unlike leisure services promotion has tended to be seen as a separate activity. Frequently, it absorbs all the marketing budget and effort. Strategic marketing has often largely been subsumed in promotional programmes, with emphasis on reaching out to users and potential users through literature, activities and media presentations.

Conversely, for social services, there has been need for a much greater emphasis on promoting the value and range of services. Promotion has tended in the past to focus on problems rather than positive aspects and considerable effort is now needed to persuade clients and donors that services are beneficial both to society and individuals.

Like leisure services, the promotional tools used by charities are integral to their activity. Services to both clients and donors would fail without them. With so much competition for funds in recent years, donors need to know more about causes and how funds are administered. Communications strategies are therefore essential to deliver accountability. Clients also need to be made aware of how to access support, and communicating with them has therefore become more significant.

The evangelical role of churches – perhaps the oldest form of promotion – means that their expertise in promoting themselves is central to their mission. Finding the right message for different target groups, and suiting the style of a particular church, has become more meaningful in an age when marketing promotions have made people more sensitive to techniques of selling. As with other not-for-profit organizations, promotion has become associated in the minds of customers with the total 'product' of the organization and is therefore significant for its impact on relationships with church members and also society at large.

Conclusion

In all the sectors we have considered, there is evidence of considerable marketing activity: some of it strategic and well planned, but some the result of expediency and in response to rapid and far-reaching changes in the public sector. For many managers, marketing has become a central issue because their funding sources have changed due to competitive tendering, the establishment of internal markets and the growth of entrpreneurialism in their operating environment. What is also evident, though, is the impetus for not-for-profit organizations to embrace the quality approaches to their service delivery which their competitors are using to deliver improved performance – and which funders and customers are demanding of all services. By combining marketing practices with effective quality management, organizations can both attract customers and funders and maintain an ongoing relationship with them. Effective marketing for the not-for-profit sector demands a multi-faceted approach which aims to sustain long-term relationships through the sensitive application of marketing in circumstances which are often ethically challenging.

References

Barnett, R. (1992) *Improving Higher Education: Total quality care*, The Society for Research into Higher Education and Open University Press.

Bullivant, J. (1994) *Benchmarking for Continuous Improvement in the Public Sector*, Longman.

Bullivant, J. and Naylor, M. (1992) Best of the best. *Health Service Journal*, 27 August, 24–5.

Debrah, Y.A. (1994) Evolution and implementation of a quality improvement programme. *Total Quality Management*, **5** (3), 11–25.

Foxall, G.R. and Goldsmith, R.E. (1994) *Consumer Psychology for Marketing*, Routledge.

Kinnell, M. and MacDougall, J. (1994) *Meeting the Marketing Challenge. Strategies for public libraries and leisure services*, Taylor Graham.

Kotler, P. and Andreasen, A.R. (1996) *Strategic Marketing for Nonprofit Organizations*, 5th edn, Prentice Hall.

Kotler, P. and Roberto, E.L. (1989) *Social Marketing: Strategies for changing public behavior*, The Free Press.

Lynch, J.J. (1993) *Managing the Delight Factor*, IFS International.

Manoff, R.K. (1985) *Social Marketing*, Praeger.

Miles, C.(1993) Market values. *Health Service Journal*, 12 August, 32–5.

Wistow, G. and Robinson, J. (1993) *All Change. No Change? Community care six months on. A second report of development in the health and social care divide*, Kings Fund Centre.

CHAPTER 12

Cases and issues

Introduction

In this section four case studies are presented of organizations which needed the application of marketing principles to resolve particular issues. The cases represent different complexities, but all demonstrate that not-for-profit organizations share similar problems with those of for-profit businesses. Two come from one county, Nottinghamshire, which illustrates how an environment can affect organizations in related but different ways: the impact of recession and the collapse of the mining communities had a direct effect on both the school and the cathedral discussed here. Balancing organizational goals, available resources, and people and systems as well as dealing with a complex and turbulent environment requires a strategic and customer-focused approach. The second two case studies follow the marketing developments over five years in different local authority services – a leisure services department and a library service. The effects of compulsory competitive tendering, budget restrictions, unitary status, convergence of departments and the cultural environment on marketing practice are highlighted. Each of the cases would consider themselves to be a 'quality' organization engaged in marketing as the means to achieving specific long-term objectives; they all placed emphasis on aspiring to best practice, even in contexts where customers and stakeholders may not have formalized their expectations. What distinguishes the cases from the business sector is the special emphasis that had to be placed on the ethical and professional elements of their activities and the need for managers to address those cultural issues which meant that a marketing approach was often not comfortable for members of the organization or its clients.

Garibaldi School, Mansfield

Garibaldi School in Forest Town, a former mining village near Mansfield, is a school which has been described as one of the most rapidly improving in the country' (Driscoll and Scott-Clark, 1996). The school is an 11 to 18 comprehensive serving Mansfield, Forest Town and Clipstone, a depressed area which has seen the disappearance of its traditional employment opportunities for young people through the virtual demise of the Nottinghamshire coalfield and the decline of the hosiery and textile industries. The school was built in the 1960s and is sited next to a council estate; over 90 per cent of pupils come from within this immediate area. By 1993, unemployment in the area was 3 per cent higher than the national average. Economic decline had reached unacceptable levels and funding through economic development grants was initiated. Clipstone benefited from the Neighbourhood Renewal Programme, a housing investment programme providing £4 million for the district. The local economy is staging a slow recovery, with industrial estates being developed to house new businesses through funding from the European Development Fund. North Nottinghamshire Training and Enterprise Council are also supporting business development by consultancy assistance, investment in the community and advice, information and training for the unemployed. The recent reopening of its railway station (Mansfield had the dubious distinction as the largest community without its own rail link) has given a further boost to the area's social and economic revival. Providing for the educational needs of communities struggling to regain economic and social control over their destinies is part of this revival, one which benefits the community as a whole.

In 1989, though, when the current Headmaster Bob Salisbury took over the school, it had problems related to this wider socio-economic context. Hopelessness characterized the ethos of the school. The sixth form numbered only eight pupils, vandalism was rife and truancy was accepted as an undesirable but inescapable norm of behaviour. Around seventy pupils a year were lost to other local schools, with poor exam results a sign to parents that it could not deliver the standards they expected for their children. Originally intended for a roll of 1100, by 1989 the numbers had dropped dramatically. Expectations of the school were low in the community when the new head teacher arrived. Community involvement in the school was largely non-existent and parents perceived the school to be lacking in sufficient resources to educate their children effectively. The school was seen to reflect the poverty and decline so evident in the rest of the local area. There was a clear link between this impoverishment in the community at large and the lack of confidence in the school to deliver the skills needed by the pupils to help them exploit further education and employment opportunities.

The previous management of the school had been largely traditional in character, with a head teacher who had operated a hierarchical staffing structure and formal management style. There were three deputy heads and pastoral care was delivered through a chain from year heads, deputy year heads to class teachers. A rigid management structure had developed, with low motivation and limited capacity to respond quickly to circumstances, let alone to seize opportunities for development. The poor state of the buildings and lack of technical equipment were examples of the results of a culture which denied staff the opportunity to change their environment and build an adequate resource base. Pupils were dealt with in a similarly rigid manner: for example, they were excluded from the school buildings at lunch-time and breaks, creating a sense of a school in a siege with its own customers.

The tasks facing the new Head were therefore complex:

1   Relationships with the local community had deteriorated to such an extent that there was no confidence in the school to deliver the basic skills and competences required for the job market. Building trust within the community was a key issue.
2   There were no additional resources available to support the school, given the budgetary restrictions on all schools. The Education Reform Act 1988 had introduced Local Management of Schools and lessened the budgetary controls of the local education authorities. While this enabled schools to manage their own destinies to a greater extent than ever before, it also forced the pace of change through the competition it encouraged between schools for pupils, the setting up of league tables of examination performance and the independent Office of Standards in Education (Ofsted) inspections. Schools were increasingly thrown onto their resources to capture more pupils, generate income and deliver on quality in educational performance.
3   The organization of the school was rigid and both staff and pupils suffered low motivation. The culture was one of high dependency on rules rather than norms of behaviour, and there was lack of initiative evident in the behaviour of staff, who were unwilling to take actions unless specifically instructed by the head teacher. Effective human resource management was regarded as key to developing the school.

The head teacher has described the context as one in which change was feared and the school had not faced up to the problems of education in a competitive world:

In my view we will not have the luxury of simply maintaining the status quo in tomorrow's schools. Rapid technical innovation and millions of well-educated people coming on line in India, Argentina, Mexico, Brazil and the Philippines, will surely challenge existing global trading patterns. For us in schools, the future will be about trying to equip all of our young people with a portfolio of skills which will make them 'marketable' as individuals whatever the world throws at them.

Bob Salisbury (1993) therefore set about developing this vision within Garibaldi School and helping pupils to achieve their full potential. Enlisting the active support of the community and freeing the energies and talents of his staff were key to the success of his venture. On taking up his post, he discussed the issues with children, their parents and the staff to pinpoint the specific problem areas and identify areas for growth and change. Changing the culture by a variety of methods was an important first step. From their experience of a more traditional head teacher who wore academic robes to meetings and assemblies, he offered an open door and an approachable manner to pupils as well as to staff. He also initiated a new policy with regard to the treatment of pupils, who were now allowed to enter the school at break and lunchtimes. They responded by showing a greater respect for the school and its premises and staff were relieved of the tensions associated with excluding children from their school. Two new deputy heads were recruited when two of the three in post left for jobs elsewhere, and the third who was already in post enthusiastically embraced the new ethos.

It was felt essential to motivate the staff in order to encourage a more proactive attitude to change, and to move away from the negative culture of the past. His introduction of an appraisal scheme which has evolved over a period of six years was part of the school's planning processes of staff development for both teaching and non-teaching staff. It has been assessed under the Investors in People Initiative and achieved accreditation in 1995. Appraisal became recognized by staff as a vehicle for their professional development. Departments use the School Management Plan, formulated annually, as the basis for their own Plan and from this the staff each has a Self Development Plan. Every member of staff has a mentor, usually their line manager, and the mentor meets with each member of their team to review their role description and to set personal targets for the next year, with a Self Development Planner as the outcome of this process. Mentoring continues throughout the year, with a formal review at mid-point. At each stage of the planning process training requirements are identified, resulting in a twelve-month training plan for the school.

School Management Plan – organizational level
Departmental Plan – team level
Self Development Plan – individual level

The School Management Plan first sets out the mission of the school and its aims:

WHAT ARE WE ABOUT?
Learning for life
Opportunity for all
High expectations
Dignity and respect
Developing people
Preparing our students for the 21st Century.
HOW DO WE DO THIS?
Building confidence and self esteem
Emphasizing communication skills
Encouraging flexibility
Taking account of changing technology
Encouraging a positive attitude
Encouraging a global outlook.

It then details the projects to be undertaken over the next 12 months by each Department, the staff involved, training required, cost, time-scale, method of evaluation and the links to the school's aims. The level of detail is important, to ensure that the school's aims become embedded in actions.

The appraisal of staff is carried out by the head teacher for teaching staff and deputy head for non-teaching staff, during an interview held in the summer term. There is considerable time and energy devoted to the process, which is a measure of the importance placed upon it. The reasons for undertaking such an extensive and integrated planning process result from the desire that:

- appraisal be part of the process of professional development, not a 'bolt-on activity' which takes place out of context;
- staff think about their performance every day;
- planning and evaluation be linked on a personal, team and whole school level so that all are working towards the same goals;
- managers are encouraged to 'coach' their team members and to take an active role in the professional development of their team members;
- appraisal be constructive, not threatening.

Appraisal was also seen as an important means of measuring the effectiveness of the school in conjunction with reviews, pupil feedback sheets on the quality of teaching and regular SWOT analyses with parents to identify what they felt about the school.

Winning the support and enthusiam of his colleagues through effective and individual attention in this way was an important initial and
continuing element in the regeneration of the school. Winning that of
the community was equally important. The school had been a target
for vandals to the extent that damage, including arson, had been common. Pride in the school and its integration into the life of the community had to be developed. Because the stated aim of the school is to
identify and cater for the needs of pupils for the next thirty years and
to focus on future rather than on past educational goals and attainment
levels, the needs of the wider community became a natural focus for
action. There were clear gains as a result of this approach. By 1993
there were 800 pupils attending the school, and an increase to about
1000 is expected to be sustained over the next two years. With the belief
that learning is a lifelong process all members of the community were
encouraged to develop their skills within the school. There are at present
around thirty adults retraining in the sixth form on a variety of courses,
at no charge. An 'under-fives centre' has been built on the school site to
enable parents and carers to join the sixth form. A drop-in centre for
adults to learn computing skills, homework clubs and breakfast facilities
were some of the other means of breaking the barriers between school
and community. Inventive partnerships with the local community were
also initiated, resulting in:

- a new Sports Centre for the school and local community;
- an all-weather football pitch and tennis courts with floodlighting;
- a European Studies block with language laboratory, which also
  houses a local language services company;
- computer rooms;
- a completely refurbished and re-equipped technology suite.

Much of this success has resulted from the cultivation of relationships
within the community at large, including especially those businesses
which the head was able to convince of the mutually rewarding partnership possibilities. Use of the media to develop community perceptions of
the school and listening to and informing the community about the
school became an important element of school management. The pupils'
perceptions were equally significant. Research conducted in the school
had identified the following as issues for problem pupils:

- being branded a failure;
- unsettled home background;
- general disinterest at school;
- pupil psychological or emotional instability;
- inability to work;
- revolt against adult authority;
- lack of self esteem;
- dislike of adult/teacher;

- use of drugs or alcohol;
- lack of interest in the subject/lack of relevance of the subject.

Controlling disruptive behaviour and thereby enhancing both the experience and perceptions of such pupils were dependent on an entirely changed school philosophy based on mutual dignity and respect, an emphasis on rewards rather than punishment, close mentoring and monitoring of individuals and constant evaluation of teaching materials. Computer-assisted learning, for example, was found to be effective in improving behaviour and raising the standards of the least able pupils.

In order to implement many of the actions which would raise the level of performance of the school, generate the enthusiasm of staff and pupils and enhance community involvement in the school, specific marketing activities were undertaken. By using the contacts of a local brewery a 'free day' was set up when their marketing consultants discussed the possibilities with the head and introduced the basic strategies available to him. Communicating effectively with parents, raising funds and improving the 'atmospherics' of the school were identified as priority targets. An entrepreneurial approach was enthusiastically embraced by the head teacher and communicated to his staff. At first, there was some reluctance on their part to take initiatives but by encouraging colleagues to learn by their mistakes and providing incentives to staff for successful projects the head successfully transformed the school into a thriving organization engaging in for-profit activities to enhance revenue and to develop the school's portfolio. An initial project developed by the head involved negotiating with a local theme park to sell tickets on an agency basis, selling over £17 000 worth in the first three months. This purchased a school minibus. An even larger theme park was alerted to this success and Garibaldi then took on the Alton Towers ticket agency for north Nottinghamshire, with a better share of profits on sales than the previous contract.

A manufacturer of scientific and educational equipment was also contacted by the head with the offer to build a showroom at the school which would enable the school to have new equipment (a modern language centre; new science laboratory; new home economics room) and would promote the company's products. The school showed its commitment by offering half of the refurbishment costs – which they then obtained from the Greater Nottingham Training and Enterprise Council (TEC). This was successfully negotiated and Garibaldi School also gained a 3 per cent commission on orders. Once the language centre was established, a link with a language service company was made through the TEC and this now has a base at the school and provides evening and weekend courses for local companies, using school facilities. The school has also developed a role as an exhibition venue for companies targeting the education market, with the school's own administrative staff largely taking over the management of events.

The physical appearance of the school has also been transformed in ways other than through the purchase of expensive equipment. A local brewery chain donated old signs which became distinctive notice boards, and waste bins were recycled from another organization. The school's entrance hall became a warm and welcoming space and the school's achievements were displayed prominently and professionally in the corridors through photographs, press cuttings and pupils' work. New decor, hall curtains and the resiting of the library to provide for a sixth-form centre were some of the other changes to meet the needs of pupils and their community.

The achievements since 1989 have been recognized nationally and internationally and have resulted in a number of awards:

The Chartered Institute of Marketing Midland Company of the Year Award 1992 and 1995
IBM Excellence in Management Award 1993, Paris
Entrepreneurial Award 1993, Belfast
Modern Languages Award 1992
Investors in People Award 1995
DTI Innovation Award 1995.

Additionally, the school hosted a visit from HRH Prince Charles in 1994 and was featured in Sir John Harvey Jones's BBC2 *Troubleshooter Returns* series in June 1995.

Promoting the school has also been achieved through the participation of the head in marketing education. As well as mounting successful courses on fund-raising techniques, and marketing for schools, he has published a guide to managing school marketing. This glossy publication is yet a further example of local business partnership with the school through East Midlands Electricity sponsorship of its production.

The principles underpinning the marketing planning undertaken by Garibaldi are set out in this document, beginning with the Success Factors for the school (Salisbury, 1993):

1 *Test and examination results*
Do all individuals achieve their potential?
What is the position of the school in the league tables?
2 *Quality of teaching*
How is this viewed by parents?
3 *Appearance of buildings*
Are they attractive and well maintained?
Are signs clear?
Is display work fresh and interesting?
4 *The caring school*
Is the school sincere in its care of pupils and parents?
Are relationships between pupils, teachers and parents positive?
5 *Organization of parents' meetings*

6   *Extra-curricular activities*
Does the school have activities which attract pupils?
7   *Length and arrangement of school day*
Do parents and children find the arrangements attractive?
8   *Children's behaviour inside and outside school*
How do children seem to behave?
Are there any complaints from the public?
Is the atmosphere in the school calm?
9   *Links with feeder schools*
Are these well established and effective?
10   *School uniform*
Is there a policy on school uniform?
11   *Unofficial grapevine*
What is the perceived image of the school?
12   *Media coverage*
Does the local press, radio and TV make favourable comment?
13   *Community involvement*
Does the community feel part of the school?

References

Driscoll, M. and Scott-Clark, C. (1996) Class action. *The Sunday Times*, 18 August, 1.8 Focus.

Salisbury, B. (1993) *Managing School Marketing: Promoting a positive image*, East Midlands Electricity.

Issues

1 The school's methods of developing and sustaining relationships with stakeholders.
2 How to change the expectations of the varied groups of customers: pupils, parents, employers.
3 The roles of the head teacher through leadership and motivation to manage quality and meet the needs of customers and stakeholders.

Questions

1 How should a marketing plan address the Success Factors developed by Garibaldi School?
2 Identify the elements of the marketing mix evident in the case study and consider their significance in the school's performance of its mission.
3 What pitfalls would you regard as threats for the future?

Southwell 2000: campaigning for a parish cathedral

Southwell Minster is one of the hidden, lesser-known ecclesiastical gems. It serves as the parish church of Southwell, a large Nottinghamshire village which is famed for its racecourse and lies some eight miles from Newark – noted for its Civil War connections. Despite its considerable beauty and unique situation in a still largely unspoilt and undeveloped village, Southwell Minster has never attracted the numbers of tourists of the larger cathedrals despite equalling them in architectural and historic merit. The building is also the Anglican cathedral for Nottinghamshire, with the Bishop's residence situated next to it. Southwell is a recent bishopric created in 1884 out of the dioceses of Lincoln and Lichfield to provide a diocese for the East Midlands. Nearby the Minster are also the ruins of the medieval Archbishop of York's palace, and a magnificent Great Hall which remains intact as part of the original fourteenth- to fifteenth-century building. The Minster history can be traced back to AD 956 with evidence of a large Roman settlement in paving found beneath the floor of one of the aisles and in the cemetery. The building seen today is mainly from the three periods of 1108 to 1234, 1234 to 1287, and 1288. Its interior has been described as a 'composition which combines in a remarkable way the robust with the lively' (Pevsner, 1979).

There are many important features to the Minster: its facade with the 'pepper pot' towers is unique; the two-storey nave is unusual for its date; and the Chapter House is celebrated for its rich, naturalistic carvings of foliage, birds and beasts. A relatively undecorated church, with few grave monuments and brasses, its character as a living parish church as well as cathedral is very evident.

Close by is Vicars' Court and the Residence of the Minster Provost, a group of well-proportioned seventeenth- to eighteenth-century brick houses occupied by the present clergy. Set back on the surrounding roads are fine prebendal houses, formerly the residences of the non-resident canons who held livings from the Minster.

This architectural heritage of the Minster and its surroundings is key to an understanding of its wider importance: not only to the diocese but also to the county. Nottinghamshire is relatively lacking in fine, large buildings. The only large National Trust property is at Clumber Park, where just the stable block and church remain. In the other 'Dukeries' to the North of the county there are a few remaining large houses, but none is remarkable. Wollaton Hall in the city of Nottingham, a well-preserved Elizabethan mansion, is now a museum, but it lacks furnishings from the period to set it off adequately. Nottingham Castle is in such a restored state that the original medieval building has been mostly lost, and the twelfth-century Worksop Priory is the only other large, early ecclesiastical building of note, but its location to the far north of the county and poor situation in the town detracts from its potential for wider religious as well as secular significance. Compared with the adjacent counties of Leicestershire and Derbyshire, Nottingham therefore has a limited number of architectural focal points and heritage sites to which the community can relate. Southwell Minster is one of the few buildings of its kind in Nottinghamshire which potentially can command broad commitment for both religious meaning and historic significance.

As a cathedral, Southwell Minster is of lesser importance than Lincoln, its nearest neighbour, and York to whom it owed allegiance for many centuries. Consequently, it has not received the kind of large sums to support restoration which had been raised for more obviously nationally prestigious buildings. By the early 1990s it had become clear that there was a lack of funding to support urgent building work, particularly for the Chapter House which is recognized internationally as a unique expression of naturalistic art (Pevsner, 1945). The Minster is a focus for pastoral work throughout the county and an important expression of its ministry has been the work of the choir school and resident choirmaster. Supporting this musical tradition of choir and organ music had become a well-established part of ministry; critically acclaimed recordings were sold in the Minster bookshop, organ recitals were regularly performed and national and international tours undertaken. It was therefore decided in 1994 to launch a coordinated funding drive – 'Southwell 2000' – to provide a focus for supporting the wide-ranging remit of the Minster as a centre for religious worship, as an important building architecturally and historically, and for its contribution to the Anglican tradition of church music. The aims of the campaign were:

1 raising money to ensure the restoration of the fabric of the Minster, especially the Chapter House, by the year 2000;
2 replacing the organ and supporting the musical life of the Minster;
3 establishing a Visitor's Centre (the need for which had been identified in the Bishop's visitation during 1994).

These aims were set by the Provost (who has responsibility for the Minster as a building and a parish church), the Bishop (whose role is the pastoral care and management of the diocese) and the Minster's Administrator. A target of £1.25 million was set: £750 000 for the fabric; £250 000 for the organ and £250 000 for the Visitor Centre. It was recognized at the outset, though, that the new organ would not be seen as a priority by some donors and that the Minster would need to use its own resources to augment funding for this.

In the early stages the Provost and Administrator were most active in planning the fund raising, but it quickly became evident to them that professional expertise was needed to launch an effective marketing campaign. A consultancy organization specializing in fund raising was therefore employed at an early stage to provide initial advice on structuring the appeal and to give a blueprint for action.

The three-pronged aims of the funding campaign were addressing very different aspects of the complex role of the Minster: as historic building; as focus of religious worship for Anglicans in Nottinghamshire and further afield; and as a centre of excellence in church music. An Appeal Director was first appointed on a contract basis by consultants with experience of marketing in similar large organizations, and after the initial period of team building it was decided to appoint a full-time Director to manage the difficult task of meeting each of these aims. To support this work, an Appeal Office with Appeal Secretary was established, and a computer system installed in order to facilitate database development. A traditional fund-raising structure was set up, of a two-tier committee – fifteen in all – with President (Lord-Lieutenant of the County), Vice-Presidents and a Chair from a high-profile financial background (a senior partner in a locally based firm of international accountants) to give credibility, and the Provost and members representing functional interests who also had responsibility for targeting different geographical areas of the county. The remit of this committee was extensive: to develop and oversee the whole campaign, and to manage the fund-raising activities. However, the administration of the funds raised and the spending decisions in pursuit of the objectives of Southwell 2000 were matters for the Provost and the Cathedral Council. The accounts, which were operated quite separately from those of the Minster, were maintained by the Cathedral Council and independently audited.

Organizing an appeal committee for the purpose of fund-raising was in itself a difficult task. Inevitably, as with all committees, there were varying agendas and perspectives at work, and different degrees of commitment. The culture of the Church had to be worked within and accommodated by the committee in developing a marketing strategy for the campaign. The Church is probably the last bastion of the establishment after the armed services and also the least well adjusted to the business practices of the twentieth century. Relating to the dynamics of change was therefore an inevitable difficulty for both the clergy and lay people of the Minster congregation. The mission of the Church is essentially spiritual as well as dealing with the practical problems of running a large organization whose members have a range of needs and agendas. This makes for tensions in maintaining the central role whilst developing a marketing function that seeks to tangibilize intangibles and to bring business values to bear on problems. Changing the culture of the Church sufficiently to allow for the implementation of marketing practices in the service of its main goals and to convert the vision of the campaign into business realities was a key role of the Appeal committee and the Appeal Directors. Ensuring there was a minimum level of team work to achieve this was essential, but also difficult at times. As well as the committee members, volunteers were needed to support the work, and managing their input and maintaining motivation was important.

The first task was to build the team, from the Chair of the committee through to flower arrangers and the individuals who were offering to run small activities. Listening skills were particularly important, as well as a disciplined approach to organizing individuals. The full-time Director's previous experience in a senior military post, as well as in marketing, was a considerable asset here. It was also important, though, for him to have a level of freedom to act, which was unlike the usual decision-making pattern in the Church, where an established hierarchy was in place to deal with requests for actions. Answering requests by the usual route took too long, and this had to be short-circuited so that the Provost and the Chair could decide on immediate actions.

The first task was to appreciate the overall job that had to be undertaken. While the consultants had provided – and continued to support throughout the campaign – a 'blueprint for action', local factors had to be taken into account. There were several issues which needed to be addressed:

1 The geography of the diocese. Nottinghamshire is a long, thin county with Nottingham in the south and an extensive hinterland stretching to the north. Southwell lies closer to Newark than Nottingham, the major population centre.
2 The recession. The campaign was launched at a time when the Nottinghamshire coalfields were being run down and the recession was biting, in an area which had previously escaped large-scale economic problems.
3 The local targets for funding (which firms should be approached for corporate support).
4 Available resources for the campaign (an audit of the people and skills available to the Appeal committee).
5 The low profile of the Minster in the county as a cathedral, despite its historic significance.

In order to meet the three aims and to take account of each of these issues, a wide-ranging programme was developed, with both longer- and short-term actions and a recognition that each aim of the campaign required a different target, with varying marketing tools. Weeding out ideas which could not be supported and only running with activities that met the overall aims of the Appeal and that also met the quality criterion which was seen as an essential means of sustaining the profile of the Minster were important in the initial planning. As each of the funding targets had appeal for different segments of the donor population, it was vital to provide assurances that a gift could be earmarked for a particular project. Funding the organ, for example, was not a priority for many of the donors who wanted to support the fabric of the Minster.

The key actions were identified as:

- approaching charitable trusts;
- targeting personal benefactors;
- approaching business donors;
- organizing activities;
- developing a covenanting campaign.

First, a sweep of charitable trust databases was undertaken, and the contacts of the committee members used to the full. These were major activities and were undertaken at national as well as local level; they took several months of sustained effort to complete. The Church Commissioners had to be thoroughly convinced of the professionalism and worthiness of the Minster project in order to provide support. Their perception of the ability not only of the Appeal committee to raise funds but also of the Minster to administer the programme effectively had to be a positive one. Support at county and at local level was canvassed. One committee member, for example, was a respected retired local GP and chair of school governors and had many contacts within the village and throughout the county. Identifying the key people in the community and approaching charities resulted in important benefactions as well as support for specific activities: English Heritage gave matching funding to support restoration; influential individuals agreed to take responsibility for activities; and Nottinghamshire County Council provided grant aid of £50 000 to develop a prestigious concert programme involving established professional artists, 'The Southwell Season'.

Business donations and personal benefactions were less successful. Many large companies have long-established charitable trusts which are accustomed to dealing with fund-raising campaigns and these had to be contacted through those mechanisms developed to distance the commercial arm of the business from its charitable donations. A professional approach in dealing with these was essential. Some national companies with local bases (e.g. Boots plc) gave generously, but for others the recession was a problem. Brochures were printed and distributed to publicize the personal covenanting campaign, but this was similarly not as successful as other elements of the Appeal.

The Southwell Season of concerts was successful on two counts. It was profitable and developed a high profile for both the Minster and the Appeal. The emphasis on a quality product which was necessary as part of the overall image of the Minster and its role in the life of the county was considerably helped by the appearance of leading singers and musicians and the superb ambience created in the Minster. Corporate hospitality was available in the Great Hall, and audiences travelled from around the region to the performances. Other activities were targeted across the interest range and involved all sections of the community, organized and coordinated by the committee. A racing day was held at Southwell Races and a music and antiques evening in Newark (recognized as a centre for the antique trade); a Nottingham philanthropist who was also a well-respected and influential charity worker organized a performance of the Beijing Opera at the Nottingham Playhouse; a postal auction which raised several thousand pounds was run; and 'candles for Christmas' were sold to Nottinghamshire schools.

The geographical coverage and involvement of the whole county were seen as important for ongoing relationships, and a deliberate balance was struck in the provision of activities and targeting of donors across the area. It had been decided at the outset in consultation with the Bishop not to involve the parishes directly in fundraising, as they had financial difficulties of their own, so that the involvement of the whole county through other means was seen as important.

The results of the campaign were impressive. At its close on 31 December, 1995 a total of £1.8 million had been raised, including the matching funding from English Heritage (the outstanding amounts of which will be received as work on the fabric is completed). The excess over target was used to pump-prime further projects, including an educational centre with audio-visual facilities to develop the educational role of the Minster and to encourage greater participation by schools. The Appeals office has continued its work through the Capital and Projects Fund, charged with the role of raising additional funds needed for the educational centre and future fabric and other capital projects. The Appeals Director has now moved on to similar work in another cathedral and the committee has been wound down.

There has also been a continuing effort to sustain the goodwill which the Appeal engendered, an aspect of the campaign which had been recognized as essential at the outset and which informed the thinking of the Appeal Director and the committee throughout its life. 'Time spent saying thank-you' was seen as an important means of developing longer-term relationships and investing in giving for the future. Every donor, no matter how small the gift, received a letter of thanks. It is still too soon to estimate the full impact of the Appeal on the profile of the Minster nationally and locally, but the short-term aims of the project were achieved, and the financial targets exceeded.

References

Pevsner, N. (1945) *The Leaves of Southwell*, Penguin.
Pevsner, N. (1979) *Nottinghamshire*, 2nd edn, revised by E. Williamson, Penguin, pp. 319–33.

Issues

1 Developing a culture within the Minster which enabled a marketing approach to be implemented successfully.
2 Balancing short-term gains and longer-term relationships in the planning and running of the campaign.
3 Targeting donors effectively by segmenting the potential donor market.
4 Maintaining the momentum of marketing at the end of a successful campaign.

Questions

1 How can the concept of marketing be marketed in an organization whose values and aspirations are not related to business objectives?
2 What might have been done to improve the giving from personal and business donors?
3 What marketing planning should now be undertaken to build on the success of the Appeal, and how might the marketing function be organized?

Leicester City Council Leisure Services Division

Leicester is one of the ten largest English cities and is situated in the East Midlands forty miles north east of Birmingham. A population of approximately 290 000 includes 30 per cent Asian, West Indian, Chinese, and other racial groups with a wide range of languages and cultural backgrounds. The city's traditional industries comprise a range of textile and clothing manufacturers with engineering and service industries also large employers. The city has two universities and a wide range of arts and entertainment facilities including arts centres, and concert halls. There are eight museums and 3000 acres of parks and gardens, a variety of leisure centres, sports grounds and an international athletics and cycle stadium. Leicester is Britain's first Environment City, awarded in 1990 by the Royal Society for Nature Conservation and the Civic Trust in recognition of the city's pioneering environmental programmes. The council has been under Labour control since 1987 and has a national reputation for its radical approach to equal opportunities and focusing on the customer in local service delivery. In 1996 Leicester was pronounced one of the new unitary authorities but preparation for this status had begun years earlier. Recreation and arts have always been given a high priority in terms of improving the quality of life of residents and total expenditure in 1991/ 2 was £33 million (gross), £22 million (net).

The appointment in 1990 of a new Deputy Director of the then-named Recreation and Arts Department provided an opportunity to reassess priorities and issues affecting the Department. On appointment Martyn Allison conducted an analysis of the organization based on observations and discussions with staff. He identified ten key issues affecting the city, the council and the department:

Issues affecting Leicester
- Race relations in a growing multi-cultural city – arts and recreation have a major role to play.
- Quality of life – the department plays an important part in improving life quality and promoting personal and community development at a time when variations between the affluent and the less well off are increasing.
- City image – Leicester needed to improve its national profile and increase tourism but not at the expense of local initiatives designed to respond to the issues of race relations and quality of life.

Issues facing the city council
- Declining resources – the pressure from central government on capital and revenue finances was increasing and the uncertainty engendered made planning ahead very problematic.
- Political uncertainty was an issue closely linked with declining resources and the lack of clear direction to take with damaging consequences.
- Business culture had been introduced into the authority with the result of a management revolution causing major rifts between those espousing new culture and the old service culture.

Issues facing the department
- Lack of a common mission was highlighted by inherent divisions between the different areas and a lack of aims and measurable objectives.
- Task management – there was limited evidence of turning policies into positive action.
- Competition for declining resources was evident without real assessment of overall departmental needs or priorities and little cooperation or planning.
- Equal opportunities was a concern to many staff with the advent of the new competitive culture.

A SWOT (strengths, weaknesses, opportunities and threats) analysis was also undertaken of the Arts and Recreation Department which identified the following elements:

Strengths
Reputation
Width and depth of service
Size of budget
Equal opportunities
Performance orientated
Positive attitude to change
Acceptance of delegation
Friendly atmosphere
Commitment to customers
Training (skills, qualifications)

Weaknesses
Complacency
Management information
Management training
Planning

Marketing
Team work
Distrust
Understanding
Recruitment
Rewards for performance
Amount of paper
Identity/image
Procedures
Accountability
Size of plant

Opportunities
Pressure for change
Concern for customers
Changing culture of councils
Tourism
Green city
Sponsorship
Demographic change

Threats
Political uncertainty
Distrust
Poll tax
CCT
Economic recession
Demographic change
Changes in education

By identifying the elements of the SWOT analysis and relating the wider environmental concerns of the city and the council to those of the department the Deputy Director was able to develop a five-year plan based on the following five key tasks:

1   To generate greater team work with a common mission.
2   To provide a coordinated planning framework for the Department.
3   To introduce a clearer financial strategy, reduce uncertainty and enable more effective targeting of resources.
4   To improve the quality of management information as a prerequisite of monitoring performance.
5   To introduce a coordinated training strategy.

A common mission

As all staff were united in their desire to increase participation in their particular service, both to increase income and to benefit society, a common mission was identified as the increase in participation in leisure activities particularly from under-represented groups. Working as a team, all staff could work effectively by channelling their skills towards the achievement of the common aim. Marketing and good customer service combined with effective development and outreach work was necessary to attract and maintain customers. The positive management of change was envisaged as a method of ensuring the continued development of equal opportunities for those delivering the service and for those benefiting from it. Decision makers should reflect the community in that the different racial groups, women and disabled people needed to be represented in the management structure. There was a need to recognize the importance of effective management to deliver the service rather than focusing on the differences between a business and a service culture.

Planning framework

A planning framework was seen as vital to coordinate existing plans and make them simpler to understand. This would comprise:

- a departmental strategy showing long-term aims and objectives;
- corporate plans detailing key areas of corporate policy to back up the strategy and outlining the main objectives over the next 5 years;
- facility and service marketing plans to develop services in relation to the corporate objectives;
- annual action plans already in existence needed to be adapted to include annual reports and targets for the following year taken from the service marketing plan and corporate objectives;
- work programmes consisting of monthly statements of tasks required to implement the annual action plans.

The framework would only be as good as the degree to which it was monitored and reviewed and the resulting positive action taken. It was felt that more attention needed to be given to monitoring of targets and to corrective actions where these were not being met. The Corporate Management Team should be responsible for the setting and achievement of objectives and targets with managers given more responsibility for the success of their own performance. Work programmes should be used to monitor performance as well as task achievement.

Financial strategy

In order to minimize the effects of external financial uncertainty a series of key questions should be asked to develop a financial strategy for the department:

1 Will the overall budget grow by the rate of inflation or less?
2 Should priority be given to maintaining existing services or developing new services?
3 Should priority be given to certain service areas such as arts, sports, parks, play, neighbourhood centres?
4 Should priority be given to the whole community or to certain sections, i.e. women, black and Asian community, people with disabilities?
5 Should additional resources be created by reducing expenditure or increasing income?
6 Should additional income be created by increasing usage or increasing prices?
7 Should additional resources be generated from the private sector?
8 Should additional resources be created by reducing existing support to the voluntary sector or by increasing further the use of the voluntary sector?

In this way decisions based on the strategy and corporate and service plans could be taken to manage change and, for example, to transfer funding from areas of low priority to areas of higher priority. The Corporate Management Team would identify areas for development and areas of saving based on annual reviews of budgets and savings. Good performance would be rewarded with increased resources.

Management Information

Accurate and up-to-date management information would be essential for the successful implementation of this approach. This information would be either quantitative (statistical and financial) or qualitative (performance measures). A major review of quantitative information systems, a clear strategy, increased use of modern technology and better coordination was seen as critical. Equally important was the development of performance measures and methods of monitoring the degree to which objectives are met. Such measures should be appropriate to specific services and those services which are essential to the overall aims but necessarily require higher subsidies than others are equally valuable.

Training strategy

Effective management in local authorities now requires new skills which can be learnt through training and retraining and benefit the whole organization. A clearly defined management training programme was seen to be essential for the development of existing staff and to encourage new initiatives. Positive action towards under-represented groups would assist in developing the equal opportunities policy.

Communication, identity and image

Poor communication within the department was evidenced by the amount of procedures and paperwork at the expense of verbal contact. Effective management and increased confidence and mutual trust was seen as one method of overcoming these barriers.

The lack of a real corporate identity or image for the department was seen as another weakness undermining the effective marketing and running of the department. Suggestions to solve this problem included a change of name, a new logo and consistent themes running through publicity materials to link together the various activities of the department's work.

The strategic plan

In 1991, as a result of the analyses described above, the strategy document *Leisure in Leicester 2000* was approved by the Recreation Committee of the council. The strategy provided a clear framework within which coherent political and management decisions could be made to develop the provision of leisure services in Leicester over the next few years. The two principal aims on which the strategy was based were:

'to improve levels of participation and access to leisure opportunities having particular regard to the needs of those sections of the community experiencing discrimination' and

'to achieve effective and efficient service delivery through total quality management' (Leicester City Council, 1991, p. 3).

The emphasis of this long-term strategy was placed firmly on increasing opportunities for participation and on cost-effective service delivery. Marketing was seen as an integral part of the whole process with all staff making a contribution to marketing the service. Marketing practice and techniques were at the core of the planning process rather than treated as a separate function. The strategy set out the core values of the city council and stated that 'effective marketing is the key to the successful achievement of these aims'. Marketing strategies would be produced for each facility and service identifying objectives and targets for the next five years. The strategy document looked at the future provision of leisure services in Leicester within the context of corporate and service aims and the need to operate within a static or declining resource base.

Corporate aims

Under corporate aims the financial strategy was laid out on the basis of central government cutbacks and constraints. It was emphasized that future development of leisure services was, nevertheless, essential for the effective functioning of the department but that this would be arrived at not by increase in the overall budget but from other methods:

- the transfer of resources from areas of less priority or relevance;
- increased usage and charges;
- grant aid;
- voluntary sector support;
- increased support from the private sector in sponsorship and partnerships.

Equal opportunities were addressed in terms of lack of access to services caused mainly by financial and cultural barriers. There was a need to differentiate between those least able to pay and those able to pay for services, while marketing research shows that even the poorest leisure users did not equate quality with free or low-priced services. It was important to evaluate pricing policy to ensure value for money and that those in greatest need received greatest help while those who could pay were required to make the largest contributions. Cultural barriers were recognized as existing for women, black, Asian and disabled people even though substantial progress had been made in recent years. Apart from encouraging equal opportunities in employment, especially in senior management, clear targets for improving participation in leisure activities over the next ten years by these groups would be set. Each service manager would concentrate resources on each group in turn over a number of years to ensure maximum effort was made to meet their needs.

Improving and maintaining customer service was an essential part of the strategy and implementing the customer care code formed a vital component. Quality assurance was seen as the method of achieving the best customer care standards and the department aimed to have quality assurance certification by 1995. Clear procedures as well as effective management and motivation for all staff was the framework in which good service for customers would be achieved. Staff development and training, support from managers, good communications, involvement in decision making, delegation of responsibility, and equal opportunities would form the major part of this new approach. Total quality management would be achieved through positive team work and the involvement of all staff in reaching the department's objectives.

Preparation for local government reorganization and the possibility of unitary status was considered in the strategy, as well as the importance of improving the corporate image and developing a coordinated environmental strategy to contribute to Leicester's Environment City award in 1990.

Compulsory competitive tendering (CCT) had already made a fundamental impact on the department and the city council wished to continue to provide its services through its own direct service organizations (DSOs). An all-purpose Leisure DSO had been created to cover grounds maintenance, leisure management and catering and cleaning contracts. The strategy document noted that value-for-money services would be ensured only through effective working practices and overall improved efficiency. CCT was also considered in relation to each of the service areas, where appropriate.

The role of community groups and organizations was considered in relation to the grants from the council and through central government funding programmes. The importance of this sector was recognized particularly to the extent that services could often be provided in a more cost-effective manner and that it encouraged community involvement and development. However, it was also more difficult to ensure quality of services, to maintain accountability and responsibility, and to cease funding where needs have changed. The strategy proposed that organizations be supported only where they sought to achieve objectives set out by the department's marketing strategies, new projects would be funded for a limited time span, and projects would be subject to the same evaluation and monitoring processes applied to in-house services.

Service aims

The long-term aims for each section of the department were set out to provide a framework for the specific marketing plans for each area including, sports, parks, cemeteries and crematorium, entertainments, play, neighbourhood centres and community work, the arts, youth and projects work, Leisure DSO and support services. For example, in the area of arts the department provided grants to two theatres in addition to running its own Arts Section including arts development in the community, advisory services, and arts promotion and exhibitions. Marketing strategies and development priorities to improve the arts services were outlined in the strategy document:

1   Improving accessibility to the arts for the whole community and especially in terms of equal opportunities for women, ethnic groups and the disabled would be achieved through project developments such as an Asian dance development scheme, disability arts projects and animation projects.
2   Consideration needed to be given to the relative priorities between the performing arts, visual arts and technical and craft skills.
3   Facilities for arts, such as galleries, studios and training centres, needed to be developed and improved. Access and programming should also be considered.
4   More self-help initiatives should be considered by developing the training and advisory services in conjunction with community venues, schools and other organizations.
5   The voluntary sector should be supported in partnerships and in kind.
6   Educational links could be developed both formally and informally.
7   The animation role of artists with the community should be assessed.
8   Specific needs for arts provision in terms of geographic areas and areas of interest needed to be assessed and gaps in service identified.

Implementing the strategy

Between 1993 and 1996 the budget for Leisure Services was reduced by 12 per cent, which has meant considerable efforts have been made to cut costs and increase income generation without drastically reducing the quality of services. The establishment of a single Leisure DSO was a unique response to CCT and in 1991 the contract to run the city's twelve sports and leisure centres was won. A strategy for maximizing income, effective marketing and an effective management structure was the major priority. Compulsory competitive tendering, which had the effect of dividing Leisure Services into client and contractor sections, has caused more debate in the Department than any other issue. However, both sides acknowledge the importance of the service overall and the impact is on the management rather than the delivery of services. The effectiveness of the marketing strategy is often influenced by the success of the working relationship between clients and contractors. Both sides need to recognize their respective roles and a working partnership must be developed in each case. The reductions in budget have had a greater overall impact on service delivery than the effects of CCT. In 1996 it was decided not to reduce the quality of services but rather to reduce quantity instead. The need to maximize income and reduce costs perhaps at the expense of service causes friction in the department and emphasizes the need to set out the correct specification for the level of service concerned. If the client cannot afford a particular improvement in the quality of service then the contractor cannot be expected to deliver it at their own expense.

The responsibility for marketing services lies with the individual managers who all receive training through regular programmes. Unlike many authorities, training has not been cut as this was seen as counter-productive. Managers and other staff need to be equipped with the skills necessary to perform their tasks effectively. All staff undergo an annual development review from which training needs are assessed and priority needs are identified. The training strategy was being reviewed in 1996 with the aim of equipping staff for future developments. All service centres have marketing plans which are updated every year or every three years as appropriate. Overall the marketing strategy is designed to work within the corporate framework leisure strategy as set out in 1991. While some aspects were obviously outdated by 1996, the strategy overall has stood the test of time and the aims of the department remain basically those of increased participation in services and total quality management and which the department continues to work to achieve.

The Leisure Pass scheme encourages under-represented groups and especially those on low pay to participate in leisure activities effectively providing half-price admission to many centres. Targets are set which monitor the uptake of the scheme. Whereas budget restrictions have meant a reduction in the amount of market research carried out, a MORI survey is conducted every two years and local surveys of use and non-users are carried out regularly. Changes in service delivery as a result include, for example, improving the quality of play areas by reducing the amount of dog mess. Public concerns identified in surveys led directly to new dog byelaws imposed on all parks and open spaces. Increasing activities for children and young people was another area of public concern being addressed by the department.

Annual service plans are compiled for each service, which identify priority areas and targets for the year ahead, enabling managers to plan for the year within the resources available. This is done in conjunction with line managers and teams or networks representing geographical areas and arts, sports, children and young people and parks to coordinate with the overall service strategy and marketing plans.

Income generation and pricing strategies were also under review in 1996 and the department had commissioned an independent analysis of sponsorship policy. It is hoped to obtain increased sponsorship and develop more partnerships with the private sector, reflecting the need to increase resources. Other areas under review were fees and charges and other income-generating opportunities such as investments in new equipment which will pay for itself in the longer term. Rationalizing property owned by the department and optimizing use of buildings provides more scope for cutting costs without reducing services.

With unitary status announced in early 1996 preparation work had increased and a new strategy document was being developed, *Leisure in Leicester 2005*. Unitary status would include the transfer of arts, museums and libraries from the county council to city council control and become part of the Leisure Services framework. A programme of work was developed to produce a series of strategies for the four areas linked to unitary status – libraries, museums, arts and children and young people. These will be coordinated with the strategies for each area (north, south, east and west) and with those for arts, sports, children and parks. These documents were used to generate a range of priorities for development in each of these areas and, in turn, will be used to develop the new strategy document for the department incorporating new marketing plans and budget strategies. Individual centre plans would then be developed from that.

In conjunction with the new strategy document a quality strategy was developed using McKenzie's 'seven S's model' to identify outputs, outcomes and performance indicators under the headings shared values, strategy, structures, systems, style, staff and skills (see also Chapter 6). One aim was to achieve the quality assurance standard ISO 9002. This has already been achieved for Leisure DSO, Support Services, Grant Aid and Leisure Schemes. The work programme together with the revised strategy and the quality strategy documents were being developed in parallel in preparation for unitary status in April 1997. However, extensive budgetary cuts again in 1996, with the prospect of even more severe cuts in 1997, combined with the practical work of preparing for unitary status, has meant a curtailing of work on strategy development. It is seen as a priority area for the first six months after unitary status.

References

Leicester City Council Leisure Services Department (1991) *Leisure in Leicester 2000*, Leisure Services Department, Leicester City Council, Block A, New Walk Centre, Welford Place, Leicester LE1 6ZG.

Torkildsen, G. (1992) *Leisure and Recreation Management*, 3rd edn, E & F N Spon.

Issues

1 The role of total quality management in developing and implementing marketing strategies.
2 Developing a marketing strategy to incorporate measures to deal with budgetary cuts.
3 The effect of devolved management on developing marketing strategy and planning for quality services.

Questions

1 What are the constraints to marketing for quality leisure services?
2 How should the marketing strategy be adapted to allow for the changes involved in assuming unitary status?
3 How do changing council politics affect marketing strategies?

Birmingham City Council Department of Leisure and Community Services – Library Services

Birmingham is Britain's second largest city with a population of approximately one million, comprising a wide range of cultural and ethnic groups. It was at the heart of the Industrial Revolution and continues to be a major manufacturing centre. With excellent road, rail and air communications to all parts of Britain and abroad, it is a major international city and boasts the International Convention Centre, the National Indoor Arena and the National Exhibition Centre. There are three universities and it is a national centre for the arts with internationally renowned opera and ballet companies, the City of Birmingham Symphony Orchestra, theatres, and a cultural complex in the city centre which houses one of the largest public libraries in Europe, a gallery and a museum. There are also problems of increasing poverty, especially in the inner city areas, 15 per cent unemployment, and evidence of poor reading levels among children and adults.

Birmingham City Council has for several years been concerned with the whole issue of marketing and promoting a positive image of Birmingham. The political agenda of the council featured strongly in the strategic decision making of the local authority departments. The task for Library Services was to respond to that corporate drive and, in addition, to define the service in terms of relevance to the community as whole. The Director of Library Services in 1991, Pat Coleman, instigated a policy of research and strategic review to carry out the council's aims. A statement of aims and objectives formed the starting point for an overall strategy statement for services in 1991–2 but without a separate marketing strategy. The Director of Library Services viewed the integration of marketing within other management functions as a positive outcome of the planning process.

The strategy report identified specific areas of concern where services should be targeted and/or particular needs catered for. These included

- a significant increase in the number of elderly residents where there were implications for the housebound service as well as services for the active retired with increasing leisure time;
- the peak in the number of pre-school children in 1991 and the consequent rise in the number of teenagers at the end of the decade pointed to changing levels of demand;

- the needs of ethnic minority communities needed to be more fully assimilated into the library service recognizing the wider dispersal of groups within the city, the need for more emphasis on English-language skills, while provision of ethnic language material was also important;
- service delivery to the areas of deprivation in the city should be reviewed;
- the library service had an important role in addressing the issues of reading problems among children and adults as well as the need for new skills in a time of high unemployment.

In the light of these and other changes in the social and economic environment, the strategy report recognized the need for the department to reassess its role and purpose in order to contribute to the strategic development outlined in the city council's strategy document. Marketing planning for the library service was therefore closely linked to the key elements as set out in the city strategy which encompassed economic regeneration, quality services, the national and international role, and efficiency and effectiveness.

Economic regeneration

Information services for business, science and technology contributed directly to economic development while other well-resourced and responsive library services could be marketed as a feature of the city attracting people to live, work and visit. The potential markets for expanding the information services include specialist community services and ethnic minority businesses, for example. Extending the libraries' role as a centre for informal learning to increase open educational opportunities, helping people to acquire basic skills especially in reading and writing, was essential. The development of cooperation and new partnerships with external organizations and training bodies, both private and public to assist in achieving these objectives was also recognized.

Quality services

Providing quality services was seen as essential especially in reflecting the specific needs of individuals and groups in the community and particularly in the inner-city areas. A marketing strategy had to be developed to target these groups and to promote the services provided. Further research was needed to identify the needs of individuals, particularly those disadvantaged in various ways, and of groups with special needs. Services targeted at these groups needed to be developed and integrated into the library service generally. The development of integrated strategies should include cooperation with other departments in the authority and services aimed at minority ethnic communities should be reviewed and improved.

International and national role

There was a need to develop a more positive contribution to the international and national image of the city by exploiting appropriate services and collections of material. The image of Library Services should be updated and improved and the Central Library developed as the focal point in the city centre. Existing services should be extended and new services initiated to support the development of the single European market and the activities of the International Convention Centre.

Efficiency and effectiveness

More management information was required to facilitate effective strategic decision making and policy development in Library Services. Increased marketing research was necessary to identify the needs of existing and potential library services. This would be achieved through a new culture in the department of questioning the deployment of resources and maximizing their use. It was felt that a greater emphasis on customer care was needed and that cooperation with other council departments would assist in this process. Performance measures to assess efficiency and effectiveness in the department should be introduced which reflected the role and purpose of library services. Methods of income generation would be investigated to aid the development of core library services.

Implementing marketing strategies for individual service areas and promoting services overall were central to this strategy with the emphasis very much on the need to conduct more extensive market research. The systematic integration of marketing information into management decision making was thought to be necessary given the increasing emphasis on performance and value for money in the public sector. A programme of systematic community profiling was developed in 1991 to enable the service to become more responsive to community needs and more effective in the planning and delivery of activities.

Community profile strategy

In order to establish the library service at the heart of community life service plans were prepared based on a process of information gathering to define the needs of the public. The process of community profiling involved three key elements:

- Area profiling – an annually conducted assessment of needs, priorities, and opportunities within the context of specifically defined geographical areas as well as an identification of the characteristics of the communities. To facilitate the planning and marketing process it is essential to identify these characteristics and how they affect service delivery and effectiveness. Examples of these elements include the existence of priority funding for a district or a motorway dissecting a residential area;
- User profiling – a bi-annual assessment of the characteristics, needs and priorities of service users. This included details of age, sex, ethnicity, disability, economic status, language, mode of access, address, frequency and purpose of visits, extent of library use, and satisfaction levels;
- Forward planning – an annual process of planning activities geared to meeting the needs and priorities of users and the wider community as identified in the profiling process.

The community profile strategy aimed to provide information on community needs in relation to library services to facilitate the development of relevant action plans to meet those requirements. The determination of priorities to enable effective targeting of service development and resource allocation was another essential element of the process. The profiling process entailed

- identifying the market;
- identifying community area needs and key issues;
- identifying users;
- identifying users' needs;

- identifying priorities for medium- and long-term action from market research.

The area profiling exercise has been very valuable in the long term and was used to create statistical reports giving a detailed profile of the population for the catchment area of each of the city's libraries. This information has been used extensively in the planning of services and in the allocation of resources. The level of the book fund is also informed by area profiling. Allocation is decided by turnover rates and levels of use (75 per cent), but a proportion (25 per cent) is retained and then allocated to each library according to the level of disadvantage identified in that particular catchment area. These policies again reflect the key council policies; for example, the needs of the under-fives were targeted recently in a particular part of the city because the area profiles revealed an area of disadvantage. This information is fed into the marketing plan and in 1996 it was planned to conduct the exercise again to provide an updated view.

Convergence

In April 1994 the three existing departments of Libraries, Museums and Recreation and Community Services were converged to form one new department of Leisure and Community Services. Previously each division had marketing and public relations personnel which were merged under a new marketing function for the whole department. The recognition of the value of marketing has increased with a new Assistant Director of the Libraries and Learning Division, Vivien Griffiths, who is very supportive of marketing practice. The pressures of convergence, staff changes and budgetary restrictions, however, meant that marketing resources were now redistributed across the department, and whereas Library Services had previously had a dedicated marketing unit of four and a half staff other divisions have not had the same level of investment in marketing. Even so, Library Services can now call on the support of a new Marketing and PR Team of fourteen staff.

A new Libraries Strategy was compiled to take a three-year perspective on development between 1995 and 1998. The document aimed to provide a framework of priorities for managers in planning for the years ahead. Strategic objectives and priorities comprised the following:

1 To deliver high-quality services by (for example)
   - continuing to improve services within the resources available;
   - measuring performance against strategic objectives and key

performance indicators which emphasize quality and equity of service;
- communicating to citizens the quality and quantity of services achieved.

2 To meet needs equitably and sensitively by
- meeting the needs of the widest cross-section of people and to ensure the needs of people experiencing disadvantage are met appropriately and in a sensitive way;
- improving the quality and range of materials and services available in libraries, ensuring they reflect the diverse composition of the city's population;
- continuing to develop and implement programmes of positive action to improve the representation of women, black and ethnic minorities and people with disabilities.

3 To improve access to and take-up of services by all groups by
- ensuring the service is responsive to the needs and preferences of local people;
- encouraging high levels of take-up of library services by all communities within the city;
- developing programmes of customer research, consultation and feedback to identify the needs of users and non-users;
- continuing to promote the use of library services through a sustained city-wide campaign;
- targeting provision of services effectively to distinct groups within the city and encouraging take-up by those groups.

4 To network with the wider library and information community, so as to enhance the contribution of the service to the local community by (for example)
- ensuring that Birmingham develops its role as a centre of excellence and innovation in public library provision.

5 To improve the quality of life of local people by (for example)
- further promoting literature and the related arts, encouraging reading in particular;
- providing information and other services to support the commercial and industrial sector;
- improving access to information for those seeking work, training opportunities and developing their skills;
- continuing to promote the community libraries as important focal points for local activities.

The priorities for 1995–6 included a wide range of specific measures designed to develop quality services, increase research and levels of responsiveness to targeted groups, and promote the services more extensively. Providing more choice and opportunities for the public within resource limitations remained at the core of the strategy.

Developing a communications policy

The need to focus attention on the department's role in improving quality of life (health, education, environment), tourism (sports facilities, arts, museums) and economic development (business information services, tourism) was highlighted in a department corporate communications plan in 1996. The discretionary nature of services provided can encourage the view that Leisure and Community Services are not as valuable as other services. The Marketing and PR team therefore drew up a set of key messages to ensure that the value of Leisure Services was communicated through PR and marketing strategies. The key messages were designed to reflect closely the council policies as set out in the Policy Framework for 1995/6 referred to earlier in Chapter 6. The objectives of the communications plan were

- to improve the negotiating position of the department in the situation of reduced budgets;
- to correct the existing negative perceptions of the department;
- to improve understanding that Leisure Services are essential services.

The target markets for the communications plan were Birmingham City Council taxpayers, elected members, members of parliament and opinion formers.

In the case of Library Services a process to involve library managers in identifying key messages and priorities was undertaken which was then developed into an action plan to implement the key messages. These were identified in relation to their role in:

- lifelong learning (e.g. IT facilities and multimedia services);
- the education and development of under-fives (e.g. the Centre for the Child);
- tackling inequality, disadvantage, and discrimination (e.g. mental health packs, disability information).

Within the marketing strategy these messages would be reviewed over the longer term so that other relevant areas could also be considered and prioritized to minimize the problem of a wide dispersal of resources failing to achieve maximum impact. Due to the diverse nature of library services and the large number of buildings involved, the marketing budget has been very stretched in the past. The effects of diminishing financial and staff resources means that focusing on these key messages concentrates attention and resources on current priority areas.

Targeting customer needs and priorities

The importance of market research is well established in Libraries and Learning and user surveys and other research studies are conducted for even the smallest project. A team of managers, meeting every two months, coordinated an annual programme of research. They are planning to look at the cycle of activities in terms of users and particularly non-users of libraries. Overall there has been a gradual change in the marketing focus from promotion to research, increasingly looking at the choices people make and why. Detailed user surveys are conducted every two years alternating between the central library users and community library users. From this information trends are detected and management decisions on service delivery taken.

At the time of convergence library services tended to lead the way in the department in terms of customer-care policy as some of the other services did not operate the same system of response to comments and suggestions. The marketing team hope that a standard system of suggestions from the public will be developed. The libraries receive around 1300 suggestion forms a year plus letters, which managers regard as a positive dialogue with customers.

In the face of continuing budgetary cuts a new approach has to be sought to marketing quality services. A library customer charter which was developed some years ago is now out of date and under review. A growing public scepticism towards charters has been compounded by severe budgetary cuts which mean that some of the promises made can no longer be upheld. For example, a promise that there will be a library within a mile of your home in Birmingham can no longer be kept due to the closure of six community libraries as a result of funding cuts. Marketing policy now has to consider a fresh approach of developing, within the resources available, those services which are based on customer needs. Birmingham Libraries are currently looking at the needs of young people and students and how they can best be met within the resources of the central library. In this way the principles of quality service provision is being revised based on customer needs and resources available. Another example of developing services within resource limitations was the provision in the central library of women-only tables. This was a need identified as a result of a user-satisfaction survey which showed the need for tables reserved for women only to use especially at busy exam times when 6000 users a day can contribute to a stressful environment. This was a response to maintain a feeling of security for women and promote the view that libraries are a secure place. Only thirty-two out of 950 tables were so allocated but some of the media reacted with charges of overt political correctness. The department's response agreed by the Committee Chairman, the Director of Libraries and the Marketing Officer suggested that as over 52 per cent of the population of Birmingham were women and more women than men use libraries, why should services not be geared to their needs? Here is an example of user surveying leading to management and service response, followed by media reaction, with the Marketing Officer, Manager and elected member being involved in one event. The initiative has been a success with only a few complaints from men.

A marketing handbook aimed at staff particularly at community level has been drawn up by the marketing team recognizing the need for staff to carry out marketing tasks on a day-to-day basis. The involvement of all staff in the marketing process is also recognized in the monthly seminars in each region to disseminate the results of the research conducted and to engage in the interpretation of the data. Workshops have also been held in conjunction with the Library and Information Statistics Unit at Loughborough University on the use of statistics in developing library services.

A major development in recent years has been the opening in 1995 of the Centre for the Child in the central library to replace the old children's library which was destroyed by fire. This includes a children's library as well as extensive facilities and information on child care, education and all aspects concerned with children of all backgrounds. This service development emphasized the role of the central library as a major recreational, cultural and educational centre for Birmingham.

Further reading

Birmingham City Council, *Policy Framework 1995/6.*

Birmingham City Council Department of Leisure and Community Services, *Birmingham Libraries Strategy 1995–98*, Libraries and Learning Division. Birmingham City Council Department of Leisure and Community Services, Central Library, Chamberlain Square, Birmingham, B3 3HQ.

Kinnell, M. and MacDougall, J. (1994) *Meeting the Marketing Challenge. Strategies for public libraries and leisure services,* Taylor Graham.

Issues

1 The importance of market research and management information to service development and resource allocation.
2 The impact of convergence on marketing strategy development.
3 The influence of political policy making on marketing planning.

Questions

1 How would you assess the effect of budget cuts on marketing strategies and service development?
2 What are the benefits of community profiles for the development of marketing strategies?
3 How should the communications plan be implemented and developed?

Selected bibliography

Aldridge, M. (1996) Dragged to market: being a profession in the post-modern world. *British Journal of Social Work,* **26** (2), 177–94.

Anheier, H.K. and Seibel, W. (eds) (1990) *The Third Sector: Comparative studies of nonprofit organizations,* Walter de Gruyter.

Ansoff, I. (1957) Strategies for diversification. *Harvard Business Review,* September-October, 113–24.

Aslib (1995) *Review of the Public Library Service in England and Wales for the Department of National Heritage,* Final Report. Aslib.

Barna, G. (1988) *Marketing the Church,* Nav Press.

Barnett, R. (1992) *Improving Higher Education: Total quality care,* The Society for Research into Higher Education and Open University Press.

Blois, K. J. (1996) Relationship marketing in organizational markets: when is it appropriate? *Journal of Marketing Management,* **12,** 161–73.

British Standards Institution (1992) *BSI Handbook 22. Quality assurance.*

Bullivant, J. (1994) *Benchmarking for Continuous Improvement in the Public Sector,* Longman.

Burnett, K. (1993) The challenge of relationships. *Fund Raising Management,* July, 44–54.

Buttle, F. (1996) SERVQUAL: review, critique, research agenda. *European Journal of Marketing,* **30** (1), 8–32.

Cabinet Office (1992) *The Citizen's Charter: Charter Marks scheme 1993. Guide for applicants,* Central Office of Information.

Castles, F.G. and Pierson, C. (1996) A new convergence? Recent policy developments in the United Kingdom, Australia and New Zealand. *Policy and Politics,* **24** (3), 233–45.

Christy, R., Oliver, G. and Penn, J. (1996) Relationship marketing in consumer markets. *Journal of Marketing Management*, **12**, 175–87.

Clark, G. (ed.) (1990) *Managing Service Quality*, IFS Publications.

Common, R., Flynn, N. and Mellon, E. (1992) *Managing Public Services: Competition and decentralization*, Butterworth-Heinemann.

Cowell, D. (1984) *The Marketing of Services*, Butterworth-Heinemann.

Cronin, B. (ed.) (1992) *The Marketing of Library and Information Services 2*, Aslib.

Davies, B. and Ellison, L. (1991) *Marketing the Secondary School*, Longman.

Davies, D. (1991) *Church and Religion in Rural England*, T&T Clark.

Foxall, G.R. (1989) Marketing's domain. *European Journal of Marketing*, **23** (8), 7–22.

Foxall, G.R. and Goldsmith, R.E. (1994) *Consumer Psychology for Marketing*, Routledge.

Gaucher, J.G. and Coffey, J.C. (1993) *Total Quality in Healthcare*, Jossey-Bass.

Goodlad, S. (1995) *The Quest for Quality: Sixteen forms of heresy in higher education*, The Society for Research into Higher Education and Open University Press.

Gronroos, C. (1983) *Strategic Management and Marketing in the Service Sector*, Marketing Science Institute.

Gronroos, C. (1990) Relationship approach to marketing in service contexts: the marketing and organizational behaviour interface. *Journal of Business Research*, **20**, 3–11.

Gummesson, E. (1987) The new marketing – developing long-term interactive relationships. *Long Range Planning*, **20** (4), 10–20.

Henwood, M., Wistow, G. and Robinson, J. (1996) Halfway there? Policy, politics and outcomes in community care. *Social Policy and Administration*, **30** (1), 39–53.

Johnson, G. and Scholes, K. (1989) *Exploring Corporate Strategy: Text and cases*, Prentice Hall.

Kenneson, P.D. (1993) Selling [out] the church in the marketplace of desire. *Modern Theology*, **9** (4), October, 319–48.

Kinnell, M. and MacDougall, J. (1994) *Meeting the Marketing Challenge: Strategies for public libraries and leisure services*, Taylor Graham.

Kotler, P. (1986) *Principles of Marketing*, 3rd edn, Prentice Hall.

Kotler, P. (1988) *Marketing management: Analysis, planning, implementation and control*, 6th edn, Prentice Hall.

Kotler, P. and Andreasen, A.R. (1996) *Strategic Marketing for Non-profit Organizations*, 5th edn, Prentice Hall.

Kotler, P. and Levy, S.J. (1969) Broadening the concept of marketing. *Journal of Marketing*, **33** (1), 10–15.

Kotler, P. and Roberto, E.L. (1989) *Social Marketing: Strategies for changing public behavior*, The Free Press

Laing, A. and Cotton, S. (1995) Towards an understanding of healthcare purchasing. *Journal of Marketing Management,* **11** (6), 583–600.

Lovelock, C.H. (1992) *Managing Services: Marketing, operations and human resources,* 2nd edn, Prentice Hall.

Lynch, J.A. (1993) *Managing the Delight Factor,* IFS International.

McCort, J.D. (1994) A framework for evaluating the relational extent of a relationship marketing strategy: the case of nonprofit organizations. *Journal of Direct Marketing,* **8** (2), 53–65.

McDaniel, S.W. (1986) Marketing communication techniques in a church setting: views on appropriateness. *Journal of Professional Services Marketing,* **1** (4), 39–54.

McDonald, M.H.B. (1995) *Marketing Plans: How to prepare them, how to use them,* 3rd edn, Butterworth-Heinemann.

McIntosh, D. and McIntosh, A. (1984) *Marketing: A handbook for charities,* Directory of Social Change.

Manoff, R.K. (1985) *Social marketing,* Praeger.

Oakland, J.S. (1995) *Total Quality Management: Text with cases,* Butterworth-Heinemann.

Pardey, D. (1991) *Marketing for Schools,* Kogan Page.

Payne, C.M. and Ballantyne, D. (1991) *Relationship Marketing,* Butterworth-Heinemann.

Pollitt, C. and Harrison, S. (eds) (1992) *Handbook of Public Services Management,* Blackwell.

Powell, W.E. (ed.) (1987) *The Nonprofit Sector: A research handbook,* Yale University Press.

Preedy, M. (ed.) (1993) *Managing the Effective School,* Paul Chapman/Oxford University Press.

Shapiro, B.P. (1973) Marketing for nonprofit organizations. *Harvard Business Review,* **51** (5), 123–32.

Sheaff, R. (1991) *Marketing for Health Services,* Open University Press.

Stevens, R.E. and Loudon, D.L. (1992) *Marketing for Churches and Ministries,* Haworth Press.

Taylor, L.T. (1992) *Quality: Total Customer Service,* Century Business.

Taylor, L.T. (1993) *Quality: Sustaining Customer Service,* Century Business.

Taylor, M. (1996) Between public and private: accountability in voluntary organizations. *Policy and Politics,* **24** (1), 57–72.

Tooley, J. (1988) *A market-led alternative to the curriculum: breaking the code,* Institute of Education.

Torkildsen, G. (1992) *Leisure and Recreation Management,* 3rd edn, E & F N Spon.

Walsh, K. and Davis, H. (1993) *Competition and Service: The impact of the Local Government Act, 1988,* HMSO.

Wilson, J. (1994) Competitive tendering and UK public services. *The Economic Review,* April, 31–5.

Wistow, G. *et al.* (1994) *Social Care in a Mixed Economy,* Open University Press.

Worthington, S. and Horne, S. (1993) charity affinity credit cards – marketing synergy for both card issuers and charities? *Journal of Marketing Management,* **9** (3), 301–13.

Wright, C. and Whittington, D. (1992) *Quality Assurance. An introduction for health care professionals,* Longman.

Index

Brook
street

Cantley

brookstreet.co.
uk

MKT Asia
12-22